Rethinking Marxist Approaches to Transition

Studies in Critical Social Sciences Book Series

Haymarket Books is proud to be working with Brill Academic Publishers (www.brill.nl) to republish the *Studies in Critical Social Sciences* book series in paperback editions. This peer-reviewed book series offers insights into our current reality by exploring the content and consequences of power relationships under capitalism, and by considering the spaces of opposition and resistance to these changes that have been defining our new age. Our full catalog of *SCSS* volumes can be viewed at https://www.haymarketbooks.org/series_collections/4-studies-in-critical-social-sciences.

Series Editor
David Fasenfest (Wayne State University)

Editorial Board
Eduardo Bonilla-Silva (Duke University)
Chris Chase-Dunn (University of California–Riverside)
William Carroll (University of Victoria)
Raewyn Connell (University of Sydney)
Kimberlé W. Crenshaw (University of California–LA and Columbia University)
Heidi Gottfried (Wayne State University)
Karin Gottschall (University of Bremen)
Alfredo Saad Filho (King's College London)
Chizuko Ueno (University of Tokyo)
Sylvia Walby (Lancaster University)
Raju Das (York University)

Rethinking Marxist Approaches to Transition

A Theory of Temporal Dislocation

Onur Acaroglu

Haymarket Books
Chicago, IL

First published in 2020 by Brill Academic Publishers, The Netherlands
© 2020 Koninklijke Brill NV, Leiden, The Netherlands

Published in paperback in 2021 by
Haymarket Books
P.O. Box 180165
Chicago, IL 60618
773-583-7884
www.haymarketbooks.org

ISBN: 978-1-64259-613-7

Distributed to the trade in the US through Consortium Book Sales and Distribution (www.cbsd.com) and internationally through Ingram Publisher Services International (www.ingramcontent.com).

This book was published with the generous support of Lannan Foundation and Wallace Action Fund.

Special discounts are available for bulk purchases by organizations and institutions. Please call 773-583-7884 or email info@haymarketbooks.org for more information.

Cover design by Jamie Kerry and Ragina Johnson.

Printed in the United States.

10 9 8 7 6 5 4 3 2 1

Library of Congress Cataloging-in-Publication data is available.

Aileme

∴

Contents

Acknowledgements XI

Introduction 1
1 The Curious Neglect of Transition in Left Theory 1
2 The Structure of the Book 5

PART 1
The Theoretical Heritage: Transition in Classical and Western Marxism

Introduction to Part 1

1 'Poetry of the Future': Marx and the Problematic of Transition 15
  1 The Primacy of Production 16
  2 Production and Alienation 18
  3 The Separation of the Political and the Economic 22
  4 The Tasks of Social Revolution and Non-contemporaneous Contemporaneity 23
  5 Communism as Positive Supersession 24
  6 Marx and Transition 25
  7 Towards a Theory of Transition 26

2 Interlacing of Times: the 'Althusser Effect', Temporality and Transition 28
  1 Expressive Totality to Ruptural Unity: Althusser Reading Marx 29
  2 Temporal Dislocation: Balibar Reading Althusser 39
  3 'Revolution against 'Capital'': Gramsci Reading Marx 47
  4 Time of Times: Althusser Reading Gramsci 54

3 The Discursive Turn: the Post-Marxist Gramsci of Laclau and Mouffe 60
  1 Class, Popular Interpellations, and Populism 61
  2 Discourse and Hegemony 68
  3 The Impasses of Discourse Analysis and the Melancholy of Radical Democracy 73

Summary: The Marxist Transition Debate and the Notion of Plural Temporalities   79
 1 Transition and Historical Materialism   80
 2 Transition Problematised: Althusser, Balibar, and Gramsci   82
 3 Post-Marxism: the Discursive Turn and the Disappearance of Transition   84
 4 Temporality, Transition and Debates on the Left   85

PART 2
Transition as Hermeneutic: the Dichotomy of Melancholy and Utopia

Introduction to Part 2

4 Left Melancholy: Obstacle or Resource?   90
 1 Mourning and 'Left' Melancholy   91
 2 Melancholy as Obstacle   94
 3 Melancholy as Resource   97

5 Through the Melancholic Impasse: Utopia   103
 1 Anti-utopianism and the Neoliberal Closure of the Future   104
 2 Reformulating the Utopian   109
 3 Marx, Engels and Utopia   110
 4 Bloch and the Not-Yet   118
 5 Spatio-temporal Utopianism as Method: Harvey and Levitas   123
 6 Timelessness of Utopia   126

Summary: Melancholy Utopia, and Transition as a Hermeneutic   127

PART 3
Enacting Transition: Substantive Left Visions

Introduction to Part 3

6 Lineages of Postwork Theory   132
 1 Antiwork Politics: the Critique of Productivism   133
 2 The Autonomist Corollary   141

    3 Accelerationism   145
    4 Postwork Departures   149

7 Postwork: a Contemporary Left Vision   151
    1 The Postwork Agenda   151
    2 Postcapitalism: Mason on the Information Economy   155
    3 Inventing the Future: the Post-accelerationist Techno-utopian Strain   164
    4 Techno-utopian Futurity   167

8 Demands, Agency and Strategy   170
    1 Postwork Demands: Non-reformist Reforms   172
    2 Social Reproduction and the Agency of Transition   179
    3 Organising Transition: Prefiguration after Occupy   190
    4 Transition as Prefiguration   195

    Summary: Transitional Politics and a Prefigurative Left Vision   197

Conclusion   199

Bibliography   203
Index   224

Acknowledgements

The following pages carry marks of many people who have empowered me to put this book together. While it is not possible to acknowledge each and every one, I shall nevertheless address some the brightest navigating lights in this journey.

Over the many years we have spent traversing the gritty Ankara landscape and beyond, Ozan Siso and Arda Karabalık's presence in my life has been indispensable: I owe you both immense gratitude for your unwavering support and meticulous help every time I needed it. I look forward to standing shoulder to shoulder with you for many more years.

I would like to thank my supervisors, Will Leggett and Justin Cruickshank: Your patient guidance, help with the bumps on the road, and faith in my capacity have made this possible. It has been a privilege to be part of the Birmingham postgraduate community, with its spirit of solidarity. I must especially thank Ilaria Bernardi: for your kind support and generous hospitality; Francisco López-Santos Kornberger: for your impeccable sense of humour and companionship; Darcy Luke and Melany Cruz: I am not so grateful to you, because you have set the standard of anti-revisionist vigilance too high.

The Centre for Social and Political Thought has been the domain of many scintillating discussions, which have shaped and refined my outlooks. My comrades, friends and intellectual sparring partners from there deserve a very special gratitude. Neal Harris, Ployjai Pintobtang, Malcolm Macqueen, and Angus Reoch: Knowing you all is a joy.

With a warm mention to Will Stronge: Thank you for the exclusive peeks at your cutting-edge research, and making time discuss its contents. You have been of great help and a solid colleague.

Needless to say, I owe so much gratitude to my family: You have supported all of my endeavours, and never interrogated why I go down these roads.

Last but not least, Greta Nonni: You are a safe haven from all the troubles, outside and within. Thanks to you, this book mirrors my best self.

Introduction

1 The Curious Neglect of Transition in Left Theory

For all of its analysis of social continuities and political convulsions, left theory has relatively little to say about their overlap: transition. Classical Marxism gestures towards a theory of transition, yet falls short of elaborating a coherent theory that treats the concept as a problem in its own right, as opposed to an element of a wider conceptual apparatus. This observation has inspired this investigation of transition, as a qualitative transformation from one kind of society to another. The notion has a troubled history within left theory, otherwise intellectually and politically invested in constructing a different world out of the detritus of the old. A systematic theory of transition could reinvigorate debates on the 'Left Hemisphere', preoccupied with exposing underlying currents of change within seemingly stagnant historical intervals (Keucheyan, 2013). Semantically, transition also implicates a finitude to historically constituted modes of production, providing groundwork for departures from the dominant ways of seeing the world. Thus, I have elected to theorise transition and its place in historical materialism to reactivate a debate. As this presentation will explain, this has a direct relevance in our political moment that, through its unpredictability, makes it necessary to revisit the topic.

This book was written in the context of a financial crisis, turning into a social and political crisis of global dimensions (Streeck, 2011: 5). Parties of the centre have suffered heavy setbacks where they are seen to be administering austerity policies and tax cuts for the better off, with public participation in elections decreasing most sharply in countries with high levels of inequality (Schäfer, 2013: 169–170). Considering that economic recovery has been dismal even after extensive quantitative easing and bailouts, the key tenets of the neoliberal paradigm have certainly been questioned (*e.g.*, Crouch, 2011; Dardot and Laval, 2013; Mirowski, 2013, among a growing body of literature). But despite the consistent fall in real wages and living standards, the possibility or desirability of systemic change is also met with scepticism. Even on the left, the desideratum of revolution and the critique of capitalism have not been straightforwardly compatible (Schecter, 2007: 22).

The twentieth century bifurcation between social democracy and communism has further stifled debates on the question. The Third International had arisen partly as a response to social democratic confidence in the evolutionary progress towards socialism. The Bolsheviks insisted on the need for a political seizure of power and revolutionary mobilisation, marking a break from the parliamentarianism of continental social democracy. On the other hand, the ossification of a Marxist-Leninist doctrine in the Soviet Union throughout the ensuing decades culminated in a similar teleology, this time with the belief in the infallibility of the Party as the achiever of socialism in one country (Cole, 1958: 846–856). Thus, both currents came to severely downplay the crucial role of the agency of the masses as the source of transition, relying on a determinism of productive forces as the harbinger of a classless society, and working on behalf of the classes in question. Transition was thereby effaced from left political debates, now marred in parliamentary realpolitik or decorative bureaucratic doxa. The glaciation of global superpowers and spheres of influence also had a role in making the question of transition appear as a far-fetched, abstract consideration, and one to be decried as 'adventurism' or 'left deviation'.

In this context, some creative interpretations of historical materialism found expression in Western Marxism, most of whose practitioners were distanced from mainstream politics. The following chapters will trace the concept of transition through classical and Western Marxism, as the latter have engaged with the former in productive directions. It would be unfeasible to address every paradigm, and less theoretically productive than prioritising depth over breadth. Omission of other approaches within the welter of left theory – the decolonial Marxism of C.L.R James and W.E.B. Du Bois, or innovative South American voices such as Álvaro García Linera come to mind – is bound to have an element of arbitrariness. However, the currents considered here are foundational for contemporary engagements, and merit a close reading for their stances on transition.

Of course, there are some notable examples of transition being paid sustained theoretical attention. It has come under sharp focus within different contexts, such as being the key concept in groundbreaking debates in left historiography over the twentieth century. The transition from feudalism to capitalism, and crucially, why this first came about in the West while there were signs of its possibility elsewhere, has been a subject of ongoing controversy. Accordingly, the Dobb-Sweezy debate in the 1940s and 1950s engendered a settling of accounts amongst historians associated with Western communist parties, followed by the Brenner debate among New Left historians through the 1970s, both of which continue to provide illuminating insights into specific historical transitions (Hinton, 1978; Ashton and Philpin, 1987). Such debates have informed historical materialist treatments of necessity and contingency. As Ellen Meiksins Wood (2002) has meticulously argued following Robert Brenner (1977), the transition to capitalism was not inscribed into trade and commerce in embryonic form. The debate on the origin of capitalism further suggests that by virtue of having once been a historical novelty, its future obsolescence is within the realm of possibility. In other words, the debate on the origins of capitalism reveals the contingency of its emergence, and the precarity of its sustenance. The investigation of its inception sheds light on the broader question of how transitions have taken place, and how this can help to conceptualise future transitions. Moreover, this debate indicates a tension between the formal proliferation of capitalist relations, and their real instantiations. A theory of transition thus needs to balance theory with lived history, informing the former with the latter. In this way, a non-reductionist yet universal theory of transition can be devised by integrating local peculiarities into *historical* materialism. While I acknowledge the importance of the empirical discussion of past transitions, my focus here is on the theory of transition. This study is therefore an exercise of theory building rather than theory testing, deriving its statements on transition from classical and western Marxism.

A recent volume on 'The Transition from Capitalism' has broached the subject through a series of interviews with leading academics and activists, signalling transition as a research agenda (Rahnema, 2017, reviewed in Acaroglu, 2019). While historical debates have addressed past transitions, contemporary ones look to its future modalities. Furthermore, Alberto Toscano's (2013) article 'Transition Deprogrammed' draws attention to rival conceptions of transition within classical and structural Marxist theory, highlighting Balibar's (2015) essay 'Elements for a Theory of Transition'. The latter is pivotal to this book since it represents a rare systematic effort to explicitly conceptualise transition, away from scheduled stages. Balibar postulates different axes of social reproduction fractured along temporal lines. Prior to this, and arguably since, theories of transition have received scant attention. The aim here is to build on Balibar's insights, arguing that the notion of multiple temporalities is an overlooked factor in historical materialist analysis. In turn, addressing transition as a phenomenon to be explained, as opposed to an *explanans*, is necessary to interrogate such temporal multiplicity.

A residual determinism issuing from an understanding of transition as a legislated stage, or as a series of lineside signals along a forward march of modes of production, has led to a persistent under-theorisation, and consequently an undervaluation, of its complexity. Addressing this gap in left theory, I problematise transition, arguing that it is both an ontological tendency in society, and an analytical tool explaining the multi-layered paths of social change and continuity. Balibar's work is important to answering the question of whether a general theory of transition, one that holds across space and time, can be constructed. Such a theory would shed light on ruptural moments, such as the French Revolution, and help to distinguish those features that are 'ruptural' about them. This book argues that such a theory can be devised, introducing theoretical and political nuances to historical materialism, with implications for contemporary left strategy.

The Marxist theory of transition developed in this discussion self-consciously avoids direct engagement with the idea of revolution. This may be a disconcerting omission, yet it is warranted due to the nature of the concept. The desideratum of revolution is not intrinsically objectionable, but impatient expectations of a complete break with the state of affairs can lead to a submissive reformism once this fails to materialise. Conversely, such an all-or-nothing mentality can paint the postulate of revolution as a straw man, and be used to justify an unprincipled reformism. To put it in polemical terms, left deviation and right deviation, as excoriated by Lenin (1974), make up two sides of the same coin. While the former insists on a maximal revolutionary break, the latter postpones it into oblivion. Both approaches engender a doctrinaire lack of engagement with the concrete situation. This semantic and historical baggage makes it difficult to appraise revolution without being embroiled in these logics. Thus, revolution is invoked only indirectly and sparsely throughout this book, while transition takes centre stage as it denotes the break without hampering a grasp of the continuities on either side of it. In sum, I theorise what Marx (1972: 15) surmised as the 'birth marks of the old society' following the rupture, and what Bloch (1995a) regards as the Not-Yet before the rupture.

In the following chapters, it will be shown that understanding transition as an embedded societal tendency should be central to a critical social theory, providing the analytical means to theorise postcapitalist futures. Through a temporally attenuated theory of historical change, grounded in the primacy of productive activity as a determinant force on the social formation, transition can be formulated as a sociological concept. Theoretically overlooked and politically effaced, transition as an actuality, or as a fixture of social life, is a notion that left theory can bring to salient debates in sociology and political theory. As a theoretically-driven study, this book aims to contribute to the field of philosophy of history, understood as the theories of historiography that examine approaches to the past, and conversely, the ways in which the past intrudes in the present. More specifically, the notion of transition invokes an overlooked conflict inscribed in historical change: temporal lag. This is particularly relevant to historical materialism. Though class struggle is central to this enterprise, temporality as a sociopolitically constructed and contested reality introduces an additional fold to its instantiations.

The book moves from the theoretical underpinnings of transition, towards its substantive manifestations, and culminates in a practical look at its potential enactment. Moving from the general question of what transition means, to a more specific discussion of its manifestations, ensures that the conceptualisation of transition in the first part traverses the book. To avoid a solely internal discussion, the final part shall put the theoretical frame in dialogue with current approaches to postcapitalism, such as the postwork paradigm or the proliferation of left populist parties. These approaches synthesise various strands of Western Marxist theory and put forth positive, twenty-first century left projects, providing a window into present-day initiatives and a fertile ground to put a theory of transition into action. Salient left viewpoints are brought to bear on the preceding arguments on transition and indicate how this perspective can provoke new considerations, on questions including the utility of reforms, or coming to terms with the tribulations of the past.

2   The Structure of the Book

The book is organised in three Parts. These move from the intellectual lineage of the concept of transition in Marxism, through its recent manifestations in contemporary leftism ('melancholic' and 'utopian'), to its actual and potential application in substantive contemporary debates over 'postwork'. Each of these organising Parts is sub-divided into chapters, as detailed below.

Part 1, 'The Theoretical Heritage: Transition in Classical and Western Marxism', is a broad survey tracing the concept of transition along these currents. Chapter 1 primarily considers the writings of Marx, as the first thinker to outline the parameters of historical materialism – a foundational reference for leftist theories of transition. Here I shall discuss first the theoretical account of productive activity as the lynchpin of this enterprise, positing that this allows us to devise some form of an identifiable narrative linking past, present and future societies. Once the incarnations of productive activity are considered, it is possible to recognise how its alienation is a historically specific condition, and one that distances humanity from its essential capacity to produce and innovate. Marx devotes much of his attention to the critique of political economy, only haphazardly addressing transitional points between modes of production. In fact, the earlier Marx is partial to a Eurocentric, stagist model of historical evolution towards capitalism. However, his journalistic and political writings, along with some of his later correspondences, evince a different picture. Marx's necessitarianism evaporates in view of the praxis of the Paris communards.[1] Similarly, in his analyses of France, Marx notes the differences

---

[1] The Paris Commune was transformative of Marx's philosophy. I have analysed the Commune and the lesser known 1979 Fatsa 'Commune' of Turkey as part of a study on transition in Acaroglu (2018).

between historical transitions to capitalism, and the future one to socialism, arguing that while the bourgeoisie was economically organised prior to its political domination, the opposite holds for the proletariat, as they may capture the levers of power, but this would only be the beginning of a wider socialist reconstruction of the economy. Finally, Marx's correspondence with the Russian political and intellectual figure Vera Zasulich reveals a striking revision to his earlier stagism, maintaining that the ancient Russian village arrangement of *mir* could not only survive a socialist transition, but catalyse a transformation that surpasses a capitalist phase. These sporadic intimations of transition are then developed further.

Chapter 2 turns to the 'Althusser effect', forming the basis of the temporally attenuated theory of transition. This chapter foregrounds Balibar's temporal contributions by way of his work on transition. This is presented against a backdrop of Althusserian theory, to substantively discuss how the social formation is reproduced along distinct political, ideological and economic lines. These are coextensive, as they are present at every turn of social reproduction. I take up the insight that these trajectories are stratified temporally, based on a direction of temporal progress according to the mode of production. The present is a contradictory unity of the past and the future, overdetermined by the workings of the mode of production. While the political level of reproduction may move ahead temporally in the shape of intentional communities or utopian movements, the economic level may stagnate. This example shows that Balibar's concept of *décalage*, or a temporal lag, is intrinsic to the social formation, placing a temporal tension at its centre. That said, it remains to be shown how these levels interact and overlap. For this, Gramsci's conceptual repository, particularly the theory of hegemony, is pertinent. As a supreme theorist of the 'superstructure', Gramsci elaborates a historically informed and sophisticated account of the interactions and tensions between the economy and politics. This is further commendable for its granting a level of autonomy to the political, at once avoiding a facile reductionism as well as watertight separation. In sum, while Althusserian theory effectively addresses ontological questions about the content and nature of the social formation, Gramscian theory excels at accounting for how its different moments of reproduction affect one another. While these paradigms may not appear to be compatible at first sight, I argue that they are complementary *vis-à-vis* a versatile theory of transition.[2]

---

[2] A brief rehearsal of the broader treatment of hegemony here is in press as part of an introduction to Gramsci's thought (Acaroglu and Stronge, forthcoming). Additionally, for an examination of hegemony as it pertains to left strategy, see Acaroglu, 2016.

Marxist theories of the state, a well-trodden field, are indirectly broached within these discussions on the copresence of the economic and ideological within the field of the 'political'. While not the focus of this study, what is and is not considered within the ambit of the political traverses the discussions of temporal lag and its manifestations.

Finally in Part 1, Chapter 3 considers post-Marxism, part of the 'discursive turn' in social theory. The contingency-oriented political theory of Ernesto Laclau and Chantal Mouffe is taken as archetypal of this turn. The theorists argue that the Marxist category of class has been preconceived as a privileged agent of social transformation, and that this is detrimental to New Left politics as a diverse movement of disparate political wills, held together by articulated chains of equivalence. Laclau and Mouffe's influential interpretation of Gramsci sees hegemony as central to society, as a field of discursive articulations. I argue that this is problematic due to its monadic expansion of the political at the expense of the economy and production, leaving Laclau and Mouffe bereft of a transitional horizon or direction to social progress. This chapter thus rounds off the appraisal of the classical and western theoretical heritage with a critique of the turn to post-Marxism, rejecting its core hypotheses and retaining the historical materialist benchmark of productive activity as the central dynamic of historical transitions.

Part 2, 'Transition as Hermeneutic: the Dichotomy of Melancholy and Utopia' follows the theoretical parameters of transition with the sociopolitical manifestations of temporal lag. The concept of left melancholy, spanning the works of Walter Benjamin, Wendy Brown and Jodi Dean is examined in Chapter 4. This phenomenon has been descriptive of the current predicament of left politics, straddling both the legacy of twentieth-century defeats and atrocities, and the widespread disillusionment following the normalisation of an unrestrained capitalism. The central argument is that the left has lost sight of a socialist horizon, adapting itself to social democratic compromise or negative campaigns such as anti-racism and anti-globalisation. However, looking to Benjamin's account of melancholy as a redemptive, subterranean impulse, I maintain that left melancholy is a resource. Past defeats and failures, such as the authoritarian turns in real socialisms, or the repression and co-option of non-capitalist arrangements, nevertheless make up a repository of experience. These are recalled at times of struggle, where the originary desire to build a better life, muted yet not extinguished, can redeem past failures.

At this point, utopian impulses figure in transitional politics, as a dialectical counterpart to left melancholy. Accordingly, Chapter 5 is an exploration of utopia. This is approached firstly as it has come to be understood as a sterile, or latently totalitarian disposition, among anti-utopian streams of left and right wing thought. However, this conception of utopia is challenged, referring to Ernst Bloch's formulation of utopia as the anticipation of a future society, as well as Ruth Levitas' (1990, 2013) ground-breaking defence of utopia as a hermeneutic of social change, and a sociologically viable component of cultural and political movements. The reappropriation of utopia serves to historicise the neoliberal moment as an outcome and effect of social struggles, functioning as a reproduction of the past at the expense of budding imaginaries and constructions of the future. By showing that neither Marx nor Engels themselves were as opposed to utopianism as often assumed, I seek to dispel the left undervaluation of prefigurative politics. On this note, utopian studies have a lot to contribute to the conversation on strategy and organisation. Considerations of ways to build bridges towards imminent futures can help to reinvigorate atrophied debates on the effectivity of different approaches, pointing towards the importance of prefiguration as a catalyst of germinating futures.

As a theoretical discussion of the manifestations of temporal lag, the phenomena identified in Part 2 are reformulated based on the premises of Part 1, showing how left melancholy and utopia attest to contradictory temporalities. And as an argument for positive utopian construction, Part 2 is situated as a substantive nexus between Part 1, and the more overtly political discussions of Part 3.

The final, Part 3 of the book, 'Enacting Transition: Substantive Left Visions', analyses a practical case, the 'postwork' paradigm. This is an emerging theoretical current and political tendency, centred on the limitation of work and a technologically updated welfare state. The contributions of writers and theorists in this paradigm have been the subject of intense controversy. This has been evident both within the specialist field of left theory and economics, as well as in mainstream political debates, particularly with the British Labour Party's receptivity to aspects of the postwork programme. While there is undoubtedly a widening range of global, twenty-first century left departures, postwork has been singularly appealing as an emerging paradigm, embodying the heritage of twentieth century left traditions and contemporary searches beyond them.

Chapter 6 is concerned with scene-setting, outlining the lineages of postwork with its roots in a variety of movements and theoretical currents. Postwork has antecedents in autonomist Marxism, which also deploys a selective reading of Marx, but also provides foundations for a politics premised on the refusal of labour. These approaches are considered, in conjunction with the critique of productivism in Jean Baudrillard's denunciation of Marxism. It is shown that critiques of productivism are politically valuable, with the exception of Baudrillard's account. In addition, this chapter critiques accelerationism, which casts a shadow over Srnicek and Williams' (2015) paradigmatic manifesto for postwork society. I argue here that accelerationism nullifies temporality, and thus any discernible nodes of transition, necessitating substantial revisions to restore its utility.

This anatomisation of lineages prioritises the salient works, as a more thoroughgoing analysis would be beyond our scope and merit a separate examination. This exploration is indispensable before dwelling on postwork itself. While the paradigm is an emergent property of a conjunction of approaches, these precedents indicate some limitations around questions of transition and temporality.

Following the discussion of the strands of postwork theory, Chapter 7 critically engages with its main texts. In particular, as Paul Mason's (2015) views on postcapitalism draw from the Marxist labour theory of value (LTV), the limitations of this theory are discussed at some length. Thus, I critique the LTV as a widely misrepresented account of the obsolescence of capitalism. Kathi Weeks' (2011) book on antiwork politics and postwork imaginaries is discussed as a foundational work, synthesising a variety of approaches to put forth an innovative political programme and research agenda. Weeks weaves her political statements with a utopian strain, devoting as much attention to the performative and empowering functions of emancipatory politics as their immediate policy outputs. By contrast, I argue that Mason's more media-savvy work evinces a techno-determinism, relying on an over-simplified conception of transition as a pristine postcapitalism ready to emerge out of the old, without paying due attention to the agencies implicated in such a process of construction. This critical analysis then turns to Srnicek and Williams' (2015) *Inventing the Future*. The writers critique left and right political dispositions, seeking to rectify the counterproductive tendencies of the former while recognising the effective aspects of the latter. Thus, politics and hegemony are foregrounded in this manifesto; while the unsustainability of the present state of affairs is laid bare, the writers are also wary of implying an inevitable turn for the better, imploring their readers to become politically active. This chapter contrasts techno-determinism with techno-utopianism, arguing that only the latter can provide a compass towards postcapitalist transitions.

Finally, Chapter 8 delves into the political enactment of transition. In keeping with the case study, postwork demands such as Universal Basic Income and automation are discussed, firstly by contrasting their intrinsic merits, and secondly by making observations on their performative capacities. Thus, certain demands, while seemingly unfeasible, are seen to be effective nonetheless as poles of attraction for the development of political agencies. This is followed by an overview of contemporary approaches to organisation, where the post-Occupy context has reignited discussions on horizontal and vertical modes, and their respective merits. Invoking the earlier elaboration of the imminence of agency, it is argued that a degree of prefiguration is key to left politics. Anticipating and enacting a utopian horizon can help to materialise the latent transitional futures in the present. In sum, this chapter moves through the issues of 'what' is to be demanded, 'who' is to bring changes about, and 'how' to organise most effectively, concluding with a call for more extended theorisation of prefigurative politics.

PART 1

The Theoretical Heritage: Transition in Classical and Western Marxism

∴

Introduction to Part 1

Transition is a term loaded with historiographical assumptions. By definition, it implies that a directionality is at play. This further suggests a realism regarding historical progress, as a series of objective and knowable patterns across history. Thus, the first part of this book formulates the theoretical underpinnings of transition, showing firstly that it exists in a directly practical sense, and secondly that it has a direction, albeit against a backdrop of a complex temporality.

In order to account for the ontology of transition, Chapter 1 outlines the premise of productive activity as a fundamental human trait. This historical materialist frame places the mode of production as the primary dynamic of historical change. Referring to Marx, it is argued that across historical phases, peoples' culturally transmitted creation of the means to survive and express themselves is a universal constant. The creation of such means is refined and innovated, generating novel forces of production. In turn, these forces are put to use through the relations of production. The notion of transition elaborated here thus considers it as a transformation of the ways in which society reproduces itself, including its ideological and political patterns. Having established these parameters, I turn to Marx's statements on how transition practically takes place in historical contexts. I argue that far from practicing economic reductionism, Marx casts his analytical net over the ensemble of all social relations, differentiating their political and ideological moments, and proceeds to analyse how they interlock or grate against each other, creating contradictions that compel historical movement.

Chapter 2 develops this observation to propose a theory of transition, deploying the Althusserian concepts of complex unity and social formation. Étienne Balibar (2015) has made use of this conceptual apparatus to outline a theory of transition that simultaneously takes account of the spatio-temporally provincial dynamics of transition, and retains a grounding in productive activity as a universally overdetermining factor. Following Balibar, it is argued that it is possible to devise a theory of transition, insofar as it incorporates temporality as a social and political divide. Accordingly, the social formation is reproduced along temporally fractured economic, political and ideological layers. In Balibar's terminology, this is known as *décalage*, or temporal lag, and constitutes the crux of the theory of transition as a recognition that the historical present is a complex unity of temporalities, ranging from hangovers of past epochs and anticipations of future social formations. Having integrated temporality into the historical materialist frame, it is further necessary to account for how temporal contradictions are articulated across moments of social reproduction, particularly between the three axes identified above. For this, the latter part of this chapter broaches Gramscian theory. Hegemony is a highly versatile concept that helps to explain how consent and coercion interact in the overall reproduction of the mode of production. Here the goal is to describe how hegemony is an interlocutor of temporal divides between different trajectories of transition, such as the contradiction between political revolution and stagnant economic reproduction. Additionally, this chapter synthesises Althusserian and Gramscian theory, outlining their points of contact such as their outlooks on temporality and ideology. In so doing, this chapter underscores the theoretical productivity of bridging these seemingly incompatible perspectives and provides a coherent formulation of transition from elements of classical and Western Marxist thought.

In keeping with Part 1's subject of the 'theoretical heritage', Chapter 3 pursues the theory of hegemony into post-Marxist theory, with Laclau and Mouffe's (1985) manifesto for 'radical democracy' as its political centrepiece. Following an exposition of their contingency-oriented political theory, this chapter argues that while it has thus far been possible to chronologically trace the intellectual travails of the concept of transition, Laclau and Mouffe's exhortation to jettison class as an outdated category has meant that post-Marxism loses the transitional horizon hitherto anchored in the mode of production. The theorists maintain that it is misleading to *suture* society along predefined economic – class – lines, instead advocating a vision of the social formation thoroughly imbued with political determinations, where the creation of political wills precedes their subjective existence. However, despite the best intentions of the theorists, this reading also lends itself to left accommodation with the *status quo*, seeking incremental gains and recognition within liberal democratic settings.

Left theory is definitionally inclined towards social transformation, and all of its hues from reformist to revolutionary implicate various approaches to transition. The conspicuous absences of transition are also symptomatic of attitudes towards the notion. At the same time, there are vibrant discussions of transition that directly theorise aspects of the transcendence of capitalism, such as those found in the works of Lefebvre (2009), Marcuse (1970) and Holloway (2002). That said, the choice of Althusserian theory is predicated firstly on the fact that Balibar's engagements provide a unique instance of naming the concept as a problematique. It is therefore responsible to begin from Balibar in a study of Marxist conceptions of transition. Much more importantly, I have chosen to remain with Balibar and move towards wider Althusserian and Gramscian theory, culminating in an analysis of post-Marxism because, as the following chapters aim to convey, temporal lag as an inroad into a theory of transition is cogent and valuable.

CHAPTER 1

'Poetry of the Future': Marx and the Problematic of Transition

To map transition as a Marxist problematic, it is first necessary to locate the ontological grounds for transitional tendencies in society, as laid out by Marx, and justify the normative position that transition is desirable, and indeed necessary, in the corpus of his writings. In light of this, I will first focus on conscious production as a unique human attribute, followed by an exposition of the process of alienation. Secondly, I will discuss the overcoming of alienation as a process essential to transition, and illustrate Marx's vision of socialist construction through his political writings. By providing an exposition of the theory of alienation, followed by the political ways in which it can be dispelled, I argue that Marx provides a coherent historical snapshot of transitions between modes of production, and sets the stage for further theorisation. It should be borne in mind that Marx's work is not a unified whole, nor the authoritative outlook on the theoretical framework of this investigation. Rather, the rationale for beginning with Marx is that he has developed basic historical materialist parameters, without which the directionality of transition would be unmoored from the productive underpinnings of social life and left to arbitrary value judgments. This outlook helps to show that transition is immanent to society, but it remains untheorized as a 'problematic' in an Althusserian sense (*problématique*) (Althusser, 2015c: 415–416; Brewster, 1970). This term will be used intentionally in reference to the need for a coherent synthesis of the localised pronouncements on transition, to be further systematised in Chapters 2 and 3.

There are two points to be made regarding presentation and epistemology. Marx (1993: 215) shows an awareness of his 'idealist manner of presentation' in *Grundrisse*, where the parts that make up the structure – in this case money and capital – are isolated from one another and taken up separately, as though fixed in aspic. He explains that the phenomena he considers are simultaneous processes, each containing traces of the others. The reification of social reality on paper marks its abstraction from the ongoing flow of social relations, where concepts are relationally copresent. This warning against an expectation of practical conformity from theoretical constructs is also underlined by Engels (1959: 13–14) in a preface to the third volume of *Capital*, where he denounces the expectation of 'fixed, cut-to-measure, once and for all applicable definitions in Marx's works'. Engels (ibid) further states that 'where things and their interrelations are conceived, not as fixed, but as changing, their mental images, the ideas, are likewise subject to change and transformation; and they are not encapsulated in rigid definitions, but are developed in their historical or logical process of formation'. Following this advice, it can be said that Marx holds up a mirror to society, using concepts with a definitional flexibility receptive to shifting social relations.

In an example, Marx (1959: 157) explains that the plant is not related to the sun solely through one-way causation, but in a mutually defining unity; one confirms and contains the other. The sun, even though it may appear to have an entirely independent existence, gains its characteristics from this mutual constitution. Similarly, a Marxian appraisal of transition needs to treat its concepts as in need of cross-referencing with the minutiae of lived social reproduction. This helps to ground transition ontologically into the processes of day-to-day life. Secondly, this approach blurs the separation between 'fact' and 'value'; what one is sensitive towards tends to register more in their perception, and thus there is an element of subjectivity to even the passive gaze. This is not an insurmountable epistemological problem, but a disclosure of the ontological-normative logical structure used here. 'Transition' is hereby situated as a transhistorical yet non-teleological reality of every social formation. A description of its latency is simultaneously a prescriptive defiance of the theories that oppose and deny it. The ontological and normative division is nevertheless retained. The 'facts' have an existence independent of the observer, but this does not suggest that contradictions beneath the surface cannot be grasped.

'All science would be superfluous', wrote Marx, 'if the form of appearance of things directly coincided with their essence' (1991: 956). He was thus a critical theorist *avant la lettre*, locating the objective functions of normative behaviours based on material relations (McCarney, 1990: 91–109). Understanding these underlying realities as only accessible to the reasoning mind would lead to idealism, if only Marx was not then to invert this idealism by taking the standpoint of the objective contours of production (Wolff, 1988).

1   The Primacy of Production

Every society produces means to ensure future subsistence, handed down from previous generations along with their own innovations. Marx (1968: 8, 10–18) uses the concept of the forces of production in multiple senses such as specific tools and machinery, or modes of organization and technical knowledge that are instrumental to production. These are intertwined with relations of production in which people must partake to maintain themselves.

The novelty of Marx's historical materialism, Hobsbawm (1997: 41, 190–191) maintains, is not the discovery of class nor even the economic theory of history, but the objective and observable role of the capacity to manipulate forces of nature using material or mental labour – along with its requisite organisation – across societies. In this sense, the relations of production are not voluntary but mandatory: 'In the social production of their life, men enter into definite relations that are indispensable and independent of their will, relations of production which correspond to a definite stage of development of their material productive forces' (Marx, 1904: 11). The forces and relations of production constitute the economic structure in conjunction. Marx (1962: 122) makes this point in a polemically overstated manner against Proudhon's suggestion that associative and egalitarian modes of production could evolve through a rearrangement of distribution:

> Social relations are closely bound up with productive forces. In acquiring new productive forces men change their mode of production; and in changing their mode of production, in changing the way of earning their living, they change all their social relations. The hand-mill gives you society with the feudal lord; the steam-mill, society with the industrial capitalist.

Here Marx targets a substitution of political will for the objective consequences of the mode of production, going so far in the other direction as to elicit a technological determinism. This is a reading of historical change as an impersonal succession of increasingly sophisticated means of production, prefiguring all social relations. In turn, this would obviate the need for political intervention in transition, devolving the task to the inevitable arrival of *socialist* means of production. This perspective has rationalised the standard charges of mechanical determinism against Marx. Consequently, political agency is effaced in favour of an abstract model of linear progression. The means of production thereby become stand-ins for the entire mode of production (the hand-mill is feudal while the steam-mill is capitalist). Throughout this examinations, I refute this caricature by invoking the centrality of utopian social imaginaries to Marx's thought, along with the adaptability of means of production towards different goals in the discussion of postwork theory. The present chapter, for its part, expounds on a non-determinist, temporally stratified reading of Marx, foregrounding my nuanced reiteration of historical materialism.

Instead of generalising from a non-contextual quote, it is appropriate to situate the weight Marx attaches to the mode of production within a totality of the social formation. Productive activity, of which the means to produce comprise one aspect, provides an insight into the principles of historical movement, because of its inherent dynamism and universality. It should be noted that this outlines certain bounds for historical movement, but cannot be used to explain away all social phenomena. On the contrary: the acknowledgement that modes of production have an overbearing influence on social life means that every turn of social reproduction gives rise to a need for explanation. As a result, historical materialism is less of a narrative of historical movement and more of a benchmark for inquiry.

The aforementioned passive gaze, or a purely momentary perception, does not give an insight into a social world of myriad contradictions. The workings of society can only be grasped by acknowledging the primacy of production. The conscious activity involved in production, and its intrinsically life-sustaining quality, renders a sort of knowledge that reveals the transformative potential under the superficial veneer; more senses are engaged and the output is an impetus of further activity. Marx's (1978: 145) famous Thesis 11 on Feuerbach read: 'The philosophers have only *interpreted* the world in various ways; the point, however, is to *change* it'. Apart from its injunction to political action, this thesis underlines a Marxist epistemology. In order to understand society, one needs experience of its contradictions, and productively derive knowledge from these. Within capitalist relations, production takes place in an alienated way; in Hegelian terms, as production-in-itself. The hallmark of Marxism is to illustrate the metamorphoses of relations of alienated production, culminating in the prospect of production-for-itself. In this sense, Marx's critique of capitalism is not an outright rejection based on its factual inability to fulfil a predefined moral standard, but one that sets out from its own inconsistencies (Ollman, 1977: 7). The dialectical critique of alienated society renders visible people's consciousness of their own intolerable situation. Solely negative appraisals are therefore dismissed as 'vulgar criticism' that fail to make manifest what is latent (Marx, 1974: 157). In conclusion, the lags between the apparent and the substantial, and 'fact' and 'value', are driving tensions within Marx's social science.

2   Production and Alienation

The bottom line of the quotidian production of means required for survival, and its reverberations along society, reveal a subterranean flow of history. Marx (1975a: 95) explains this position thus:

> What is society, irrespective of its form? The product of man's interaction upon man. Is man free to choose this or that form of society? By no

means. If you assume a given state of development of man's productive faculties, you will have a corresponding form of commerce and consumption. If you assume given stages of development in production, commerce or consumption, you will have a corresponding form of social constitution, a corresponding organization, whether of the family, of the estates or of the classes – in a word, a corresponding civil society. If you assume this or that civil society, you will have this or that political system, which is but the official expression of civil society.

Also, in the *German Ideology*, where Marx (1968: 8) systematically presents his worldview, he begins from the premise that engagement with nature through productive activity is an innate aspect of humankind. Refuting Wagner's supposition that people begin by 'standing in that theoretical relation to the thing of the external world', Marx (1975b) argues that 'they begin, like every animal, by eating, drinking etc., hence ... by relating themselves actively, taking hold of certain things in the external world through action, and thus satisfying their needs'.

Production is an essential human trait, because people must devise and innovate means of production in a historically specific manner, optimising tools handed down from previous generations while crafting new ones, from the skilled hand of the hunter-gatherer to the contemporary quantum computer. The exercise of creative powers reproduces the pattern of ongoing production and gives rise to new needs. Therefore, people are natural beings, but also 'human natural beings' insofar as their real activity is culturally mediated (Marx, 1959: 82). Marx calls this 'species-being' in earlier writings, and continues to contemplate the topic without the same terminology in *Capital*, explaining the purposive element saying, 'what distinguishes the worst architect from the best of bees is that the architect builds the cell in his mind before he constructs it in wax' (1990: 465). Every conscious production process also involves consumption. To wit, the individual simultaneously develops and expends their productive capacities, and by consuming means of production also creates ground for further production (Marx, 1993: 124–125). For this reason, it could be said that he sees humans as perennially incomplete and suffering beings, for they feel the need for new means outside their reach to chisel their self-realization (1959: 41–42, 56).

Marx's nuanced vision of human nature is not a denial in terms of a reduction to social relations. A non-dialectical reading of the sixth thesis on Feuerbach, where Marx (1978: 145) remarks that the human essence is 'the ensemble of the social relations', would lead to a misunderstanding that human nature is denied *in toto*. However, this thesis, which should be read in conjunction with the others, claims that while there is no abstract human nature, there is still a dynamic essence. In the guise of a total subjectivity of the human essence, the thesis can be read as a denial of agency in that everyone is merely an encapsulation of the sum of social relations. A figment of writing from Marx, taken at face value and in a literal sense, can betray the intended meaning. This one-sidedness can be overcome with the dialectical approach that Marx maintained. Etymologically, dialectics comes from the Greek roots of *dia* and *logos*, two and reason. In a simplified sense, it means to reason by splitting into two (Nicolaus, 1973: 37). In Marx's reasoning, it is analytically useful to maintain a duality of individual and society, insofar as one is aware that the two are in a mutually constitutive unity. If the distinction is not maintained, then it would misleadingly appear as though individuals are homogenised units of society. Conversely, the societal backdrop is expedient for a fuller account of individuals. After all, people can only individuate themselves in the midst of society by cultural means, and society is emergent from the sum of its individual constituents (Marx, 1993: 84). An integrally dynamic essence can solve the dilemma of a static human nature, or complete lack thereof. According to Marx's well-known formulation, 'Men make their own history, but they do not make it as they please; they do not make it under self-selected circumstances, but under circumstances existing already, given and transmitted from the past' (1972: 10). This is at once a general and a historical statement. Here Marx claims that humans make history, which, as explained earlier, is tied to productive activity. Nevertheless, this general activity takes place in historically determinate ways. Consequently, as Geras (1983: 107–108) maintains, an innate human nature can be ontologically isolated, but this is a *historical* innateness.

Conscious activity involves a mix of cognitive and physical skills. One conceptualizes and plans what they seek to create, and they do this by manipulating materials found in nature, the 'inorganic body' of man (1959: 41). This anthropological suggestion allows Marx to chart the exit from pre-history, marked by the division of labour. Furthermore, this division of labour should not be understood as a cooperative allocation of duties, but one which demarcates those who farm and toil from those who preach, rule and study. This distinction heralds the end of primitive communism (Marx, 1969: 14):

> With these there develops the division of labour, which was originally nothing but the division of labour in the sexual act, then that division of labour which develops spontaneously or 'naturally' by virtue of natural predisposition (e.g. physical strength), needs, accidents, etc. Division of labour only becomes truly such from the moment when a division of material and mental labour appears.

The separation of mental and manual labour traverses Marx's epistemology of praxis. As Balibar (1995: 40–41) argues, Marx had broken the watertight distinction between poiesis and praxis in Western philosophy by showing that one passes into the other. The servile, repetitive activity of poiesis spills over into self-realizing, original praxis; to compose a piece of music, one must go through the repetitive process of learning the techniques involved in playing a musical instrument. Conversely, all praxis is recycled in further poiesis. Thus, foreshadowing Gramsci, Marx sees the grasp of external reality as an intervention that inevitably alters it, or a 'philosophy of praxis' (Hoare and Smith, 1971: xxi). That being the case, the separation of mental and manual labour, and its crystallization into social groups, some of which predominantly engage in the one kind or the other, creates a stunted understanding of the world and sense of self across society. Ollman (1971: 132) therefore astutely points out that alienation in Marx is treated as the absence of unalienation. On this reading, alienation is a mode of existence in which dissociated 'going through the motions' – and subsequent effacement of agency – marks all aspects of personal and social livelihood, and undermines the healthy human potential to flourish on multiple levels.

In Marx's (1959: 41) eyes, alienation culminates at the point where people are at home when not working, and not working when at home. When at work, labour is externalized in the service of an impersonal force, and the product is externalized from the worker. Marx thus maps the concurrent stages of alienation as emanating from the production process. Due to the division of labour, the proceeds of production are surrendered to the capitalist, who promotes or retards production in order to sell at a surplus, some of which then goes into circulation as capital. This marks an alienation from the product. The fruits of the worker's labour is estranged from them, and furthermore stands in opposition to them as an alien entity (Marx, 1959: 39).

Labour-power, as opposed to self-realizing production in which the labourer can direct their activity by their will and imagination, is the commodified subordination of productive activity to external forces beyond their grasp. Additionally, such commodification also causes an estrangement from other workers: as they relinquish ownership of labour-power to the capitalist for wages, the labour market becomes a domain in which workers confront one another as sellers of labour-power. However, labour-power is an alienated incarnation of inherent productive activity, thus reducing it to a commodity would mean diminishing the humanity of the workers. In this sense, while it is a commodity with an exchange-value, it is a peculiar commodity distinguished from inanimate products. This contradiction pits labour and capital in an existential struggle. The tendency is to trim the historical humanity of the worker into a machine, such that the capitalist seeks the set of hands without the accompanying human being capable of thought and imagination. This is unfeasible since, as outlined above, the division of mental and manual labour fails to capture the real composition of productive activity as a mixture of both. Conversely, overcoming alienation would engender the producers' recovery of these circumstances. Following McLellan (1969: 459), work is a central site of Marx's account of alienation, and a postcapitalist transition as its transformation will be the subject of Part 3.

Another obstacle capitalism faces is its inability to reduce all activity into value, and subordinate all individuals to relations creative of value. This is also a result of the human capacity to seek innovative ways to produce and the new needs that arise from consumption (Marx, 1959: 159). In this sense, alienation is a defect on the social body, and while it may be very advanced, it cannot capture the entirety of social relations and the human psyche, since every moment of capitalist production twists its contradictions further. It follows from this that Marx views the transition to communism as one traversing the epoch of the 'man lost to himself' to an appropriation of their productive potential, where 'through the objectively unfolded richness of man's essential being is the richness of subjective *human* sensibility (a musical ear, an eye for beauty of form – in short, *senses* capable of human gratification, senses affirming themselves as essential powers of *man*) either cultivated or brought into being' (1959: 47, 163).

3   The Separation of the Political and the Economic

The separation of the political and the economic spheres of the social formation results from the dismemberment of the organic bond between mental and manual labour, reinforcing alienation. Marx (1993: 120) excoriates his contemporary economists for treating production as a neutral extra in the interplay of economic transactions, 'encased in eternal natural laws independent of history'. They thereby fail to see the historical subsumption of relations of production under an impersonal market exchange, a pained, political process. The production process, while constituting the economic base of social relations, is conditioned by political struggle among classes. However, in what Wood (2016: 20) describes as possibly 'the most effective defence mechanism available to capital', the ruling class and the political authority are separated in capitalism, so it appears that a neutral state oversees market intercourse. While this is a troublesome view of the state as an entity above social struggles, there is some truth to the suggestion that capitalism impersonalizes and 'simplifies' exploitation, and effaces what Marx (1991: 441) refers to as 'former political and social embellishments'.

The decoupling of the political authority from exploitation leads to the depoliticisation of production processes, strengthening the capitalist class by driving a wedge between struggles against exploitation and those against the power structure maintaining it. The state mechanism remains the political bulwark of exploitation, through legal and repressive apparatuses, but it is only indirectly accessible to disruptions of patterns of production. Marx's political project is thus a preoccupation with the political forms that can exploit the contradiction between the social organization of productive activity on the one hand, and the relationship of power over production and appropriation on the other.

4   The Tasks of Social Revolution and Non-contemporaneous Contemporaneity

In his study of Louis Bonaparte, Marx (2009: 3) observes that the working class and the oppressed are spectators of a power struggle between factions of the ruling class, in which neither side can domineer the regime, and remarks that the 'social revolution cannot take its poetry from the past but the future'. This attests to a recognition that contrary to the transition from feudalism to capitalism, the transition towards a society of voluntary association and democratic planning has its roots in the future. While prior shifts in social relations enabled the bourgeois takeover of political power, the proletarian revolution has to facilitate socialist relations of production that were far from mature under capitalist auspices.

To substantiate this temporal contradiction, Marx had to first settle accounts with the Hegelian inheritance of a closed teleology, in terms of an abstract 'history' guiding society following a predefined logical sequence. Marx treats history in an open-ended manner, avoiding *a priori* announcements of the succeeding mode of production. In a similar vein, Hobsbawm's suggestion that the movement through 'Asiatic, ancient, feudal and modern bourgeois modes of production' is a logical and not a historical progression is correct (Hobsbawm, 1964: 36–38; Marx, 1964). Hobsbawm (1997: 213) also states that the materialist conception of history sets out a basis of historical explanation, but cannot be substituted for the explanation. The reality of a history without a guiding logic restores agency to its participants, and makes it possible to conceptualise multiple modes of production in a contradictory unity. Thus, Marx

(1993: 150) stresses that while a predominant mode of production characterizes the epoch, processes of transition ceaselessly obstruct its totalisation:

> In all forms of society there is one specific kind of production which predominates over the rest, whose relations thus assign rank and influence to the others. It is a general illumination which bathes all the other colours and modifies their particularity. It is a particular ether which determines the specific gravity of every being which has materialized within it.

Moreover, witnessing the Paris Commune, Marx (1940: 23) even writes in a letter to Kugelmann that:

> World history would indeed be very easy to make, if the struggle were taken up only on condition of infallibly favorable chances. It would, on the other hand, be a very mystical nature, if 'accidents' played no part. These accidents themselves fall naturally into the general course of development and are compensated again by other accidents. But acceleration and delay are very dependent upon such 'accidents', which included the 'accident' of the character of those who at first stand at the head of the movement.

As Harvey (2000: 174–175) observes, this testifies to the shift in Marx's view of history towards a dialectic of 'either-or', rather than the 'both-and' of Hegelian transcendence. This is a contingent attenuation to historical unfolding, as the political and existential choices that individuals and groups make can introduce a new set of possibilities, marking an opening for a qualitative rupture. In fact, the 'ruptural' aspect of transitional moments lies in this necessarily contingent appearance of a space of possibility. Accidents can disencumber the positive supersession of alienated social relations, as the reappropriation of creative and associative capacities.

5   Communism as Positive Supersession

Building on this discussion of alienation and capitalist contradictions, Marx's vision of transition can be presented as a socially grounded tendency. The nature of transitional unfolding, however, remains to be shown. It is essential to recall that according to Marx's dialectical reasoning, the whole is a contradictory and open-ended unity of its parts. When projecting this outlook onto historical development, an upward spiral can be proposed as a simplified visualization. Left in this way, it appears that Marx had a pretension to unearth an end-goal and the signposts along its singular path. This would then make historical materialism vulnerable to charges of reading preconceived notions of transition, or a secular millenarianism, into history. It appears as though Marx recognizes this fault in other communist writings, when he remarks, 'Communism is the necessary form and the dynamic principle of the immediate future, but communism as such is not the goal of human development, the form of human society' (1959: 167). For Marx, communism was not a postulated endpoint, but a beginning of human history beyond the prehistory of class stratification. It is a *positive* supersession as the negation of the capital-labour antagonism, engendering the marks of its traversal along the long path from primitive communism, and in that way both familiar and novel (1959: 56).

Returning to the spiral analogy, Marx makes clear that historical change is not linear, but contradictory and staggered. Engels (1987: 376) had remarked that 'repulsion is the really active aspect of motion and attraction the passive aspect'.[1] This citation from the *Dialectics of Nature* refers to the natural scientific observations of Engels' time, yet a similar reasoning is in action in Marx's critique of Proudhon, regarding his desire to keep the 'good' side of capitalism while disposing of the 'bad' one: 'It is the bad side that produces the movement which makes history, by providing a struggle' (1962: 124). This provides an insight into dialectics of transition as seen by Marx and Engels, maintaining that conflict in society provokes transformations, while forces of attraction tend to mend the *status quo*.

6   Marx and Transition

In terms of transition, Marx has set forth the universality and dynamism of material reproduction as ontological indications of the tendency of transition. Although Marx has not created a theory of transition in its own right, there are haphazard observations on future society throughout his works. In early sketches of what was to become *Capital*, Marx argued that capitalism was not a totalised system. Despite its unprecedentedly global reach, capitalist relations entrenched themselves after a series of setbacks and false starts, and in

---

1   While Marx and Engels had differences in opinion, it is reasonable to represent Engels' positions as reflective of Marx's, as they maintained a productive correspondence for many decades and had much common ground. I follow Hobsbawm (1964: 53) in reading the differences in terms of the stress given to different aspects. Consequently, considering Engels in conjunction with Marx in a chapter on Marx's thought does not contradict, but amplifies, the outlines of historical materialism as its founders saw it.

societies in which it is the dominant social relation, it coexists with other modes of production. For Marx, this coexistence was far from harmonious, or divided along neat lines. Instead, the dominant mode of production weighed heavily on the rest, and stunted their developments in ways that grafted them onto the mechanism of the extraction of surplus value.

This may apply to preceding modes of production, particularly in the case of postcolonial nations who have had to adapt at inorganic speeds, but also to prefigurative social forms that have not had a chance to take root. The latter was of interest to Marx, as can be inferred from his writings on the Paris Commune and the Russian *mir* as proto-communist models. The latter is a striking example, showing that Marx went so far as to suggest that this ancient survival could vitalise socialist construction, skipping a capitalist phase. In a letter to the Russian politician and intellectual Vera Zasulich, Marx suggested that this self-governing village commune may not only survive transition, but aid to skip a capitalist phase altogether (cited in Shanin, 1983: 97–123). According to Deutscher (1955: 68–78), Marx began to study and read Russian after the age of fifty, and even planned to integrate his findings into *Capital*. While we will not know how he envisioned this, I shall attempt to develop a temporally differentiated theory of society in the next chapter to expand this element of non-linearity. Ultimately, Marx's analyses of his political environment suggest that he distinguished political and economic moments of transition, and argued that the working class shall draw from a 'poetry of the future'. The bourgeoisie ascended through granular economic shifts and the eventual imposition of market imperatives upon social reproduction. By contrast, a socialist revolution may find itself at the commanding heights of the polity – and with an unprecedented extension of democracy – but shorn of a correspondingly far reaching shift in the mode of production.

7   Towards a Theory of Transition

While the ontological grounds for a transition as the undoing of an alienated social existence is implicit throughout Marx's writings, these can be gleaned more directly in his political commentary and theories of alienation. By temporally locating the processes that produce tensions and anticipate a resolution, Marx makes a cogent case for viewing society as a whole of contradictory processes emanating from the production process, and the political struggle between capital and labour. Additionally, historical materialist premises serve to walk the tightrope between historical necessity and contingency, since the 'bad side' of history and the transition towards communism is not a predetermined endpoint, but rather a plausible reappropriation of the human essence.

However, Marx was constrained to provide specific critiques on historic events when he was not busy sketching the basis of his theory of history, and did not provide an explicit theory of transition as a problematic. While this is not a deficiency as such, looking for the principles that characterize limit cases would be a step forward in addressing a historical materialist blind spot. Beyond their particular moment, limit cases also provide an insight into how the social order survives, and how alternative arrangements fare. The following chapter shall address this gap by invoking the notion of plural temporalities as a theoretical expression of what Marx had anticipated.

CHAPTER 2

Interlacing of Times: the 'Althusser Effect', Temporality and Transition

The unorthodox Marxist Ernst Bloch opined that the communists' inability to galvanise the historically restive German peasantry issued from their unawareness of unfulfilled aspirations sprawled across history. The institutions of the past towered over their worldview; thus, the longing for equality and community over the land was susceptible to reactionary ends as well as progressive ones. It was not that capitalist modernisation left the peasantry behind as a historical curiosity, figuring in the political scene only as rural fodder to metropolitan reactionary politics. In Bloch's (1977: 26) words, 'superstructures that seemed long overturned right themselves again and stand still in today's world as whole medieval city scenes', signifying not only an outdated prejudice, but the chronological presence of the non-synchronous. While Marxists' exposition of the roots of social issues was unparalleled, this 'cold stream' of reason and disenchantment fell short of inflaming the passion and hope of the 'warm stream', made up of sedimented folk tales of struggles against the powerful (Bloch, 1996: 595). The discussion below builds on this notion of temporal differentiation to explain its modalities as part of a temporally stratified social formation, a task for which Althusserian and Gramscian branches of Marxist theory have been path-breaking.

To illustrate Bloch's commingling temporalities, this chapter investigates the theme of temporality, and develops Marx's earlier discernment that non-contemporaneous elements survive in a permutation of distinct modes of production. This defies a model of neatly legislated historical epochs, and reinforces the complexity of history as lived praxis. Seizing on this, I evaluate how non-simultaneity is conceptualised respectively in Althusserian and Gramscian theories.

Despite disagreements, there are points of contact between these orientations, specifically in their accounts of ideology, conception of continuities between the ideological and political vectors of hegemony, and the treatment of time as a sociopolitical concept. Additionally, the Althusserian theory of transition provides a backdrop for the Gramscian theory of hegemony, pertaining to politics as a struggle to bridge temporal gaps. The thematic focus prioritises coherence over chronology. Following a critical exposé, the purported discord between Althusser and Gramsci will be scrutinised, proposing that 'structural' and 'historicist' accounts of transition can be reconciled to the benefit of both. The notion of multiple temporalities is a point of convergence, considering the high regard, from distinct angles, for the role of the political as a mediator of social transition.

A note on the progression from the previous chapter, with a focus on alienation as it pertains to transition, and the current chapter, where Althusser's theories are consulted, is in order. Althusser (2005: 32) argued that in *The German Ideology*, we can see a relentless repudiation of Hegelian concepts, particular those of species-being, alienation and its supersession, all of which have comprised rudiments of a theory of transition I have sketched thus far. This notorious 'break' between the young and the mature Marx tends to be considered as Althusser's key contribution to Marxist philosophy. Based on these, it may appear inconsistent to entertain Althusserian theory alongside an account of transition that uses these concepts. Nevertheless, there is a strong case to synthesise Althusser and Balibar's theories on temporal lag with the holistic approach to Marx's philosophy in the previous chapter.

Althusser (ibid: 78) rightly identifies a 'change of elements' in Marx's thought, in the sense of a migration away from the Hegelian mysticism of the Idea leading history to its teleological endpoint, and towards political economy. Even so, the notion of productive essentialism, a theoretical stance owing much to Hegel's species-being, finds expressions in both the young and the mature Marx, up to and including *Capital*, where the Hegelian vocabulary is absent, but this productive capacity figures in Marx's descriptions of exploitation. For this reason, Althusser appears to make a clear-cut distinction between the phases of Marx's theoretical journey, from a purely philosophical left Hegelianism to political economy, whereas these inclinations can be glimpsed in every stage, and take on a potent historical materialist synthesis that redresses the shortcomings of its parts. In addition, as this analysis aims to trace the theme of transition in its various incarnations in classical and Western Marxist theory, a complete exposition and comparative analysis of each thinker invoked here is beyond the scope of analysis. Nor should there be an expectation of seamless porosity among each of these thinkers' entire theoretical corpuses, as my goal here is to marshal the most useful elements from their theories to build a temporal theory of transition.

1   Expressive Totality to Ruptural Unity: Althusser Reading Marx

Althusser (2005: 39) asserted that the hallmark of Marxism is in accounting for itself historically, setting forth a theoretical level autonomous from the historical moment. As Pfaller (2015: 32) notes, one of Althusser's 'best tricks' was to grasp a feature of ideology as the illusion of 'fullness'. Not only does it paper over the cracks between the lived experience and objective social relations, it also congeals dominant relations within its conceptual schema. The dominant ideology positions itself as the parameter of the 'outdated' and the 'utopian' as an outcome of its function of reproducing dominant social relations. This is how, for instance, the proletariat as a historically constituted class becomes an atomised aggregation of participants in the market as sellers of labour-power, freely and rationally considering their most optimal bidder among fellow specimens of *homo economicus*. This 'fullness' stems from the subsumption of ideology within the social formation as a rationalising mechanism. Ideology interpellates between the individual and their subjectivity; it positions people in categories, such as the assignment of a name, citizenship, induction into the Church, and as Butler (1990) argues, identification with 'core' genders (Althusser, 1970: 11). Social existence is inextricably bound in ideological garb.

The closed 'fullness' of ideology belies its material underpinnings which historical materialism can expose. Furthermore, the 'fullness' represents an overdetermined 'void', a point where discrete levels of social reproduction do not align, and subjective relations to the world register an appearance of foreignness. This has important implications for the question of emancipation, since the smooth plateau of ideology is riddled with real historical discrepancies.

This contradictory unity of society cannot be seen from a viewpoint of expressive totality, which postulates an imminently ensconced and transcendent 'essence' within society (Althusser, 2015a: 44). This is a residual Hegelian notion, coupled with an idea of transitive causality wherein the essence emanates unidirectionally across all parts of society. As such, the effectivity of the whole on the parts, along with the differential effectivity among the parts, is effaced in an ideologically cemented unity.

Althusser (2015b: 623–624) maintained that the social totality was stratified along real fault lines, while remaining steadfastly committed to the totality of a 'structure in dominance'. Furthermore, determination in the last instance of the mode of production anchored the effectivity of discrete levels, and Althusser (2005: 201–202) could fend off criticism on this level as such:

> So to claim that this unity is not and cannot be the unity of a simple, original and universal essence is not, as those who dream of that ideological concept foreign to Marxism, 'monism', think, to sacrifice unity on the altar of 'pluralism' – it is to claim something quite different: that the unity discussed by Marxism is *the unity of the complexity itself*, that

the mode of organization and articulation of the complexity is precisely what constitutes its unity. It is to claim that *the complex whole has the unity of a structure articulated in dominance.*

As the 'lonely hour of the last instance never comes', processes of class struggle are overdetermined by their ideological cover up (Althusser, 2005: 113). This does not jeopardize the ontological primacy of the relations of production over ideology, but suggests that 'ideology' is not simply a smokescreen around blunt exploitation. The base and superstructure are conceptually divided yet empirically co-constitutive. Althusser (2014: 236–245) emphasizes that the base-superstructure topology is 'metaphorical' since it conceptually separates moments of capitalist reproduction. While the relations of production are reproduced through processes of production and distribution, they are also immediately secured in the superstructure of law/state and ideology (Althusser, 2014: 779).

Immediacy is the operative concept here, as this conception of ideology has a materiality. Ideological processes are embedded in the relations of production, from the legal contract binding labour-power to a wage to the culturally transmitted norms of the working day. Hence, exploitation cannot simply be explained by a specific ill will on the part of the exploiter, or a conscious submission of the exploited; all actors involved act per their own beliefs and habits, and exploitation emerges as their combination. In fact, ideology as 'false consciousness', or a mere subjective inversion of the objective asymmetry in relations of production, wrongly presupposes a 'correct consciousness' that realigns what is objectively taking place with its subjective perception. On a strategic level, this can lead to a crude vanguardism of 'consciousness-raising'. The 'false consciousness' is integral to one's position within the mode of production, and more importantly, it is idealistic to envisage being able to sift through ideology to arrive at an uncontaminated kernel, to then disseminate this as the objective truth. In this sense, Althusser topples the Church and Party alike from a vantage point of privileged access to the truth by reiterating the ideological instantiation of all moments of social reproduction.

Ideology is not merely, or even primarily, a subjective conviction, although this is part of its materiality. The practices and rituals governing an ideological disposition also constitute the ideology. This reinforces the point that ideology cannot be removed like a blindfold. Althusser (2014: 605) quotes Pascal's words '[k]neel down, move your lips in prayer, and you will believe', demonstrating the fallacy of an ideological meta-social vacuum, going so far as to claim that subjective convictions are identical with their instantiations; one prays because they believe, but also believes because they pray.

A pertinent example can also be found in Althusser's (1992) autobiography, written in the 1980s after he was confined to an asylum following his tragic murder of his wife. Here Althusser recounts the events that shaped his personality and character (observing that contrary to his previous claim that education was the supreme ideological apparatus, the place of pride really belongs to the family), intertwining some of the imagined events with the externally observable reality. Following one description of an event which he was confident to have witnessed, but turned out to be a figment of the imagination, Althusser remarks that he remains loyal to 'the facts' throughout his account, with an essential caveat: 'I intend to stick closely to the facts throughout this succession of memories by association; but hallucinations are also facts'. This is not a wholesale relativisation of reality, but a recognition of its temporal fragmentation. It is misleading to try to arrive at the essential, since this is implicated in the inessential, such that effects are at least spectrally imminent in their causes (*e.g.*, acute schizophrenia and bipolar disorder, and (self-)destructiveness). There is also a temporal inversion to be gleaned from this self-deprecating autobiography. Elliott (1987: 330) calls this work a 're-writing of a life through the prism of its wreckage', which may be true but fails to fully capture the dialectic between subjective reflections and objective processes. At any point, one has a notion of the past that maintains an 'official' narrative and benchmark for current activity, which can be as suggestive as the lived experience, at times replacing or redefining it. This phenomenon extends from personal reflections to political attitudes. Althusser (2014: 607) concedes that there are various modalities of the 'materiality' of ideology, such as those of the inner conviction and its enactment. However, the fact remains that a dualism of naked exploitation and ideological veil, or a dormancy and an 'awakening', are inappropriate extensions of the topological base and superstructure metaphor to the complex unity of the social formation. In other words, the base/superstructure division is methodologically expedient, but cannot be assumed to be ontologically real, a point echoed in Gramsci's theory of hegemony.

The outcome of this approach to ideology is the permanent displacement of 'false consciousness' as the imaginary inversion of concrete processes of exploitation, such as the unfounded belief in upward social mobility and equality of opportunity. Althusser (2014: 591–598, 801–802) refers to the young Marx to tease out this negative view of ideology, where it is a 'pure illusion', a residual reflection, or lifeless by-product, of the social reality. Contrarily, Althusser argues that the stark conditions of existence are evasive, since accessing them entails working through ideological constructs. Therefore, ideology is the 'individuals' imaginary relation to the real relations in which they live' (Althusser, 2014: 597). This relation is in turn shaped and maintained by factors outside the purview of ideology, the mode of production being determinant in the final analysis. Thus, Althusser (2014: 576) advances the thesis 'ideology has no history ... *of its own*'. Its survival or eradication is predicated within the political and economic realms of social existence. Seemingly superannuated worldviews, such as white supremacism or Islamic fundamentalism, cannot only persist but prosper, despite their feeble internal consistency, as long as their existence sustains certain patterns of social relations. On a brighter note, the hailing of individuals to their ideologically interpellated posts may be challenged through the same ideological apparatuses. Hence, structural imperatives must be reinforced at every moment of social reproduction.

The theoretical consequence of this relativisation and autonomisation of ideology can be explained more clearly with reference to Lenin's (1977: 21) quip that Marxism 'is omnipotent because it is true'. Here Lenin suggests that the Marxist outlook is superior because it identifies an Archimedean point on the central knots of capitalist society, giving its practitioner the capacity to transform it. Historical materialism cannot be reduced to a political ideology, due to its grounding in objective production processes, but this does not directly give it a political omnipotence. The historical manifestations of Marxism as a political force are irreducibly ideological for the afore-discussed reasons. Here, the word 'ideological' is not used in the pejorative sense as commonly (mis)understood, but as an organic secretion of the social formation. Secondly, ideology, encompassing politics, is not a direct conveyor of the truthful explanatory power of Marxism. It is more accurate to consider this relationship between theoretical accuracy and political power as one of translation and refraction, such that something of each is lost or distorted when expressed in terms of the other. Consequently, while Marxism has a credible claim to truthfulness, its political viability is always subject to contestation, to the point that it can be socially constructed and maintained as an inferior factor in social change by dominant patterns of social relations. Still, such a marginalisation is not the same as absence. Hence, the argument here is not that Marxism loses relevance at times of a lull in social struggle, but that it is not politically omnipotent as a straightforward function of its theoretical rigour.

In Althusser's (2015a: 77–78) view, ideological misrecognition takes place as a perception of coherence, where theory 'sounds hollow' to the attentive ear. In other words, where there is an omission, a sense of things not adding up, we can expect to find this 'consecrated as a non-omission'. Conversely, scientific practice, or Marxism, is compelled to explore its shortcomings precisely to maintain its rigor, and avoid a misleading 'fullness'. Any scientific paradigm maintains itself by fixating on the blind spots that it cannot adequately address with its conceptual repository. In this sense, transition, by dint of the fact that it signifies a lacuna for historical materialism, is also a focal point of its rejuvenation as a sociologically rigorous study of historically constituted social transformations. In the same vein, Balibar (2007: 1–13, 17–19) argues that Marxism is constitutionally incomplete due to its historical grounding. Having been incubated in the confines of left Hegelianism, Marxism looked to the political economy. This is where the Hegelian heritage 'sounded hollow', and Marxism emerged as a robust methodology through its 'escape' towards political economy, and even further into productive activity.

A Marxist reading of Marx, or a 'symptomatic' reading, focuses on his conceptual discrepancies, disputing illusions of fullness. Reading Marx in such a manner situates him as the living, fallible person, into the broad field of historical materialism. Crucially, Althusser's (2005: 78) reading identifies a 'change of elements' where unlike, say, Feuerbach, Marx abandons the Hegelian terrain, and turns to political economy, where productive activity is key to a critique of capitalism as well as a historically reflexive theory of how societies evolve and transform. Althusser's ambition, from this standpoint, does not aim to un- or re-cover an 'essence' (1978: 332–333, 374). Such an attempt would be futile, as the 'orthodox' Marxism of Marx, Engels and Lenin had incorporated various strands of thought from the beginning. Rather than excavate a pristine Marxism in the wake of the 'dogmatist night', Althusser (2005: 31; 2015a: 87–90) aimed to produce scientific knowledge through theoretical practice.

As Elliot (1987: 51–54) observes, a 'detour of theory' was essential to avoid justifying or refuting Marx's political positions from his theory, much less those of the continental communist parties (Althusser, 2005:160). The strident antihumanism of Althusser should be considered within the context of de-Stalinization and ensuing controversies around the Soviet Union, and about the paths to revolution in various contexts, particularly following the violent suppression of the Hungarian revolt of 1956 and the appeal of Maoism. For the global communist movement, the 1950s were a period of euphoric confidence as well. The Soviet Union had emerged as a victor of World War II, and the second global economic and military powerhouse. China had begun its own socialist construction, while the western left enjoyed remarkable prestige following the war, building on the legacy of resistance against Nazism, and making significant electoral gains. There was also a 'thaw' in the Cold War, where cultural diplomacy between the two camps was at a high, and Khrushchev embraced a period of 'peaceful coexistence' with the capitalist bloc.

The Communist Party of the Soviet Union had declared that class struggle was resolved, and socialism had been achieved. Henceforth, the state was no longer a class state, but one of the whole people, emblematised in the slogan 'Everything for man, and respect for the legality and dignity of the person'

(Harnecker, 1994: 325–326). This belied a retention of the Stalinist doctrine of 'socialism in one country', as the purported achievement of a classless society within the confines of a single state. Meanwhile, the communist parties of France and Italy had denounced the goal of an eventual overthrow of the capitalist state, and participated in the post-war construction of liberal democracies, toeing the line of the Soviet Union (Elliott, 1987: 10–11). Althusser (1976a: 149) problematised this fading of class struggle in theoretical and political discourse, criticising the complacency of a mechanical historical process that centralised the economy or humanity in its incarnations, disparagingly referring to socialist humanism as 'bogus 'Marxist' philosophizing on man'.

This contextualisation is fairer to Althusser, as he also wrote that he was aware of the controversy of positing anti-humanism, and penned his critiques with a reluctant mindset (cf. Timur, 2007: 16). Nevertheless, the rise of humanism caused a theoretical slippage that needed to be addressed. The open critique of Stalin, for instance, was inaugurated with Khrushchev's denunciation of the 'cult of personality'. Althusser (1976b: 78–93; Gerratana, 1977) finds this to be based on premises alien to historical materialism, for it emphasises personal failings over structural causes for the excesses of this period. The retrospective Soviet criticism of the 'abuses' and 'errors' of the Stalin period was thus erroneously presented as closure. To the contrary, Stalin's once collaborators and accessories undertook the process at the expense of a wider social reconciliation, and, as Deutscher (1967: 102) argues, 'having revealed the huge skeleton in their cupboard, at once slammed the door on it and would say no more'. The official de-Stalinisation maintained the premise of history as teleology, whereas Althusser's concern was to formulate it as a process without a subject. He believed that Marxist-Leninist theses possessed the theoretical acumen to prevent a relapse into the economic determinism of the Second International, as well as humanism as its subjectivist mirror image. In this sense, Stalin's writings on dialectical and historical materialism assumed an evolution towards classless society, not unlike social democracy. In addition, both social democracy and Soviet socialism relegated class struggle to the background, the former announcing the inevitable arrival of socialism through reform, and the latter its completion. In such a conjuncture, a non-determinist critique of humanism addresses an omission, aiding the revitalisation of historical materialism. Focusing where the theory is underdeveloped, to prevent a glossing over in the manner of references to a 'cult of personality', is more important to Althusser than an aversion to humanism *per se*.

In the first lines of the essay *Marxism and Humanism*, Althusser (2005: 221) clarifies that, 'in fact, the objective of the revolutionary struggle has always been the end of exploitation and hence the liberation of man'. Althusser does not deny the role of humans in history, reiterating that socialism is a process of human self-construction. Rather, the point is that a dynamic of class struggle is inherent to transition. What is challenged, as Harnecker (1994: 334) maintains, is the view that people are subjects *of* history, on whose will history depends. On the contrary, Althusser (2007: 74–79) claims, it is a hollow platitude to suggest that men make history, as it is unclear what the word *make* is referring to; is history made the same way a carpenter makes a table, for instance? This would mean that the raw material of history can be freely manipulated with a sufficient level of expertise, positing the subject – Humanity – with a transcendental power over the object – an infinitely malleable History -. This would mean that while people are steeped in historical reality, they can step outside of it. Althusser (2007: 99) also mentions that this is agreeable to anyone regardless of their class, and lacks a political sting. In sum, it is more reasonable to see humans as subjects *in* history. History may take a specific direction depending on conscious human action, yet there are also impersonal forces at play. As Althusser has asserted the due importance of the 'motor' of history generated by class relations, his thinly veiled polemics against the Communist Party of France on the alleged classless 'socialism' in the Soviet Union, coupled with the line of 'peaceful coexistence' which effaced class struggle, come more clearly to the fore than a bizarre fetishism of structure, the staple charge against him. As Molina (1977: 243–244) argues, Althusser's approach is an 'a-humanism' rather than anti-humanism.

That said, there is a vexingly static symmetry to a fully balanced account of men and history. 'People are trapped in history and history is trapped in them', African-American writer James Baldwin (1984: 160) wrote of the legacy of race relations in the US. While this encapsulates the dialectical relation between the pre-given and the agency, particularly the persistence of prejudice, alone it falls short of explaining how historical change and transitions come about. This symmetry appears unidimensional and lacks a temporal axis, and gives a misleadingly stable impression. The temporal contradictions within and between levels of social practice, on the other hand, complicate a teleological view of history. Perceiving the political blind alleys of this approach, Althusser paradoxically distanced himself from politics, and focused on theory as a domain irreducible to quotidian manoeuvring. This was precisely intended to gain a sharper political grasp. The political trap of reducing theory to tactical navigation is indicative of Althusser's view of the role of Marxist theory within the social formation as a stratified yet connected terrain. Here it is pertinent to consider the contemporary stratification of discrete practices throughout Althusser's work.

In short, Althusser criticises humanism for effacing class struggle (2014: 662). Ideology interpellates individuals, pressing them into categories overdetermined by relations of production. This permanently decentres the historical subjectivity of humanity from Marxist theory. In keeping with this, humanism also attests to interpellation. Althusser seizes on this point to excoriate the notion of expressive totality. This superficial totality lost sight of the underlying contradictions that propel historical change, and crucially, the 'expressive' totality presupposed a temporal cohesion across the social formation: the 'spirit of the times', as it were, was inscribed in every aspect of a historical cross-section (Althusser, 2015b: 583). Thus, in a Hegelian manner, the notion of a closed teleology guided by a Subject was resuscitated and placed at the core of communist politics. This exemplifies the illusory 'completeness' of ideology. Instead, Althusser contends, the social formation is a historically contingent assemblage beyond the agency of specific actors.

In earlier writings, Althusser (1997: 153) had grappled with the relationship between the historical background and sociopolitical conjuncture in these terms:

> But since history is not over, there is no eternal transcendental logic, but rather, at every instant, an articulated historical structure which dominates the world in the manner of an *a priori*, and conditions it. The reality of history resides, from this standpoint, in the dialectical nature of the structure that conditions events, but is also transformed by them in its turn.

Here Althusser charges his contemporaries of espousing an atemporal worldview by substituting theory for political consciousness, whereas real history tampers with both. The 'social formation' is formulated more precisely, but remains broad enough to cover all instances of social reproduction, in subsequent writings (Althusser, 2015a: 111). Now, the topology appears in sharper contrast where the subterranean determinations of the economy manifest themselves in and through the legal-political and ideological structures. This point anticipates a discord between the discrete levels of practice.

In Althusser's (2005: 166) schema, social practice occurs along economic, political, ideological and theoretical lines, the connecting thread being the process (not the agent) of production:

> By *practice* in general I shall mean any process of *transformation* of a determinate given raw material into a determinate product, a

transformation effected by a determinate human labour, using a determinate means (of 'production'). In any practice thus conceived, the *determinant* moment (or element) is neither the raw material nor the product, but the practice in the narrow sense: the moment of the *labour of transformation* itself, which sets to work, in a specific structure, men, means and a technical method of utilizing the means.

Production has to remain at the core of Althusser's conceptualization of society, if he is to avoid a determinative pluralism of discrete layers of social practice.

Having jettisoned expressive totality, Althusser needs to account for the contemporaneous unity of the social formation. Maintaining that the disparate levels cannot be reduced to one another, he retains the thesis that the mode of production effectively demarcates ideological and political life, in terms of dispositions of perceiving the world and the nature of political authority. Notwithstanding, while containing traces of each other, these can and do follow autonomous trajectories: seemingly outdated views can gain traction based on the material interests of the powerful, while egalitarian initiatives can suspend the wage-labour and capital relation. In this sense, dispensing with an aggregative and linear conception of time allows for a more sophisticated grasp of capitalist society and its inherent contradictions. Contrarily, cross sections of historical moments furnish a blurred vision of intertwined and uneven temporalities. Thus, Hegelian and empiricist notions of historical time converge, because they take given cross sections to be expressive of a false sense of 'unity' in the moment. Once temporal differentiation is factored in, such unity sounds hollow (Althusser, 2015a). In *Reading Capital* (Althusser and Balibar 1970: 99), the break from these assumptions is accentuated in the following lines:

> It is no longer possible to think the process of the development of the different levels of the whole *in the same historical time*. Each of these different 'levels' does not have the same type of historical existence. On the contrary, we have to assign to each level *a peculiar time*, relatively autonomous and hence relatively independent, even in its dependence, of the 'times' of the other levels.

In Althusser's account of the social formation, it appears hard to see where a ruptural break could emanate from if all levels of social reality are complicit in inhibiting transgression. To account for transition, Althusser (2005: 211) proposes that a unique 'fusion' of practice along multiple levels, and not just the revolutionary intervention, culminates in a 'ruptural unity'. The principle contradiction becomes 'explosive' at a point when real contradictions condense around it. This fusion point, which becomes the weakest link to be severed, is the locus of a revolutionary diffusion. Referring to the October Revolution, Althusser (2005: 97) lauds Lenin for recognising that Russia was simultaneously behind other European countries while at its historical peak, and the combination of these positions enabled a Bolshevik takeover that could capture political power at the helm of a small yet militant working class. While there is cogency to Althusser's visualization of transition, he surmises himself when he remarks, in the same work, that the 'specific effectivity' between the different structures fastening together the social formation remains to be elaborated (2005: 131). For without explaining how different temporalities along ideological, political and economic practices give rise to windows of opportunity, Althusser has simply come up with a historical explanation after the event, and failed to render a regional theory of transition within the general theory of historical materialism. For this, it is necessary to turn to Balibar and his extension of Althusser's problematic to transition.

2   Temporal Dislocation: Balibar Reading Althusser

Balibar works within the premises set out by Althusser, and expands on the 'synchronic' study of the self-contemporaneous mode of production, alongside a diachronic reality of the intertwined temporalities of varied modes of production. As Chambers (2011: 198) puts it, our encounter with time reveals to us that it is out of joint, and these lapses show that time is not a solely objective phenomenon but a political concept. As Marx had anticipated, the social formation is characterised by a mode of production that domineers social practice at the expense of others, and gives them their colouring. This is elaborated more explicitly by Balibar in *Reading Capital*, an exercise of reading Marx with a view to identifying his hermeneutics, where history itself is not a temporality, but the subject matter of historical materialism.

Surplus-extraction, the key to the survival of capitalism, is constantly pieced together after the event, though its historical realization varies widely, depending on the effectivities of different practices. The conceptual workings of capitalism, taken in a purely economic sense, do not imply its inherent instability (Balibar, 2015: 911). The drive to reduce the worker to a cog in the machine does not implicate an eventual collapse, within the economic conceptual matrix. Balibar contends that ruptural moments come about when political contestation coincides with economic trauma, revealing the limits of capitalism in lived praxis. This can also be considered as a settling of accounts with the Hegelian legacy of the principle of quantity and quality, where a quantitative aggregation spills over into a qualitative break. However, since there is no guarantee of a qualitative rupture at the end of a quantitative increase, Balibar (2015: 866–873) instead stresses the importance of limit cases that suggest 'elements for a theory of transition'. The temporality of the economy may stagnate and drag behind innovations in political and ideological life (or *vice versa*). Broaching the coexistence of modes of production was a political intervention into the Stalinist ossification of Marxism, and the regressive tendencies of de-Stalinization that led to an identification of the ends of global left movements with those of the Soviet state.

Expanding on Althusser's theoretical enterprise, Balibar's account of transition articulates an ensemble of discrete levels of social reproduction out of sync with each other. Balibar contends that the articulation of social relations reveals as much as it conceals; processes of social reproduction attest to the underlying relations of production, but this is not *ipso facto* an indicator of social struggle. Rather, Balibar expounds on a generic account of capitalism and its ontological tendency towards crises, but goes on to show that only at moments of overlap between the class struggle and economic trauma is it possible to account for a transition beyond capitalism. This implies that while the empirical study of social life is a fruitful source for theoretical attenuation, a level of abstraction is required in terms of a theoretical grounding on the presuppositions of the mode of production (Balibar, 2015: 881).

History as lived praxis, Balibar (2015: 912–932) explains, progresses along a strained unity of ideological, political and economic levels. These involve irreducibly distinct raw materials and means of production. Crucially, the trajectory of historical change is nevertheless skewed according to the overdetermination of the mode of production, even, or especially, when it least appears to be salient and assigns effectivities to political or ideological processes. A historical materialist grounding in the changes in the mode of production is crucial for Balibar to avoid irreversibly detaching politics and ideology from social determinants. Yet, this description is also helpful in debunking a crude epiphenomenalism, namely in the monadic perception that every aspect of social reality is a direct outgrowth of relations of production. Alberto Toscano (2014: 765), who has provided an effective sketch of a 'deprogrammed' transitional theory, takes a cue from Balibar's staggered schema as an effective reagent of legislated transition. Toscano (ibid) describes the analytical separation of these layers as follows: The economic level refers to the structural change in the mode of production and the regime of surplus extraction; the political, to the transformation of the nature of state power; and the ideological, to the (counter)hegemonic confrontation of the worldviews of the preceding epoch. Echoing Althusser's contention that ideology 'has no history', Balibar (1977: 45) suggests that the prevalent mode of production does not necessarily correspond to the political regime, levelling a criticism against the line of the Communist Party of France that political despotism will be dispelled once the forces of production have reached socialist standards. Instead, as Toscano's (2014: 772) injunction suggests, transition needs to be taken up as a problem on its own right, and the imagination of a self-identical present dispelled.

The problematic of history then takes the form of a 'diachrony' between societies where different structures of production prevail. These in turn involve discrete temporal logics and rhythms, without a one-to-one correspondence with their political history. Balibar discusses this diachrony with respect to the differential time-frames and temporal lag across societies. This is conceived as the dislocation, or *décalage*, between the political, economic and ideological practices and their interplay during moments of transition. This concept of lag is also significant for the denunciation of positivism, since *décalage* denotes the discrepancy between the conceptual construct and the real object under study, whereas positivists had taken their identity for granted (Brewster, 1969: 312).

This perspective helps consider the historical trajectories of those countries that did not experience a transition to capitalism organically – *i.e.* the majority -, or due to internal dynamics, but experienced capitalist social structuration through external pressures. In contexts of precapitalist modes of production, the interaction with an inherently expansive system of accumulation traumatizes the local community and creates a stunted development of capitalism with precapitalist elements grafted onto it. While the mode of production is a conceptual sketch, the social formation historically articulates relations and means of production. In this respect, the French Revolution may have been an exceptional example of feudalism being entirely dismantled through social revolution and war. But ever since, regimes in the majority world – Turkey being an example – experienced a more complicated and incomplete transition to capitalism where elements of the *ancien régime* took on contemporary forms and became part of the ruling class. Another example can be found in the forced social restructuring of Ireland, marking a shift from military conquest to a conscious project of expropriation and transformation of social relations in a capitalist direction. Ellen Wood (2002: 154) maintains that the dispossession and impoverishment of masses and the repopulation of agrarian areas with English and Scottish settlers had explicit goals of introducing commercial competition and the instant eradication of precapitalist relations, thereby rendering Ireland more exploitable for the metropolitan centre.

Two observations can be made from these cursory examples. The first one is prompted by Marx's (2009: 3) earlier reflection that 'the social revolution of the nineteenth century cannot take its poetry from the past but only from the future', where he maintained that unlike the bourgeoisie, whose economic institutions had been developed prior to the seizure of power, the working class had to build its corresponding mode of production following the said seizure. In both examples, however, capitalism is not an imperative, latently or otherwise, as an imminent impulse. Rather, it is a result of integration in the globally expanding circuit of commodity production spurred by the Industrial Revolution. This indicates a temporal differentiation from Marx's context, *even though* these events were taking place at similar timescales. While the western European timeline saw the emergence of a distinct class that gradually shadowed others, this class was glaringly absent in other contexts – including Ireland -, where it was fostered by political initiative, complicating the narrative of capitalism emanating from Europe towards other shores, and remaking these anachronistic areas in its own image.

Gilbert Achcar (2013: 68–102) makes the insightful observation that insofar as he considered the rest of the world as being shaped according to the trajectory of western European capitalism, Marx is open to an imputation of Eurocentrism in an 'epistemic' capacity. Such epistemic Eurocentrism can be seen in the monolithic understanding of the temporal dynamic of capital accumulation, which had convulsed Europe, imposing itself on different geographies, threatening and distorting native frames of temporality. On the other hand, Marx was increasingly attuned to the differential successions of modes of production in his writings on the margins of Europe, namely Ireland and Russia. Furthermore, considered in totality, the political ambition traversing Marx's expositions of economic asymmetries exacerbated by imperialism evinces a desire to obliterate divides, and shed light on paths to emancipation in all societies, above all those in the majority world. This is exemplified through the corpus of his more journalistic and agitational writings, but also in *Capital*, where Marx (1990: 915) locates a racist and colonial *modus operandi* at the originary moments of accumulation:

> The discovery of gold and silver in America, the extirpation, enslavement and entombment in mines of the indigenous population of that continent, the beginnings of the conquest and plunder of India, and the conversion of Africa into a preserve for the commercial hunting of blackskins, are all things which characterize the dawn of the era of capitalist

production. These idyllic proceedings are the chief moments of primitive accumulation.

The tension between the formal imposition of capitalism and real sociocultural contexts suggests that Marx was reaching for a temporal differentiation not yet explicitly theorised, with shocks compelling the political vector of social reproduction to adapt to exogenous developments, creating hybridised social formations. This interplay of the political and economic moments suggests a further, second observation. In the case of Turkey, those that appropriated the social wealth according to precapitalist modes of production refashioned their enterprises to dovetail with the national capitalist economy (Duzgun, 2019). As a result, landlords and feudal leaders joined the ruling class with capital assets of their own. In the case of Ireland, however, the forced social restructuration from the metropolis went in the other direction, uprooting precapitalist arrangements and replacing them with auxiliary proto-capitalist settlers. Building on the blurring of the political and economic moments' prevalence in the introduction of capitalism, this also suggests a directional incertitude to the path of capitalist development. It can supplant existing social arrangements, but also assimilate them in ways that they retain a non-capitalist character and benefit from the proceeds of capital accumulation.

Capitalist development, once set in motion, was periodically restricted to maintain imperial hegemony. Through a framework of temporality, uneven and combined development – to borrow a Trotskyite turn of phrase – involves a temporal lag within and across societies, rendering transition more in need of theorization. In keeping with this variegated historical development of capitalism, Balibar distinguishes the routes of the labourer's separation from the means of production, expressing the need to explain moments of reproduction at every step. Another fold in the temporal latticework of the social formation lies in the potentials of the supersession of the dominant mode of production. Capitalist social relations prevail in tandem with non-capitalist ones, and this does not hinder, but accentuates, their domination. However, postcapitalist impulses may also challenge this dominance, introducing rival temporalities to contend with. In this sense, the progress of capitalist development is also a history of a non-economic prevention of its destructuration towards postcapitalist social relations.

Before delving into Balibar's theory of transition, it is pertinent to define temporal lag in the various ways it has been approached here. Based on the preceding discussion of Althusserian theory, temporal lag refers to the discrepancies among the multiple times in social life. It can be anatomised on three connected scales, beginning from the broadest: the coexistence of plural modes of production; the particular discrepancies between economic, political and ideological levels of social reproduction; and finally, the internal discrepancies within these levels.[1] I shall take these up in turn and briefly elaborate on their connections below.

The large-scale temporal lag is the discrepancy along times across historical geographies. This could refer to the dissonance – without marking a normative preference – between capitalist Western European countries and their still predominantly pre-capitalist peripheries (Wood, 2002). Or, this could denote a longitudinal shift, such as the transitional processes from feudal to capitalist domination within the limited domains of particular countries and regions (Duzgun, 2019). The object of inquiry at this scale is therefore the dominant mode of production within societies, considering how production occurs on the whole, and how the non-dominant modes of production come into conflict or synergise with the one in dominance.

The intermediary scale of temporal lag focuses on the disparate levels of social reproduction and their relatively autonomous interactions within a given society. As the focus of the theory of transition here, this temporal lag scales down the broader perspective of modes of production, which is represented by the economic level of social reproduction, flanked by the out-of-joint temporal rhythms of politics and ideology. While the dominant mode of production traverses society, it is not immediately at work at every turn, a notion captured in its 'overdetermination' and assignment of specific effectivities (Althusser, 2005). However, within Balibar's (2015) tripartite heuristic delineation, the 'economy', comprising of the direct instantiations of productive activity and ontologically present in the other levels, is taken here as a privileged stand-in for the mode of production which was the unit of analysis in the broader scale of temporal lag.

Further decreasing the size of the scale, temporal lag is manifested in the internal fissures among times within economic, political and ideological levels. This can be explained through the lack of direct correspondence between the analytic categories of these levels and their complex ontological articulation, which partially distils the range of historical inheritance of each level into a strained unity, such that kernels of future modes of production can manifest in the economic level, or direct local assemblies can take some political

---

1 The three scales indicated here need not be exhaustive, as they may be multiplied in each direction (perhaps adding a species-wide natural/biological scale above the mode of production, and even a cosmic scale beyond that, or the scale of the individual biography at the opposite end, are some possibilities).

decision-making processes under control, without each of these subsuming the dominant temporal rhythms of their respective levels.

In this respect, maintaining the *temporal* lag rather than mere dissonance enables a visualisation of the temporal pulls exerted by the future and the past on the socially constituted present. This is also helpful to counteract a straightforwardly linear notion of historical time, while avoiding a sheer indeterminacy to its progression. Ultimately, the novelty of this temporal dimension essentially lies in its capacity to make the 'unity' of the present sound hollow, paving the way for an engagement with transition.

Balibar (2015: 270) substantiates his theory of transition with the postulate of a 'transitional mode of production', distinguished by the non-correspondence between the forces and relations of production. He argues that production may be organised along lines that do not meet the exigencies of surplus-appropriation, to the extent that the torsion re-adjusts the forces of production. Here Balibar (ibid: 297) refers to the example of manufacturing as a transitional moment between feudalism and capitalism where the labourer, although detached from feudal ties, had been only *formally* subsumed under capital. The dislocation was ended with *real* subsumption when the yoke of surplus-expropriation was placed on labour-power. The issue with this concept is that it appears to reintroduce the necessity of quantity spilling over into quality that had been shunned beforehand. Otherwise the enigmatic gap between the non-transitional and transitional modes of production remains theoretically inaccessible, and only real historical illustrations can bring to light the outcomes of interlacing temporalities. This does not discredit Balibar's critique of evolutionism, however, since the levels of practice set out can explain how at some moments transition is crystallised, and at others dispelled by temporal strains between political revolution and economic stagnation. Furthermore, the disaggregation of the expressive unity of the essential section dissipates guarantees of the implosion of capitalism, along with assumptions of singular fetters (scarcity, private property *etc.*) that stand in the way of socialism. This thereby opens a void where once inevitability stood, and reasserts the decisiveness of class struggle.

Balibar's temporal lag postulates layers among and within the political, the economic and the ideological. These are present at every step, the difference being one of emphasis rather than opposition. To recall, the political line of reproduction refers to the nature of state power. Arguably, many other locales of social relations can be construed as 'political', particularly those involving power, such as gender and racial divides. However, the lack of strict boundaries between the political and the ideological can expand the political to include what might be categorised as 'ideological'. Since ideology contains a multitude of social practices, norms and beliefs, it is coincident with the turns of political reproduction. This infuses areas of social life not traditionally identified with political locales with an importance that bears on the nature of state power. For instance, campaigns for Wages for Housework, or Universal Basic Services, all address social grievances rooted outside of the formal political ambit, but by transforming the relationship between the citizen and the state, they carry immediate political relevance. Conversely, formal political life, involving legislative, executive, and judicial functions, can be situated within the grounds of ideology, attenuating its autonomy from the social formation as the condensation of its ideological inclinations, as well as forming a more solid redoubt flanking the key legal and economic institutions upholding capitalism. As the 'lonely hour' of the economy never comes, its overdetermination traverses the social formation, assigning a specific effectivity to the various spheres of reproduction, all the while working in the background in the ideologically imbued guise of a neutral, ahistorical state of affairs (*e.g.*, the standard work week, while a historical novelty, is entrenched in the social psyche as a permanent fixture).

Having outlined the relations of co-constitution within the discrete levels of the social formation, it is also necessary to return to Balibar's suggestion of a rift between the forces and relations of production. This had been an analytical move preparing the ground for the argument of a 'transitional' mode of production. Balibar alludes to an internal differentiation in the economic level, suggesting that these categories, while metaphorical, are subject to intrinsic tension and differentiation. In a recent introduction to Althusser, Balibar (2014: xiii) argues that this internal difference carries over into the political in terms of a 'short' and 'long' temporality. This pertains to a difference in the temporalities of the political struggle: a 'short' temporality, that of the class struggles that unfold in the public sphere, with state power at stake; and a 'long' temporality of the class struggles which, riding roughshod over the border between public and private, unfold in the materiality of ideology. This note introduces a twist into the nature of historical change as understood politically, interspersing short-term social struggles with the long-term transformations in the ideological vector. The short-term as used here would designate more narrowly political gains such as the impact of working class movements in industrial legislation, while the longer term refers to the less discernible, but more significant, shifts in norms that can effectuate transitional pressure. Legal changes may not immediately dispel the taken-for-granted ways of doing things, at times stopping short of making a dent in established patterns. However, the short temporality of struggles cascades across the long temporality of the ideological patchwork of enacted social institutions. This is exemplified in myriad struggles from the student movement to the efforts to prevent the privatisation of the NHS. Such struggles can gain traction and achieve a series of concessions, or recede after a brief explosion of discontent. On the surface, such short-term negotiations with capital appear as minor disturbances. Yet, at a more subterranean and long-term temporality, even when an initiative recedes, its participants have an experiential-epistemic gain that impacts their conduct, stripping back some of the ideological scaffolds of capitalism, and vitalising future episodes of short-term struggle. In this way, the two-tiered political temporality envisions distinct temporalities that can overlap to counteract the further encroachment of the logic of capital along social reproduction.

There are significant implications of conceiving political practice as one of binding the loose ends of uneven temporalities, the question being how to devise a strategy that ties advances along all levels in a 'ruptural unity'. This is constituted in the empirical social formation, although it reverberates in the theoretical sphere as well. It is at this level where the Althusserian framework is unclear regarding the nexus between the said theory and the empirical social formation, the temporal attenuation of the political field notwithstanding. Gramsci's concept of hegemony can translate these insights into a more elaborate political theory of transition, and furnish a concept that addresses the left predicament of our time; a caesura of rear-guard defence of existing welfare structures on the one hand, and amorphous and ubiquitous acts of occupations and riots on the other.

3   'Revolution against 'Capital'': Gramsci Reading Marx

As a practitioner of the 'pessimism of the intelligence', the failure of anticipated revolutions in Western Europe cast a shadow over Antonio Gramsci's writings. Such pessimism stemmed from the dismal prospects at the time, following the wreckage of depression and war in the beleaguered lone socialist state. The situation was exacerbated with the fratricidal bloodletting between the communists and social democrats in Germany, which gave way to a surge of reaction in the government, while in Italy the dynamism of the left in the streets and factories was defused through similar factionalism and fascist repression. On the other hand, Gramsci underlines the 'optimism of the will', a recognition of irreducible resilience against overwhelming odds. Even so, the conditions under which Gramsci developed his organic conceptions of Marxism were removed from the October Revolution, both temporally and politically, where a type of realpolitik and pragmatism had set in during the 1930s, with the notable exception of Spain. This context helped to turn Gramsci's attention to the mechanisms of control in stabilised capitalist economies, developing a notion of hegemony that variably applies to transitional movements and processes that neutralise them (Thomas, 2009: 221).

The political moment is implicated in 'the optimism of the will'. As in the October Revolution, a mixture of circumstantial fortune and strategic initiative can capacitate a rupture. The political intervention is not external to the objective situation. Rather, it is a constituent of it, shaping what is taken as possible and probable, also through its absence. The capacity to organise practical reality, and create new opportunities, shows the social character of 'truth' as a situation constructed through power struggle. As Frosini (2015: 2) argues, the truth is not a qualitative judgment, but a quantitative reflection of the political ability to connect interpretation (theory) and organisation (practice). Gramsci complements Marx's problematising of the subjective/objective divide here. According to Marx (1962), the empirical accuracy of the political economists had to do with the overlap between their 'laws' and a historically specific hegemonic project. Similarly, Gramsci's conceptualisation of ideology has an organisational-political character. Its endurance depends on its ability to sustain the subalternity of those deprived of the means to contribute to the mainstream discourse. Capitalist exploitation is tied to bourgeois imposition of a vision of the good society, seeking its acceptance as the 'natural' mode of existence. This also shows how power struggle could relegate the ruler to a subaltern position, where it cannot foster consent and acquiescence. The dominant classes must revise, reproduce or even efface the 'truth', to remain anchored to the present that is solidified as their critique of the past. In this way, hegemonic projects successfully craft a narrative of a linear string of events leading up to their inevitability. From a temporal perspective, bridging the gap between the present and the future of the subaltern classes is tantamount to consigning the capitalist class to the past, and relativizing its self-declared finality. This is linked to the political construction of the truth; a return of history is imbricated with the actuality of transition, and with it, a renegotiation of what is 'sensible', 'radical', or 'outdated'.

Temporal divides vary across geographies, and do not proceed in lockstep. While it is possible to steer public debates in less constraining liberal democracies, this is not easily achieved in repressive contexts, where insurrectionary preparation may more effectively challenge the ruling class. This quandary led Gramsci to reflect on strategy with respect to the differential forms of bourgeois political regimes, dispersing functional readings of the state solely as a bludgeon of the ruling class, and turning to the regional differences in how the ruling class continues to rule, and thus the prospects of its upending. Consequently, socialist strategy should be devised based on local peculiarities.

This would put Gramsci (1971: 240–241) at odds with the universalising formulations of both Trotskyite 'permanent revolution' and the Stalinist notion of 'socialism in one country' (Thomas, 2009: 213–217).

Crucially, Gramsci's categorization of the East and the West, much less geographical than theoretical, aims to capture the reasons behind the success of a frontal assault on the state in Russia and failure thereof in the industrialised heartlands of Western Europe. The nature of class domination in different contexts is composed of a historical combination of repression and consent, or dictatorship and hegemony. The predominance of consent over coercion, as is the case in the advanced capitalist core, is still a description of a specific mode of capitalist domination. Nor are these terms mutually exclusive, as coercive institutions have consent-building functions and outcomes, and *vice versa*. It is worth mentioning in passing that this coincidence of coercion and consent also appears in Althusser's (2014) ideological and repressive state apparatuses. For instance, education would appear to belong to the 'consent' side of the reproduction of hegemony, yet schools also act as mechanisms of embodied rituals that instil a coercive conformity on pupils. Or conversely, prisons may be categorised as primarily coercive institutions, yet the carceral system is engineered to inculcate consent for the wider mechanisms of political and economic power. Thus, Gramsci does not indicate a liberal partiality to consent over coercion in an expanded civil society, and state retrenchment as a condition of freedom. Rather, he explains that being able to forego coercion signals the power of the state. Not having to constantly exercise its rule suggests that its functions are fulfilled in civil society. Thus, public participation in political life is more effectively absorbed in political mechanisms, and undesirable 'extremes' marginalised through delineated forms of conduct. Conversely, the centralised states of the East belie a vulnerability as they are required to update their grip directly, and incapable of delegating such roles to the outer ditches of civil society. While the authoritarian core is formidable, the fact remains that it is surrounded by a society that it must constantly appease or threaten. In the event of a breach in its walls, the mystique around its omnipotence can evaporate, paving the way for an emancipatory discharge more far-reaching than in the West.

Gramsci's contradictory formulations of hegemony do not arise from a general confusion and incoherence, *pace* Anderson (1976), but rather a temporal reappraisal of his concepts (Crehan, 2002: 101–102). In the words of Buttigieg (2006: 38), attempts to systematise Gramsci's thought arise from an 'impulse to tame' an otherwise decentred 'work in progress' with noticeable leitmotivs. Every reading is a re-reading, bringing the discourse of the interpreter to bear on the author. This is particularly true for Gramsci, whose organic and dialectical concepts are open as a 'principle of inquiry' (Spanos, 2006: 24). Another reader has even suggested that the fragmented nature of Gramsci's notebooks suggest a 'poststructuralism ... *avant la lettre*', enabling a 'rhizomatic reading' (Jablonka, 1998, translation in Thomas, 2009: 45). However, an entirely untethered, haphazard application of Gramsci's concepts is as undesirable as his ossified canonisation justifying the reformism of the Italian Communist Party. The intention here is to repeat Gramsci's concepts through 'betraying' his uses, to adhere to the creative impulse of hegemony. These concepts gain vivacity in dialogue with historical realities, but they also maintain an economic grounding that prevents slippage into discourse analysis, as has happened with their post-Marxist appropriations.

Gramsci (1987: 34) observed the October Revolution as a 'Revolution against 'Capital'', where he lauded the Bolshevik's seizure of power that defied received wisdom:

> This is the revolution against Marx's Capital. In Russia, Marx's Capital was more the book of the bourgeoisie than of the proletariat. It stood as the critical demonstration of how events should follow a predetermined course: how in Russia a bourgeoisie had to develop, and a capitalist era had to open, with the setting-up of a Western-type civilization, before the proletariat could even think in terms of its own revolt, its own class demands, its own revolution. But events have overcome ideologies. Events have exploded the critical schemas determining how the history of Russia would unfold according to the canons of historical materialism. The Bolsheviks reject Karl Marx, and their explicit actions and conquests bear witness that the canons of historical materialism are not so rigid as one might have thought and has been believed.

As Gramsci grasps, per the habitually accepted reading of *Capital*, the Bolsheviks could not jump the proverbial gun of capitalist accumulation. Russia was still a vastly agrarian Tsardom with little industry and minuscule working class. Thus, scholarly forecasts did not expect a socialist rupture in Russia before a protracted consolidation of liberal democratic norms. This viewpoint signalled firstly the intellectual disposition arising from the class background of the scholars in question, who envisioned a regulated schedule of modernisation, and secondly, of a determinist reading of Marx. Contrarily, the Bolshevik seizure of power had empowered the Soviets and ushered in zealous socialist construction.

Against the codified Marx of the Second International, Gramsci espouses the Marx of the *Civil War in France*, along with the *Eighteenth Brumaire of Louis Bonaparte*, where sociopolitical agency creates new possibilities in historically specific contexts. Such an inspiration of the fluidity and contingency of historical change informs the 'optimism of the will'. Also, as Gramsci's experience in post-World War I Italy shows, the key factors in revolutionary breaks were political and cultural, while economic trauma was at most necessary but not sufficient (Adamson, 1987: 324–325). As a result, Gramsci is attenuated to the fallacy of totalising theories about the movement of history and society, and towards temporal contradictions within and between the 'East' and the 'West'.

Gramsci (1971: 163) alludes to *Capital*, or rather its crude representation by the founders of Russian Marxism such as Plekhanov, as an example of conceptual reification where the social reality is expected to fulfil the preconceived blueprint of 'historical economism' (Gunnel, 1968: 86). He then seeks to reconstruct historical materialism through and beyond Marx, in the direction of a 'more historicist, reflexive and dynamic form of political economy explanation' (Gill, 1993: 21). Otherwise there is a risk of a lapse into idealism. Echoing Gill (ibid), Gramsci's analytical strength issues from using 'limited generalisations and a conditional vocabulary'; the letter of *Capital* is less significant than its mode of inquiry. It is not necessarily the content of the work Gramsci argues against, but the abstract model of capitalist accumulation, without regard for Marx's concern for the struggle between the formal subsumption of the commodity form and the real obstacles it encounters.

The concept of hegemony is a case of the dialectic of abstraction and the empirical traversing Gramsci's vocabulary. As Anderson (1976: 13) illustrates, the term was not unknown to the international labour movement. In fact, it etymologically dates to the ancient Greek noun *hēgemonía*, designating leadership of an alliance of city-states for a common military end (Anderson, 2017: 1). It was contrasted with *arkhḗ*, meaning rule in a more general sense, and prefiguring subsequent uses (ibid: 1–5). Following a centuries-long 'peripeteia', or relative dormancy, it was reactivated as a term (*gegemoniya*) frequently used in pre-revolutionary Russia. Here it meant the leadership of the working class in 'uniting all oppressed sectors of the population as allies under its guidance' (ibid: 14). Lenin and Plekhanov envisioned a working class and peasantry alliance to forge a revolutionary front against both Tsarism and the bourgeoisie, a policy that Lenin pursued into the New Economic Policy years (Anderson, 1976: 15). These uses of hegemony are internally consistent, but reducing hegemony to rule, they lose the nuance in the original Greek sense that conceived of it as apart from *arkhḗ*. For Lenin and Plekhanov, *gegemoniya* is one version of the *arkhḗ*, as it directly refers to the seizure of political rule through a specific kind of leadership. However, Gramsci's reinvention distinguishes these categories, to underline the social and cultural implications of hegemony that surpass questions of political power.

Gramsci is the first theorist to provide an analytically flexible tool to explain both the establishment of leadership and the cultivation of consent, slightly shifting the terrain to ideological matters. Before contrasting these conceptualisations of hegemony, it is helpful to indicate that a situation of dual power was the key condition of socialist transition in Marxist debates. Trotsky (1977: 224) sees this as the situation where the ascendant class has concentrated political power in its hands, while the official apparatus of the state is still occupied by the forces of the declining order. This signifies a moment of impasse that calls for a swift capture of power from a cornered ruling class, or brutal, survivalist reaction from a regime reduced to its physical core. However, the antagonism between classes in this scenario resembles a battlefield with two neatly organised rivals. Militaristic language, while understandable against the violent backdrop of the time, reinforces this analogy yet oversimplifies the picture. A dual power situation also involves competing legitimacies for political prevalence, such as between a republic and a sultanate, or a liberal democracy and a republic of soviets. To resume in this register, the battlefield of the dual power situation is temporally undulated, with strategic vantage points for all sides within the wider historical landscape.

Gramsci's reading of the dual power situation goes beyond a stalemate between political forces. The 'effective reality', says Gramsci (1971: 172), is the domain of the 'active politician' of the present with an eye on the desired future. The 'effectiveness' of reality indicates a theoretical uncoupling of the historical backdrop from the resources and prospects available to make history. The importance of politics comes through in bold relief here, as politics in this scheme of historical movement represents the lever of transition. Gramsci (1971: 181–183) explains that the relation of forces making up the effective reality involves the material forces of production, political forces, and military forces. In most cases, the political level mediates between the forces of production and the military forces. Expanding on this, Gramsci (1971: 184) relates that the rupture of 1789 did not occur solely from 'mechanic' (*i.e.* economic) causes. Based on his treatment of the economic and political levels of the social reality, it is possible to suggest that Gramsci perceived a relatively rigid economic dynamic and allowed far more autonomy to the political field as an interface between the changes in the mode of production and the impasse where this is translated into violent confrontation.

As Lenin (1966: 84–85) puts forth, revolutionary change requires both an inability of the ruling class to rule, and a lack of consent on the part of the exploited classes to be ruled 'in the old way'. This is where hegemony is the operative process as the ensemble of modes of perceiving the world in capitalist societies. Spontaneous and voluntary consent underlies political legitimacy. By developing the concept of hegemony in tandem with exploitation in the Marxist sense, Gramsci shows how a situation of dual power is a struggle along multiple vectors. In Schecter's (2010: 153–154) words hegemony is always 'ethical-political, economic-political and political-cultural'. This would explain how the struggle of the ascendant bourgeoisie against the *ancien régime* culminated in the dismantling of feudal institutions in the French Revolution, albeit through long cycles of revolution and restoration. Ideals of freedom and equality antagonised inherited privilege, and mobilised a historical bloc of subjugated classes under the aegis of the bourgeoisie. This also shows the function of hegemony as a justification of inequality in capitalist society; there is nothing holding back those who strive to do whatever it takes, while before social position was determined from birth. As Sassoon (1987: 113) argues, we cannot speak of hegemony in ancient and feudal society, as there was no pretension that the ruled could participate in the political system and even change it in their favour. This does not mean that consent did not have to be cultivated in pre-capitalist societies, nor that the remnants of such societies do not survive and adapt in capitalism. But this point shows that hegemony is a political project shot through with class interests. Its novelty in capitalism is that the bourgeoisie and its organic intellectuals have been successful at seizing the leadership of social struggles with an overarching political-economic programme.

Ingrained patterns of behaviour and assumptions on possibilities of social change, and one's role within society, are enmeshed in social relations and ultimately reproduce the dominant mode of production. Hegemony pertains to the superstructure, removed to some degree from the moment of surplus-value production. However, it must be borne in mind that the base-superstructure model assumes a dialectical approach that considers the organic unity of both instances as opposed to unilinear causality. Hegemony is not a merely epiphenomenal reflection of the process of surplus-value extraction, but embedded in the relations of production. Gramsci (1977: 265–268) seems to intuit this, following Lenin's insistence that trade union struggles must be linked to political struggle to break out of depoliticised contractual bargains and into a process of positive construction. For Lenin (1960: 363), in keeping with the conception of hegemony as a strategy of alliance, carrying economic grievances to politics would counter 'narrow trade-unionism and to a 'realistic' struggle for petty, gradual reforms'. Otherwise, Lenin asserts, the spontaneous working class movement risks becoming an 'appendage of the liberals' (ibid).

While Lenin saw the solution in interference by a vanguard party, Gramsci (1968: 40) approaches the problem from the other side: in terms of how the working class – particularly in the organisational form of factory councils – could keep unions in check as 'a reagent dissolving its bureaucratism' from below. Another important difference between Gramsci and Lenin, as Marzani (1957: 7) observes, is that the former 'acted as a Marxist' while the latter gave voice to the theoretical outcomes of his political experience. In early political writings, Gramsci had progressively renounced the syndicalism that had stamped radical currents, arguing that the union is too susceptible to bureaucratic degeneration. In an article, Gramsci (1919) makes his case referring to the narrowness of economism in original terms that enhances Lenin's rationale for the vanguard party: 'The proletarian dictatorship can be made flesh in a type of organisation which is specific to the activity of producers and not of wage-earners, slaves of capital'. Here Gramsci reflects on post-revolution hegemony as a project of producers' self-formation, as a corollary of emancipation from wage-labour. This suggests that hegemony cannot be a generic term applicable to any class project, as a 'pallid theory of 'governance', or a 'technical', i.e. non-political, concern', as Thomas (2009: 221) puts it. It is more accurate to follow how hegemony unravels in Gramsci's (1971: 133) account, as an instigation of a 'moral-intellectual reform' that threatens existing social relations. Such 'reform', to be hegemonic, must displace established patterns of production and social life and render them temporally incompatible with its vision, creating a transitional strain.

Hegemony involves the cultivation of 'intellectual cells of a new type' that represent the 'new social grouping' on the historical stage, with its concomitant 'economic counterparts' (Gramsci, 1971: 18). Notwithstanding the flexibility of the phrase 'social groups', this suggests that Gramsci saw hegemony ultimately as a method of establishing class power. Additionally, the historical institutionalisation of organic intellectuals recalls the troubled concept of the 'hegemonic apparatus' (Bollinger and Koivisto, 2009) as a concentrated expression of hegemonic aspiration. Bollinger and Koivisto (2009: 305–306) maintain that Althusser intended to systematise Gramsci's fragmentary observations on political power, as an assemblage of consent-inducing mechanisms besides the repressive nucleus. Such commonalities between Althusser and Gramsci are discussed in the following section.

4 Time of Times: Althusser Reading Gramsci

Anglophone Marxism has done violence to the Althusserian and Gramscian paradigms by contrasting caricatures, presenting Gramsci as an empirical historicist and Althusser as the abstract opposite (Kolakowski, 1971: 119; Thompson,

2000: 168). Much of the vitriol is reserved for Althusser. He is a 'freak of intellectual fashion'; a deliberately obscure French curiosity; simultaneous representative of pretentious petty bourgeois verbosity *and* Stalinism in academia; a primogenitor of all the structuralism that echoes bourgeois sociology as 'complete bullshit' (Cohen, 2013: 94–95); the culprit of such continental thought 'shat upon us' (Thompson, 1995: 3–4, 16). This section seeks to rectify this reception, highlighting a temporal common ground. At first glance, there seems to be justification for the ire against Althusser. Returning to the earlier discussion of Althusser and Balibar (1970: 94), their criticism targeted the 'expressivist' notion of totality in the historical present. If this is understood as Gramsci's organic approach to Marxism as a derivative of local realities, *Reading Capital*, as Thomas (2012: 138) puts it, can be seen as an 'attempt at an Anti-Gramsci'. However, as Althusser was also aware, this is not a fair assessment of Gramsci (1988: 326), if for no other reason than the latter's view on the composition of the individual at any vertical cut in time: 'The personality is strangely composite: it contains Stone Age elements and principles of a more advanced science, prejudices from all past phases of history at the local level and intuitions of a future philosophy which will be that of a human race united the world over'. This calls for a reappraisal of the assumed antagonism.

The crucial commonality is the temporal complexity, *qua* theories of ideology. Both Althusser and Gramsci conceptualise the 'truth' of a time as a complexity of times, crosscut with previous ages that burden the emergence of the future with past prejudices. Ontologically however, the intuition of a future is actual. Even though it is in muted form, this is distinct from its eradication or absence. For Gramsci, as for Althusser, ideology is an immediately lived, corporal experience, besides subjective belief. However, Gramsci introduces a distinction of 'common sense' (*senso comune*) which does not neatly translate into English, where the same phrase would indicate more of a 'good sense' (*buon senso*) (Thomas, 2009: 16). Instead, Gramsci's common sense is a literal expression of the intersubjectively constructed, shared ways of seeing the world. This Italian sense is broader than the English understanding of reliable sense, and essential to social reproduction since it covers a repository of knowledge, the linguistic building blocks of a shared reality, and a set of axiomatic truths making interaction possible (Crehan, 2016: 43). This invokes Althusser's (2005: 232) observation that ideology is intrinsic to society, and that believing in its elimination in the cold logic of science is itself ideological:

> Human societies secrete ideology as the very element and atmosphere indispensable to their historical respiration and life. Only an ideological world outlook could have imagined societies without ideology and

accepted the utopian idea of a world in which ideology (not just one of its historical forms) would disappear without trace, to be replaced by science.

This shared insight, however, does not imply that 'good sense' cannot be identified. While Althusser does not propose a systematic differentiation of superior forms of ideology, he also argues that there is such a thing as 'proletarian ideology' (2014: 228). This is a distinct kind of ideology that is theoretically infused with Marxism. A 'spontaneous' proletarian ideology exists independently of Marxism. This was the case for utopian socialism and other subaltern rebellions, though it gains consciousness of its historic situatedness and function through its fusion with Marxism (ibid: 229). This is a result of deliberate theoretical practice, creating alternative interpellations to challenge dominant ones.

For Gramsci (1970: 328), similarly, grains of truth are scattered across the common sense, referring to them as 'the healthy nucleus that exists in the *senso comune*'. One can perceive this in colloquial platitudes, such as 'MPs are only out for themselves' or 'the political system is rigged' (Crehan, 2016: 48). That said, even *buon senso* is riddled with inconsistencies. These can be pernicious, as anti-Semitic inferences, or disempowering, resulting in a cynical view of inequalities as inscribed into humanity. Thus, as Hall and O'Shea (2013: 10) stress, common sense is a site of political struggle, where revolutionary agency *has to* start from spontaneous local knowledges to systematically formulate them for transition, not by their substitution for the 'correct' line, but through a common sense 'made more unitary and coherent' (Gramsci, 1971: 328). Gramsci (2000: 82) had maintained earlier that '[t]o tell the truth, to arrive together at the truth, is a communist and revolutionary act', and this should be understood as a collective bridging of temporal divides. Moreover, this refers to the construction of a 'new common sense and with it a new culture' (Gramsci, 1971: 424). So beyond combing through common sense to discard the afterlives of past societies and maintain seeds of future ones, these 'nuggets of good sense', as Crehan (2016: 48) calls them, should be synthesised within a left project.

Ideology and common sense, used as analogues between Althusser and Gramsci's theoretical toolkits here, both encompass the social formation and accompany every turn of its articulation. Therefore, the civil society and state divide is methodologically expedient, yet this cannot be observed directly in real social relations (Jessop, 1982: 147). There is an overlap here with the Althusserian dictum that 'ideology has no history'; as the state and civil society are present in each other, ideological social transformations do not take place through debates and paradigm shifts within the intellectual confines of a 'sphere', just as common sense cannot be seen solely as a discrete collection of ideas that one can step in and out of. This copresence, however, should not be mistaken for identity. Political life has specific mechanisms, as does civil society as part of the ideological vector of the social formation. Rather, ideological rifts are rooted away from the internal workings of intellectual life, and within mechanisms of power. Gramsci (1971: 8) would concur on this account, as he criticises understandings of intellectual activity confined to an abstract history of ideas:

> The most widespread error of method seems to me that of having looked for this criterion of distinction in the intrinsic nature of intellectual activities, rather than in the ensemble of the system of relations in which these activities (and therefore the intellectual groups who personify them) have their place within the general complex of social relations.

This resonates with Gramsci's (2000: 37) reiterated necessity of a political *and* economic drive in hegemonic struggle. It is not the intrinsic truth of ideas, but their social embodiment that brings them to life: 'An idea becomes real not because it is logically in conformity with pure truth, pure humanity (which exists only as a plan, as a general ethical goal of mankind), but because it finds in economic reality its justification, the instrument with which it can be carried out'.

As Althusser had argued, ideology is still present in these moments of reproduction, and it cannot be monopolised by singular groups. Althusser (2003: 17) illustrates this intertwinement of subjective intervention and objective determination in this self-referential passage:

> The person who is addressing you is, like all the rest of us, merely a particular structural effect of this conjuncture, an effect that, like each and every one of us, has a proper name. The theoretical conjuncture that dominates us has produced an Althusser-effect.

Here the 'Althusser-effect' can be read as an effacement of subjectivity, or self-erasure in favour of a rigid structuralism. However, Althusser's point is similar to Gramsci's suggestion that one carries, albeit unconsciously, a sedimented set of historically constructed viewpoints and behaviours. Going further, these determinations are biological and evolutionary at first, evoking Marx's philosophical anthropology of the centrality of productive activity. At a smaller scale, these determinations are historical-cultural. In this sense, the 'Althusser-effect' refers to the aggregation of biographical, social and political interpellations that have shaped the person of Louis Althusser, in conjunction with those of his reader, combining to create a unique conjuncture that is irreducible to its parts. Thus, writing a chapter that proposes a reading of Althusser is a microcosm of the interplay of the human as a subject in history, but not its driving force. This chapter, while possessing an internal structure, can only be fully explicated within a context of the intersections of the interpellations and temporal positionings of its author and readers. Returning to Gramsci (1971: 324), the alleged anti-Althusserian, this approach of explaining the individual as a result (out of many contingent possibilities) of an array of historical streams and interpellations has a remarkable resonance: 'The starting point of critical elaboration is the consciousness of what one really is, and is 'knowing thyself' as a product of the historical process to date which has deposited in you an infinity of traces, without leaving an inventory'.

A left political project must start from the actual transitional inclinations, and seek to amplify these. Althusserian and Gramscian theories converge on this temporal lag and its political implications. Neither take for granted pretensions to a privileged access to the truth or the transitional process, since they both relativise these within temporally out-of-joint social formations. While this has been an acknowledged point of Gramsci's work, the same has not been the case for Althusserian theory, on which scant writing touches upon the transitional temporality that is so crucial to the enterprise.[2]

Gramsci's theories of hegemony and common sense provide more robust explanations of the political processes that replicate capitalism than those of the Althusserian persuasion. That said, the difference is one of degree, as there is an overlap between the two outlooks' emphases on the social diffusion of ideology. While the term ideology is used in a variety of contexts without much analytical flexibility, prompting Althusser to continuously qualify his usage, Gramscian conceptual tools are more fine-tuned, as the common sense/good sense distinction testifies. The 'short' and 'long' temporalities of political struggle in Balibar's terminology can be explained more clearly, and put to better analytical use, through Gramsci's nuanced concepts. However, based on their reconstruction in this chapter, Gramsci's work serves as a regional translation of reproduction at the political level within the larger theory of the ideologically, politically, and economically differentiated social formation.

This temporal complexity lies at the core of the notion of transition that this book proposes; the present is a contradictory mixture of the past as well as the future in a direct sense, such that the 'present' in itself is not a real concept. The present is shorthand for a socially intercalated temporality, with temporal

2 For a notable exception, see Chambers (2011).

lag is its displacement onto itself, such that the folds in the progression of time simultaneously negate and repeat the past, and anticipate the future. From this perspective, the hegemonic becomes synonymous with a temporal suspension that serves the interests of the powerful, while counter-hegemony is successful insofar as it can fissure this false 'unity' of the present and restore a sense of futurity to politics, centring itself at the nexus of a becoming. As Gramsci (1971: 276) remarked: '[T]he crisis consists precisely in the fact that the old is dying and the new cannot be born; in this interregnum a great variety of morbid symptoms appear'. This can be read not just as a local observation, but as a statement of the perennial tension at the heart of social reproduction, in which dominant structures endure by repeating the past and suppressing transitions.

CHAPTER 3

The Discursive Turn: the Post-Marxist Gramsci of Laclau and Mouffe

The concern with the relative autonomy of the political and desire to break from economic reductionism culminates in a departure from Marxism in the controversial work of Ernesto Laclau and Chantal Mouffe, *Hegemony and Socialist Strategy: Towards a Radical Democratic Politics* (Henceforth referred to as HSS, 1985). The crux of the problem with Marxism, they contend, is the preconception of class and closure of the social around explicable laws. Classical Marxism underwent shifts in the autonomy afforded to non-economic and non-class determinations, yet remained committed to the teleological resolution of social contradictions through working-class agency, an expectation more tightly maintained the more it was frustrated. While this teleological motor was in motion, the seizure of power and socialist transition were eventual points on the evolutionary process (HSS: 16). Laclau and Mouffe stake out a *post*-Marxist departure, seeking to radicalise Gramscian and Althusserian concepts in ways that unhinge them from determinism and essentialism. However, they also affirm a commitment to an inclusive and egalitarian society in a radically democratic form, proposing apposite strategies against the New Right and retaining a post-*Marxism* (HSS: 4).

This chapter argues that in light of the preceding discussions of strands of Marxism, the post-Marxist project of 'radical democracy' is a provocative interpretation, but lacks novelty. It is ultimately a political program reflecting its own historical conditions, accommodating to the political climate of neoliberalism. It is also emblematic of the theoretical moment of the 'death of the subject', supplanted by an 'infinite intertextuality of emancipatory discourses' between slippery subject positions and indeterminacy (HSS: 5). These traits lead to a melancholic vision in terms of a drastic scaling down of the left project. Following a survey of mainly Laclau's notable works leading up to HSS, I will discuss the rejection of class determination, contrasting it with the differential use of the concept of hegemony and interpellation. This will lead to a qualified reiteration of historical materialism as a viable perspective on postcapitalist transition that is found-wanting in radical democracy.

It should be emphasised that prioritising Laclau's theories does not imply an underappreciation for Mouffe's contributions, particularly in HSS, which has been wrongly seen primarily as a fruition of Laclau's ambitions (Desmoulieres, 2017). While Mouffe has been a prolific theorist of the political, the focus is on Laclau as his theoretical trajectory follows explicit Althusserian leanings, particularly in his theorisations of ideology and interpellation.

1 Class, Popular Interpellations, and Populism

Laclau's political formation took shape during the Peronist regime in Argentina, whose discourse involved assertions of national sovereignty and proletarian militancy, enjoying substantial working class support. Laclau came of age in the student movement of the 1960s as a member of the Socialist Party of the National Left, a splinter group of the Argentine Socialist Party (Critchley and Marchart, 2004: 2). As the name suggests, this was a period of intense negotiation of the reactionary nature of the 'national' that Marxist currents associated with false consciousness. Laclau's impression from Argentinian populism was that popular-democratic demands should be formulated through and beyond class discourse. This is theorised in his first (1977) published work, *Politics and Ideology in Marxist Theory*.

For Laclau, the eclecticism of left populism attests to the falsity of direct translations between classes and ideological elements. By 'elements', Laclau (1977: 91) refers to discrete ideas and concepts (such as the 'myth of the ladder' and 'fetishism of the state') that make up a discernible ideological perspective. In line with Gramsci's analysis, the dominant ideology deploys elements that may have emerged at diverse points in the social topology. The predominant ways of framing reality are not the results of conscious machinations by the ruling class in favour of their interests. Rather, they enclose aspects of folk wisdom that cross class lines, congealed in the hegemonic discourse. Also, 'concrete ideological discourse' is a noun phrase loaded with Althusserian inflection as well as a post-structural openness, contributing to the unstable fixity between ideological elements and class connotations (Laclau, 1977: 99). Here Laclau refers to the precise discursive production of ideological elements in every moment of social reproduction. They are ideological insofar as there is a dislocation, and as per Althusser, they pertain to the subjective perceptions of objective capitalist relations. The social formation is riddled with the contradictions this process entails, taking shape as their condensation. For this reason, it has been possible for socialist ideological elements to be welded to nationalist rhetoric. A strategic conclusion for the left is that the national and patriotic are not inherently right-wing concepts, but can, and at times should, be inflected with a left perspective. Shifting the terms of the debate regarding national sovereignty in the popular imagination disarms reactionary appropriations, and reinforces the notion of popular power central to left politics.

Since ideological elements cannot be reduced to objective class interests, the impact of discourse cannot be discerned from the linguistic utterance *per se*, but the context of its emergence. For instance, the contemporary slogan 'Black Lives Matter' has been challenged with the counter-slogan 'All Lives Matter'. At face value they both express a normative common ground, *i.e.* that lives matter, yet asserting that 'All Lives Matter', while agreeable, serves to downplay the systematic destitution of a racialized community while ignoring historically ingrained white privileges. The Black Lives Matter slogan, as Butler (2015) maintains, derives its impact from its obviousness that has not been historically realised. Contrarily, the 'All Lives Matter' slogan, which appears innocuous, can belie a conservative rear-guard reflex against inclusion and empowerment. Thus, statements embody ideological functions based on their discursive context. This is why Laclau (1977: 115) maintains that dismissing the ideological field as a realm of 'bourgeois' politics aided the rise of fascism, engendering a failure of the working class to 'hegemonise popular struggles and fuse popular-democratic ideology and its revolutionary class objectives into a coherent political and ideological practice'.

The preliminary observation that workers of distinct countries have irreducibly specific local traits, as 'condensations of a multiplicity of interpellations', is central to Laclau's account of ideology and class (1977: 109). Althusser had delineated interpellation as a process of subjectivity-formation. Ideology 'hails' the individual, relationally bestowing them with an identity. This process at once gives the 'bearer of the social relation' a veneer of autonomy, but also creates an opportunity to negotiate the ideological makeup of the interpellation. On this, it is noteworthy that theorists such as Nicos Mouzelis (1978: 46–47) contend that Althusserian structuralism effaces agency due to its claim that the individual's sovereignty is illusory. This is objectionable because, as discussed, individuality can only be constructed in the midst of society, and Althusser's interpellation is one of the ways of explaining how this comes about. Also, there is reason to suggest that interpellation does not simply clamp down the agent in a predefined ideological matrix. Because it is an *articulated* mechanism, interpellation evades institutional reification, as individuals are interpellated in variegated concrete ways. This may not be tantamount to agency as such, signalling a limitation of interpellation as subjectivity-formation. Even so, that mass mobilisation can activate contrarian interpellations, dividing society in new ways, is foundational to the early

Laclau's case for a *national* working-class struggle, along with his later theory of populism.

Laclau retains determination in the last instance, positing that class interpellation is rooted in the mode of production, even arguing that 'the 'people' do not, obviously, exist at the level of production relations' (1977: 108). Balibar, despite his formulations of the distinct layers of social reproduction, is charged with sublimating the 'specificity of the political to the economic' (ibid: 72–78). This sets the limits of the irreducible popular-democratic interpellation, where Laclau embarks on a theory of the ideological superstructure beyond an epiphenomenal account (Howarth, 2015: 8). The organising concept of Laclau's political ontology is populism, as the articulations of a historic bloc and its popular-democratic legitimacy. Given that there are interpellations outside of the production process, which has now been confined to a region in the social with endogenous mechanisms, Laclau (1997: 108–109) can propose 'non-class interpellation' as the articulation of an antagonistic relation to the dominant power bloc, as well as a consummation of class objectives (Torfing, 1999: 29). 'Bloc' is the formative subject of the revolutionary project as opposed to class. Populism refers to the mobilisation of ideological elements, covering a span of appeals, rallying slogans, demands, representations and identities, around the historic bloc, constructing a divisive category of 'the people'. The non-class interpellation also serves as a point of inflection where class objectives gain coherence as part of a popular struggle.

While Althusser saw historical change as the articulation of class struggle through the ideological realm, for the early Laclau the mode of production is a vague backdrop to the political project. Althusser had attempted to reconcile the autonomy of the political and ideological with economic imperatives by utilising the base-superstructure topology as a conceptual metaphor for the complex unity of the social formation. For Althusser, historical materialism was an investigation of the specific effectivities that derive from the mode of production, which is determinate in the last instance not least because it is never explicitly visible. Laclau (1977: 73) however finds the Althusserian approach 'descriptive' in a pejorative sense, finding it unclear on how the political or the ideological can be deduced from the social formation, or why there are only these realms and not more (or less). In contrast, Laclau insists on the specificity of the political against the temptation to sublimate it in the economic, which the Althusserian aversion to pluralism had amounted to. The political is further demarcated as a decisive terrain of competition between contrasting visions of the nature of society and struggle between condensations of multiple interpellations. The determinant role of the mode of production is rehearsed by Laclau (1977: 135) in unambiguous terms, but with an important proviso:

> What we wish to say is that the process of social reproduction is not just the reproduction of the dominant mode of production but also of its conditions, one of which is ideology; and that the greater the importance in a social formation of those sectors which do not participate directly in dominant production relations, the greater will be the importance and relative autonomy of ideological processes for social reproduction as a whole.

As it turns out, even the performative nod towards the mode of production could mean a relapse to economic reduction. The postulate of non-class interpellations and ideological elements requires a more radical break, which will be found in the concept of discourse when Laclau collaborates with Mouffe to propose a new political imaginary bereft of economic reductionism or essentialism.

To make sense of the versatility of ideology, Laclau jettisons the class connotations of ideological elements, leaving them open to contingent appropriations. Following this decoupling of ideas from socially fixed determinants, Laclau (2005) has more recently developed analytical tools to study hegemonic discourse in *On Populist Reason*. Here what is called the 'logic of equivalence' politicizes interpellation, designating a discursive move that drives a wedge between two groups to create a new antagonism. Thus, a collective identity of discrete agents is shaped in opposition to a designated other. Reinforcing a uniformity along demands and groups is essential for hegemony. For Laclau (2005: 18) this is exemplified in the 'politico-ideological frontier' that General Perón created when he claimed that the choice was between himself and the US ambassador. Conversely, the 'logic of difference' includes different elements as a minimally differentiated mass, thereby limiting the potential of social division into antagonistic camps (Laclau, 2005: 189). This is exemplified in 'one nation conservatism' in the UK, whose proponents in government purport to lead by balancing and reconciling the interests of all citizens regardless of class (Lind, 1997: 45). These discursive movements attest to the unfixity of society that figures in post-Marxism, with politics as a practice of articulating placeholders to mobilise and furnish popular aspirations. Laclau (2005: x) draws from interpellation theory, maintaining that 'the impossibility of fixing the unity of a social formation in any *conceptually* graspable object leads to the centrality of *naming* in constituting that unity'.

There are various nominations for the ruling bloc and the underdog. For instance, the 'caste' (*la casta*) figures prominently in the rhetoric of the Spanish left-wing party Podemos to refer to the two-party domination of the Popular Party (PP) and the Socialist Worker's Party (PSOE) in the post-Franco political landscape, mockingly merged as 'PPSOE' (Valdivielso, 2017: 4). It is fortunate that the leading cadre refers directly to Laclau and Mouffe as their influences, because the party's policies and style of organisation suggests what political action along their lines may look like. Íñigo Errejón, the campaign manager, has also written on 'constructing the people' with Mouffe (2015). Podemos experienced a meteoric rise following its foundation in March 2014, following the 15-M movement that convulsed the country in a series of occupations and mass rallies against inequality and corruption. Errejón stresses the need for a new political subject and hegemonic electoral majority, calling for a consideration of 'discursive frameworks that give an antagonistic meaning to social reality' (Errejón, 2011: 77–78; Valdivielso, 2017: 4). Consequently, Podemos seeks to formulate its categories organically from the existing social movements. Pablo Iglesias (2014), the leader of Podemos, explains that this contradicts the approach of raising consciousness to meet pre-defined conclusions. For Iglesias, the esoteric students of Marxist classics lamented that people failed to understand them, leading to demoralisation and an inability to form an outlet for popular-democratic demands. Iglesias (2014) maintains that this has played into the hands of the powerful, who have a grip on people's attention, and refers to Lenin:

> There was that bald guy – a genius. He understood the concrete analysis of a concrete situation. In a time of war, in 1917, when the regime had crashed in Russia, he said a very simple thing to the Russians, whether they were soldiers, peasants, or workers. He said: 'bread and peace'. And when he said 'bread and peace', which is what everyone wanted – for the war to be over and to have enough to eat – many Russians who had no idea whether they were 'left' or 'right' but did know that they were hungry, they said: 'The bald guy is right'. And the bald guy did very well. He didn't talk to the Russians about 'dialectical materialism', he talked to them about 'bread and peace'. And that is one of the main lessons of the twentieth century.

This inference suggests an understanding of politics as the capacity to be seen as the interlocutor of basic aspirations. Doctrinal purity and analytical rigour have subsidiary roles in success; what counts more is the construction of a bloc that delineates political frontiers. The evasiveness of the 'people' is a mobilising strength, as the indeterminacy of the goals of social movements creates a terrain on which the logic of difference can be carried over to a chain of equivalence.

If Iglesias is correct that affective resonance can bring one closer to power, then promoting populist interpellations would be in order. That said, Iglesias' example itself suggests that a *left* populism involves class connotations, appealing to basic material needs, which are felt most acutely by the exploited. While this is a viable approach, the detachment from economic determinants makes it difficult to conceive of it through Laclau's theory, as this may have been met with a charge of crude reductionism. Arditi (2014: 24) imputes to Laclau the view of populism as an 'Esperanto of politics', amenable to left and right appropriations. This is a valid observation, and consequential for a project of transition. Populism appears to signify the *modus operandi* of the political for Laclau, not least because of its versatility as a tool of political analysis. He goes so far as to say that 'there is no political intervention which is not populistic to some extent', therefore operating as the matter of *'political* reason *tout court'* regardless of left or right politics (2005: 154, 225). Laclau (2005: 44–45) further asserts that 'populism is an ontological and not an ontic category'. This is a statement of the primacy of the political and its discursive monism. These terms are used purposefully to refer to the concrete, immediate and hence transitory reality of the ontic, and the global form of doing politics ontologically grounded in society. In keeping with the form and content separation, Laclau (2005: 87) proceeds to demonstrate that the construction of social division – not its *discovery* as an objective phenomenon – takes on an ontic content. Movements can reach for ontic attachments across the political spectrum. In Laclau's (2005: 87) words, 'given the indeterminacy of the relation between ontic content and ontological function – this function can be performed by signifiers of an entirely opposite political sign'.

This conceptualisation of the political affords a problematic flexibility to political signals. After all, the label of populist has been applied to figures as diverse as Hugo Chávez, Hassan Nasrallah and Viktor Orbán without much variance in its semantics.[1] If the term can explain such a range of diverse actors, this would show its substantive poverty. Nevertheless, Laclau provides an account of how voting behaviour can favour marginal options on the left and right in unpredicted ways, in a more sophisticated fashion than liberal theses

---

1 In a quantitative study of speeches by international figures, Hawkins (2009) reports of having found forty cases of populist discourse from a variety of countries based on common understandings of populism.

of deep affinity between socialism and fascism. Referring to the example of the remarkable swing in the 'protest vote' from its traditional left-wing base to the far-right in France over the 1990s, Laclau (2005: 86–88) explains how the notions of 'left-lepenism' and 'worker's lepenism' issued from a situation where Socialists were entrenched in the ruling coalition, blurring the left-right division. The votes of those denied a political voice, particularly the working-class, migrated to the xenophobic far-right from where they were thought to 'belong'. Laclau's (2005: 88) explanation is highly pertinent today: 'The ontological need to express social division was stronger than its ontic attachment to a left-wing discourse which, anyway, did not attempt to build it up any longer'. This merits consideration as a theory of political behaviour, despite falling short of illuminating the causes of the 'ontological need to express social division' itself.

Herein also lies a kernel of the post-Marxist departure that assimilates class to the people as a discursive construction. This is built upon a dualist reversal of the monism of economic determination that Laclau sought to avoid. By privileging the political moment in ever sharper relief, beginning with the non-class interpellation, Laclau (1977: 166) compartmentalizes relations of production at a region of the social, impervious to popular-democratic interpellations which arise from a 'complex of political and ideological relations of domination constituting a determinate social formation'. This is a step backwards from the co-determinant approach of Althusser and Balibar, and with that of Marx, since Marx envisioned societal transition as an interplay of political and economic factors as opposed to a substitution of one sphere for another in ruptural moments. For Laclau, however, the 'social formation' makes up the realm of non-class interpellations in a concrete sense, while the mode of production is relegated to an analytical level with little relevance to which interpellations prevent its transitions. In other words, as the political and ideological struggle has a primary role in interpreting historical change and socialist strategy, any reference to material bases, not to mention a grounding in capitalist imperatives, looks like determinism. It therefore stands to reason that the left-right distinction would be blurred at best, as nominations of oppressor and oppressed are left to the mercy of the historically localised judgments of political actors, bereft of a lens of the economic stakes involved.

The poststructural focus on articulation and conscious construction of the people come at an expense of effacing the repetitive, enduring patterns of social life. Laclau correctly speaks of the ontological function of populism, but he nevertheless fails to show how the necessary outlet for the voice of the socio-economically disenfranchised comes about. Leaving aside this dearth of explanation for the origin of the protest vote, its fluidity is also questionable, notwithstanding extensive shifts in political alignment. Those that have reason to be disillusioned with the state of affairs, as logical subjects of transitional politics, could be located within the workings of capitalism. The denial of overbearing determination to capitalism shows how the shift in 'ontic attachment' away from left parties testifies to a displacement of concrete conditions of exploitation, rather than their obstinate maintenance. This does not mean that the promotion of a hegemonic agenda that exposes the historic redundancy of the ruling bloc and articulates the democratic legitimacy of the ascendant bloc has a 'natural' constituency. Objective measures of exploitation do not directly lend credence to the case for a transition. They do, however, warrant Mouzelis' (1978: 53) protest alluding to the stability within the social formation: 'Once an ideological discourse takes a specific place and form within a concrete social formation, it becomes relatively fixed and organised within limits'.

The subsumption of the economic within the discursive construction of the political, is a gateway to post-Marxism, to which I turn below.

2   Discourse and Hegemony

HSS can be read as an attempt to hegemonise the discursive field of Marxism, as it charts a history of Marxist thought in terms of an expanding problematisation of essentialism and necessity. The basic categories of 'classical Marxism' were assumed to have explanatory power, yet their inadequacy was revealed in attempts to analyse society and formulate strategy. Particularly, the issue of political representation of class interests was inhibited by the absence of a 'sutured' entity whose interests could be projected onto political struggle. This resulted in a constitutive deflection of class interest towards a vanguard. Universalist and objectivist pretensions of Marxism unravel with hegemony, 'a fundamental nodal point of Marxist political theorization' (HSS: 3). Marxists had simply read in the working class an 'objective destiny' apparent to the trained eye (HSS: 85). The endogenous workings of the economy would intensify its contradictions and lead to a point where the forces of production cannot contain the relations of production. In HSS, the workers at the centre of the contradiction between social production and private ownership of the product are relegated to a discursively formulated 'subject position', and one with diminishing importance, since contemporary society has become increasingly complex, comprising many irreducible political actors.

Laclau and Mouffe direct an unambiguous criticism at the orthodox Marxists' simplification of transition in the following words:

> What is now in crisis is a whole conception of socialism which rests upon the ontological centrality of the working class, upon the role of Revolution,

with a capital 'r', as the founding moment in the transition from one type of society to another, and upon the illusory prospect of a perfectly unitary and homogeneous collective will that will render pointless the moment of politics (HSS: 2).

The notion of a move beyond political society is at odds with the ontological grounding of politics in society, implying that it will be a fixture of any post-capitalist social formation. The prevailing understanding of transition, Laclau and Mouffe explain, rests in the assumption that an undifferentiated mass will eventually coalesce into a revolutionary force that will restructure society, such that divisions sustained by capitalism will become redundant. Communism, in other words, stands for a teleological projection of a self-identical society, but this ideal vision does not match up to its complexity, nor to the multifaceted nature of subjectivity. Society cannot be transparent to itself such that certain social actors with a privileged vantage point can consciously manipulate it to a preconceived final state. Classical Marxist pretensions to be able to do so have historically stifled pluralism and inaugurated totalitarianism. The closure of the social should therefore be avoided, in favour of an open-ended field of articulations. Moreover, the concept of society is problematic, and to formulate a new understanding of the social 'we must begin by renouncing 'society' as a founding totality of its partial processes' (HSS: 95). Discursive articulations, as sequences of signifiers that renegotiate meanings, negate the 'essence' of the social, nullifying the totality of 'partial process' making up a coherent whole.

Subsequently Laclau and Mouffe shift the terrain of transition to the efficacy of hegemony, a concept that has been a milestone in Marxist theory yet remains anchored in class. Gramsci's innovative use of hegemony had afforded a degree of autonomy to the political from class determination that was hitherto denied. Kautsky, for instance, attempted to foreclose the plurality of the social by positing an identity between the social and class struggle, while Bernstein put forward a notion of the 'ethical subject' as the working-class subjectivity that would actualise the potentials of historical evolution (HSS: 16, 34). While the ethical judgment of the superiority of socialism is appropriate for Laclau and Mouffe, they take issue with the attribution of its execution to a 'transcendental subject, constituted outside every discursive condition of emergence' (HSS: 46). Here Gramsci is commended for refraining from referring to *a priori* collective identities, and postulating hegemony as the construction of such identities and their alliances (HSS: 65–67). Discourse is thus central to the articulation of collective wills, which cannot be deduced from economic categories. This in turn imputes contingency to social struggle, removing guarantees and beating a path to a 'new political imaginary' of mobilisation beyond class positions. The working-class as the subject of history is dissolved into intermeshing subject positions, be it assembly line worker, pacifist, disabled person, or single mother.

The economic level, for Laclau and Mouffe, remains as the last impenetrable 'rational substratum of history' (HSS: 76). Following the disaggregation of the working-class as a homogeneous, corporate unit (or its 'dethroning' as Forgacs (1985: 43) calls it), it is unfeasible to speak of a distinct economic level that outlines the terms of social struggle and identity. The economy is described as the 'last redoubt of essentialism', and 'threshold which none of the strategic hegemonic conceptions manages to cross' (HSS: 76). Gramsci formulated the economy as the articulatory core of a historical bloc, creating room for an interpenetration of the economic and the political. Accordingly, one's economic position does not implicate political leaning, as this is receptive to a cultural-ideological leadership impervious to class position. However, such leadership, to establish hegemony across society, cannot avoid elaborating an economic policy that it can show to be beneficial for all. Gramsci thereby retains the 'rational substratum' of the workings of the mode of production, and its generation of fundamental classes. The historical bloc traverses class lines, but eventually solidifies with the objective interests of the fundamental class. Radicalising Gramsci means to take a further step and jettison the economic level of discrete class demarcations, subsuming this content in hegemonic struggle.

Now, the historiography of ever-expanding contingency in Marxist theory has opened out into a post-Marxist rejection of social totality. Along with Gramsci, this has theoretical consequences for Althusserian categories, social formation being an obvious casualty. The term had been used to refer to the complex totality of economic, ideological and political practices, designating society in real terms. Historical materialism, as the science of social formations, takes these as its objects, viewing them from a dislocated – as opposed to empiricist – theoretical angle. Dislocation among different levels of the social formation was an inspiration for Laclau's earlier work on the irreducibility between class, politics and ideology, which makes it clearer why Torfing (1999: 16) considers him as more sympathetic to the Althusser of *For Marx* than of *Reading Capital*. While Althusser maintained the staggered and uneven development of levels in the social formation, he nevertheless avoided a pluralism of these levels by retaining determination in the last instance. Laclau and Mouffe's work carries an imprint of the dislodging of coexisting differential rhythms and temporal logics within one singular social formation, yet they renounce the social formation and overdetermination for a perceived essentialism (HSS: 97). Althusser's stances are brought to conclusions that suggest a post-Althusserian departure.

What tied down Althusser's otherwise liberating insights was his adhesion to a Marxist theoretical purity, symptomatised in the elevation of the economy to the status of an 'abstract universal object' (HSS: 99). Laclau and Mouffe are peculiarly unsparing in their judgment of Althusser's 'essentialism', considering that he had challenged the 'expressive totality' of historicism, *i.e.* the notion that history was guided by a 'spirit', where every part revealed the stamp of the whole. By maintaining a universal referent in the economy, Althusser allegedly makes the mistake of smuggling pre-discursive objects to a social reality where every object is constituted as an object of discourse (HSS: 111). The commitment to the ubiquity of discourse undermines not only the topological account of the social, but also the notion of a coherent 'society'. Alongside the assertion of the constitutive role of discourse, the lack of an overbearing determination signals a rejection of Althusser's 'social formation' in favour of the 'impossibility of society'. Not only has society become increasingly complex, the notion of society as an 'intelligible totality, itself conceived as the structure upon which its partial elements and processes are founded' hints at an arrogance in determinist theories (Laclau, 2014: 122–126).

The desacralisation of the economy is carried out in terms of theoretical scrutiny as well as references to the post-industrial makeup of contemporary western societies. The theorists take to task the sociologists of class, particularly Nicos Poulantzas (1975), Eric Olin Wright (1985, 1989) and Harry Braverman (1974), for their somewhat panicked search for a 'working class' whose interests can be linked to socialism. But in the process, whether speaking about the nature of productive labour, contradictory class positions, or consequences of deskilling in the labour force, they cannot but make political and ideological claims regarding the economic necessity of a naturally antagonistic working class. Laclau and Mouffe aver that these debates are so fixated on the differentiation between social groups that they lose sight of the incorrigible differentiation *within* them (HSS: 80–85). Fragmentations within the working class show that the thesis of homogenisation, namely that society is bound to be increasingly polarised into two camps of haves and have-nots, has turned out to be unfounded. They (HSS: 81–84) also point to the ways in which the production process has transformed through interventions of the working class as well as the internal fissures along gender and racial lines aggravated by their traditional political institutions. Such differentiations signify a working-class of collective will, echoing E.P. Thompson's (1980: 19) injunction to save the historical personalities of working people from the 'enormous condescension of posterity'.

It is worth noting that Mouffe later develops this poststructural critique of suture by formulating what Leggett (2017: 119) refers to as a 'politico-centric' account of society. Mouffe rejects the possibility of defining a prior, objective social terrain in which politics can intervene, as such definitions are inevitably absorbed in discursive contingency. Instead, Mouffe (2005: 18) argues that the social is constituted by power relations, suggesting the impossibility of society as an object of knowledge:

> Power is constitutive of the social because the social could not exist without the power relations through which it is given shape. What is at a given moment considered as the 'natural' order – jointly with the common sense which accompanies it – is the result of sedimented practices; it is never the manifestation of a deeper objectivity exterior to the practices that bring it into being.

The coextension of all social deliberation and power relations with politics are paramount to Mouffe's own theory of the political, but the pronounced anti-realism of HSS can be glimpsed in its pages. Society does not exist outside of discourse, and social identities are created through perennially agonistic political processes. Mouffe thereby refines the thesis of the impossibility of society with a positive suggestion of the instantiation of social agents as causes and results of infinite political decision-making. According to Leggett (2013: 311), this amounts a neglect of the *social* terrain in which subjectivities are constructed *prior* to entering the political field, and is consequently missing a 'thicker sense of how social and cultural forms of association are a source of identity'. However, for Mouffe and other post-Marxists, the contingent nature of social life facilitates a new paradigm of left strategy and analysis.

The subsequent section in HSS is appropriately titled 'Facing the Consequences'; instead of casting nostalgic glances towards the consistency of classical Marxism, it is now necessary to discard privileged subjects and homogenised agents (HSS: 87). Proposing a 'new political imaginary', Laclau and Mouffe explain that in a discursive terrain without guarantees, it is necessary to leave behind privileged points of rupture, decentring the ruptural unity overdetermined by economic relations (HSS: 152). Transition is made possible with hegemonic practice, and cannot be presupposed as a social latency. Moreover, hegemony is the sole political method that presupposes the openness of the social (HSS: 142). Despite lapsing into some references to prediscursive concepts, such as imperialist exploitation in the Third World (HSS: 131), and making numerous statements on capitalism as a pregiven social order, Laclau and Mouffe are adamant that 'objective and intelligible patterns of relations empty empirical society of specifiable content' (HSS: 126).

The plurality and indeterminacy of the social can only be navigated by hegemonic practice, widening the democratic sphere to include multiple collective wills in an antagonistic unity. Antagonism is a consciously chosen word here, as 'contradiction' would indicate a logical impossibility while antagonism can accommodate coexistence (HSS: 125). Indeed, Mouffe subsequently elaborates on this aspect of HSS at length. Her project argues for the necessity to a healthy democracy of both competing antagonisms, and their domestication into co-existing 'agonisms' which respect each other's right to exist (see, for example, Mouffe, 2005). In sum, Laclau and Mouffe make a call to extend the democratic field and move on from the hubris of presumed, eventual socialist triumph. Instead, their theoretical architecture aims to build discursive chains of equivalence in a bid for radical democracy.

3   The Impasses of Discourse Analysis and the Melancholy of Radical Democracy

Laclau and Mouffe's privileging of the political moment heavily depends on discursive openness. The production process is seen as politically instantiated, denying autonomy or even distinctiveness to the economy (HSS: 84). Laclau's earlier insistence on the irreducibility of politics, coupled with the distinctive operations of the economy, has given way to a continuity of the former over the latter.

Laclau and Mouffe (HSS: 2) have taken hegemony, which had been a 'complementary and contingent operation for classical Marxism', towards post-Marxist conclusions. The pivotal role of the concept rests in the unfixity of subject positions (HSS: 85–86), and their chains of equivalence that bind progressive subjectivities in a 'radical democratic' enterprise. Accordingly, the class struggle analytic is a non-viable essentialism that posits a homogeneity among insolubly diverse social strata. It is more fruitful, in their opinion, to approach political subjects not as classes but 'collective wills' (HSS: 67). This action-based approach to the working-class resembles Hindess and Hirst's (1977: 7) epistemological rejection of 'correspondence' between our preconceptions and the way the world is, explained as follows: 'We do not deny the existence of social relations – that would render our very project absurd. What we reject is the category of 'concrete' as object-of-knowledge. It is the relation of 'appropriation' or of 'correspondence' of knowledge to its objects which we challenge'.

Hindess and Hirst (in Cutler, et al., 1977: 128, italics in the original) take issue with templates of causality as such: 'What we are challenging is *not merely* the economic monist causality of Marxism, *but the very pertinence of all such general categories of causality and the privilege they accord to certain orders of causes as against others*'. This has great importance *vis-à-vis* transition. As in the early Laclau, an Althusser-inspired detachment of class position from political agenda arrives at a point where it is not possible to discern a confluence between the object and the object of knowledge. Consequently, aside from the working class losing its 'ontological centrality' (HSS: 2), positing goals that are in line with the advancement of the working class becomes an arbitrary and ahistorical assertion.

Laclau and Mouffe would diverge from Hindess and Hirst in that the former maintain that political grievances can refer to material circumstances, whether in the production process or elsewhere, so that there is a degree of correspondence, even if vague. For the authors of HSS, however, the material circumstances would only be a point of contention if they are discursively articulated as such, overturning the causality of the lived exploitation to its political expression. Thus, Laclau and Mouffe oppose the existence of a social reality independent of discourse. They do not uphold an idealist view that the object does not exist save for its discursive construction, a view they articulate clearly in their response to Geras' (1987) criticisms (Laclau and Mouffe, 1990). That said, there is no stable point linking prediscursive social reality with people's opinions of it, as the nature of the connection between symbols and referents is obscured. If there is no prediscursive objectivity, then the discursive formulations of observed phenomena all hold equal merit. Such a perspective is compatible with the hegemony of the dominant order, as exploitation, for instance, is obfuscated as 'a matter of opinion' that while possibly having empirical referents, depends on where one chooses to look from.

Wood (1986: 61) claims that the principle of non-correspondence is pivotal in the turn to discourse, and if discourse is fundamental, 'a caveman is as likely to become a socialist as is a proletarian – provided only that he comes within hailing distance of the appropriate discourse'. While this is a polemically overstated *reductio ad absurdum,* Wood's criticism does point to a deficiency in Laclau and Mouffe's account of western societies, wherein class differentiation does not explain social behaviour any longer. Indeed, while one could not expect to find the condition of the working class in England as it was in Engels' time, it is hardly a case of conceptual imperialism to refer to 'capitalist society', albeit in an evolved form, when referring to these societies. Arguably this would also be a normative common ground for a card-carrying Conservative, who may have an entirely different stance as to its virtue yet would agree with an anti-capitalist on a minimal definition of capitalism. As a matter of fact, HSS is peppered with what could only be described as orthodox Marxist phrases such as 'the advanced capitalist social formations', 'an intensive regime of accumulation', 'capitalist periphery', and 'imperialist exploitation', among others (HSS: 137, 66, 131, 160, respectively). A certain practical solidarity in language undergirds social existence, since there could be potentially catastrophic consequences if two people used the same words to refer to entirely different objects, or different words to refer to the same. This does not endanger the left project, as taking a basic definitional agreement to then articulate to the adversary the problems with their subscribed positions could make for a powerful discursive strategy. However, this appears less feasible with the elusive conceptual repository of radical democracy.

The formulation of discourse takes a tautological turn as discursive elements are produced within the same monistic circuit, with reference to one another. An upshot of this is the ironic disappearance of ideology as a concept referring to a gap between the way things really are and their subjective perceptions, as to refer to ideology it is necessary to have an at least provisionally non-ideological referent. Laclau (2006: 114) has expanded on his views on ideology, saying that it should not be abandoned, but retained without the 'slightest pejorative connotation' as a descriptor for discourses which attempt to reify and universalise their contingent character, to engage in the hegemonic game. The 'objectivist' vision of Marxism, Laclau (2006: 104) contends, does not have any purchase on contemporary societies. As the class struggle and its role in historical change encountered empirical and theoretical refutations, the social parameters of the political were also eroded, making way for the theory of discourse as the central explanation of social life (Laclau, 2006: 112).

Laclau's (2006: 111–112) later clarifications do not suggest that the concept of the mode of production is redundant, but he maintains that capitalism does not *ipso facto* provoke resistance. This aligns with the view of the political construction of subjectivities. For example, a working-class collective will may participate in the radical democratic program as a *political* agent whose identity is informed by surrounding labour processes. Yet the point remains that this is not an expression of an economic determination, and definitely not a lag between the political and the economic. This would leave little room for a definition of ideology, though Laclau (2006: 114) proposes an adjustment that places ideology at the centre of discursive constructions of meaning and the limits of all possible representation. This view builds on the proposition that all representation is 'catachrestical' and 'tropological', *i.e.* there is always a mismatch between the utterance and its object. Discursive forms operate through 'absolute metaphors' that invoke other forms (2006: 114). As a result, the failed closure in stabilising meanings is in itself ideological. This expands Laclau's (1997: 206) earlier formulation of ideology as a self-referential 'belief that there is a particular social arrangement which can bring about the closure and transparency of the community'. Here Laclau alludes to real socialism, where nationalisation of basic industries was seen as synonymous with a transparent society, exemplifying a suture. The social subsumption of the economy also generates ideology, as Laclau (1997: 206) has argued that 'there is ideology whenever a particular content shows itself as more than itself'. This would further emphasise that ideology is ingrained in articulations; as Laclau (1997: 212) concludes 'the illusion of closure is something we can negotiate with, but never eliminate. Ideology is a dimension which belongs to the structure of all possible experience'.

Imbuing ideology into the fabric of discourse has underwhelming consequences. A strategic gain from the account of ideology without pejorative connotations is in allowing for a revaluation of dominant discourses, without dismissing people as passive receptacles or cultural dupes. However, this diffusion of the ideological into social life can also jeopardise its analytical utility. The obfuscation of ideology is an upshot of the tampering with realism and objectivity discussed above. The dispersion of discourse is chosen somewhat arbitrarily as the location of the ideological, but this simply displaces the problem of how to build a hegemonic bloc without reference to the non-political. Laclau's reformulations only generalize the impossibility of closure towards an inescapable incoherence, and inability to link concrete demands with their causes and consequences regarding material interests.

The theories of discourse surveyed here enact a closure themselves, coming from the opposite direction to the economic, and vastly expanding the discursive field. This is acknowledged in HSS and some of Mouffe's later work (*e.g.*, 2005: 15). It is questionable whether things can even be said to exist if they escape the purview of discourse. The disappearance of ideology also undermines hegemony in the original sense. Gramsci (1971: 18) had argued that the ascendant historical bloc secures its leadership over society when it develops economic superiority simultaneously with its cultural-political justification. Moreover, organic intellectuals produce theoretical and cultural works that are formally incompatible with the dominant ones, such as the novel genre as part of the flourishing culture of the secular bourgeoisie. Hegemony therefore involves economic and cultural leadership, to legitimise itself as an interlocutor of all social groups. Relations of production continue to impose limitations on civil society, which is nonetheless autonomous from the non-economic areas of the social formation. As Geras (1987: 49–50) argues, the post-Marxist outlook cannot accommodate relative autonomy, seeing the economic 'post-and-chain' as determining all or nothing.

Geras' point is apt, yet it does not elaborate on how economic determinants shape the 'superstructure'. In this respect, it is helpful to follow Eagleton's (1991: 83) suggestion that the superstructure should be seen in 'adjectival' terms rather than substantively, echoing Althusser's use of the base-superstructure model in metaphorical terms. The superstructure is no more or less 'real' than the base, the designation being relative, as opposed to a fixed locale in the social formation. Eagleton (ibid: 83) explains this in the following terms:

> You can examine a literary text in terms of its publishing history, in which case, as far as the Marxist model goes, you are treating it as part of the material base of social production. Or you can count up the number of semicolons, an activity which would seem to fit neatly into neither level of the model. But once you explore that text's relations to a dominant ideology, then you are creating it superstructurally. The doctrine, in other words, becomes rather more plausible when it is viewed less as an ontological carving of the world down the middle than as a question of different perspectives.

The distinction between the superstructure and the base needs to be understood as a dialectical unity, rather than separate spheres. Their determination is not unidirectional, as opposed to Laclau and Mouffe's political world of open-ended contingency. Additionally, imputing to Marxism the view that the working-class is a homogenous and corporate entity is erroneous. Using categories relationally, capital cannot be separated from wage labour, but has the quality of being capital insofar as it congeals labour as surplus value. The political potential of the working class comes from their capacity to sublimate this relation. This picture more cogently explains the world-historical affinity between the working class and socialism than discursive proficiency.

Laclau and Mouffe have sought to undo the last bulwark of essentialism at the economic level by exposing it to the workings of hegemony, but lost the material bearings of the hegemonic project. As Leggett (2013) has argued, post-Marxism would have benefited from allowing for the prior subjectivation of agents before taking part in the hegemonic game, yet this would also raise the question of what exactly would remain 'post' of Marxism. In a similar vein, Rustin (1988: 172) argues that hegemony is a compelling theory because it 'encourages reflection on the actual causes and conditions which make collective redefinitions possible'. The post-Marxist reformulation loses sight of such limitations, ending up with a political agenda with more to say about accommodating to the *status quo* than moving beyond it. While radical democracy can be placed in left-of-centre politics, its premises engender left-liberalism. The acknowledgement of problematic aspects of Marxism, while a daunting task in the face of rigidified orthodoxies, has failed to revitalise the subversive character of transitional politics, offering a new explanatory model that is inferior to the Marxist paradigm.

The project of expanding liberal democracy to include marginalised groups in a popular struggle is symptomatic of the victories of the New Right and neoliberal social engineering that have left fragmented struggles in their wake. A sense of resignation can be discerned in radical democracy, since it avoids statements of truth, and punches hardest towards its left. In the meantime, the New Right has transparently waged class warfare by isolating and diminishing working class bargaining power and dismantling entire industries to ensure profitability and a shift towards a financialised model. The working class was thus deprived of its securities, not to mention the real drop in wages from levels that had once surpassed inflation rates. As Wood (1986: 9–10, 182–183) suggests in her withering criticism of post-Marxism, the turn away from organised labour as an agent of socialist transition ironically coincided with the 'winter of discontent' of 1978–9 and the miner's strike of 1984–5, pivotal points in British history where the rhetoric of class struggle was used not just by organised labour and the left, but would be utilised by the Thatcher regime itself. The goal of rolling back the gains of labour was often voiced in direct terms by the right. Per Wood's explanation, the discursive turn was stimulated by the setbacks in these working-class struggles, not to mention the academic allure of discourse theory.

The influence of such developments can be inferred from the pages of HSS, but Wood's speculation is nevertheless cynical, considering how much purchase an alternative thesis of left melancholy could have in enlightening its motives. The efficacy of the New Right in garnering support from a hegemonic project of its own cannot be explained solely with the ebbs and flows in industry relations, and Wood takes a reductionist attitude when she dismisses the 'authoritarian populism' of the Thatcher regime as an insignificant façade over bourgeois domination. Such an explanation would also need to consider the general demoralised accommodation of the left, which has demoted a founding vision of postcapitalism to 'realistic' piecemeal concessions from capital. While Laclau and Mouffe have the best intentions for rekindling the left imaginary cornered between decaying social democracy and calcified Soviet doctrines, radical democracy embraces the state of affairs, striving for its improvement without a view to its overthrow. It is unclear, as Laclau and Mouffe pull the rug of ontological-normative grounds for socialism from under its feet, how to gauge gains against the rule of capital, and precipitate socialism. This is another symptom of the disappearance of the communist horizon, and scaling down of revolutionary project in the late twentieth century. *Hegemony and Socialist Strategy* is a forerunner of left melancholy, a phenomenon to be tackled in detail in Part 2.

SUMMARY

The Marxist Transition Debate and the Notion of Plural Temporalities

Having set out the parameters for the ontology of transition within the dynamic and contradictory nature of capitalism, this book has thus far explored the notion of multiple temporalities, their relevance to historical epistemology, and the reactivation of a neglected concept. Beginning from the ontology of transitional tendencies in capitalism and the ways in which they suggest postcapitalist social arrangements, I have traced the concept towards its more explicit elaboration in Althusserian theory, as well as analysing its subsequent demise in the throes of post-Marxist deconstruction. The argument developed throughout these chapters is that it is worthwhile to retain transition as a sociologically grounded concept, and that among various strands of Marxist theory there is evidence of its efficacy in explaining the perpetuation and disruptions of social processes. Conversely, it has been argued that the undervaluation of transition has driven and reflects a melancholic left accommodation to the existing order, and an inability to develop analytical means to theorise postcapitalism. Given the range of theoretical traditions and concepts that this critical survey has necessarily entailed, the following extended summary draws together the key analytical and substantive features and implications of Part 1, as a platform for advancing the rest of the argument.

Part 1 has traced the concept of transition as it has been understood – or effaced – in prevailing strands of Marxism. The salient approaches were identified, bringing historical materialist theories to bear on the problematic of transition. This treatment thus differs from approaches to socialist transition that consider it as a legislated moment in schedules of modernisation, and instead places it at the forefront of historical and social analysis. In practice this has meant reading Marx and Engels with a view to drawing out the attitudes they have taken towards a prospective theory of transition, and placing an explicit focus on Balibar's writings as a rare historical materialist engagement with this question. As Balibar has been a first-hand interlocutor of Althusserian Marxism, Althusser and Balibar's groundbreaking efforts towards a view of society as a complex and strained unity of temporal fissures merited sustained attention. The notion of multiple temporalities adds a new layer to our understanding of social change, reinforcing the historical as an actual force for political programmes that seek ways transform capitalist society. On the other hand, the structural emphasis in the Althusserian paradigm suggests a much-needed theorisation of the possibilities of contingency. Here Gramsci's theories on hegemony have presented themselves as a way of politicizing the ruptures that permeate structural Marxism. In turn, this has been seized as part of a post-structural turn towards anti-essentialist theories of discourse that jettison the predefined categories of Marxism in a post-Marxist direction. The main positions of this trend are encapsulated in the works of Laclau and Mouffe, who are wary of what they perceive as an insufficient appreciation of the hegemonic construction of subjectivities as the primary node of left strategy. In individual writings and in conjunction, they advocate an unprejudiced approach towards political agents beyond class interests and towards popular-democratic interpellations.

The outcome of this investigation was that transition was a casualty in the turn away from productive activity as a material underpinning to society. Through the lens of post-Marxism, the content of transition ceases to be specifiable, and suggestions towards postcapitalist blueprints of the future are redundant and irrelevant in a political imaginary devoid of social determinations. Discursive processes ride roughshod over different trajectories of social change and inundate the domain of struggle, making it needless to discern points of rupture. Similarly, they become irrelevant since radical democracy does not envision an endgame to the state of affairs and the structures of power that sustain it.

A more detailed synthesis of this process of tracing the implicit invocation, explicit discussion, and the curious disappearance of the concept of transition in historical materialism is provided below.

1 Transition and Historical Materialism

Directionality is necessary for a cogent theory of transition, as the term semantically implies a progression through a liminal passage between two stages. Deploying a historical materialist outlook provides the parameters to distinguish qualitative transition between social formations, or judge whether the changes solely reproduce the past embodied in existing structures. Additionally, usage of the concept indicates that in terms of historical epistemology, the transformations of human societies can be systematically assessed using objective measures. This would contradict what may be called the twin threats of relativism and of determinism (of an economic stripe or otherwise). The former rejects what it terms grand narratives with purportedly universal measures of historical change, and seeks to deconstruct Marxism as one of these culturally specific explanatory models. This being the case, historical change cannot be conceived as linear progress, nor can it be grasped as an object of knowledge, since this would signify conceptual imperialism. Determinism replicates this one-sided viewpoint, but instead of irreducible cultural mediations, the economic level, and the forces of production in particular, are treated as engines of societal transformation. The Soviet economy under Stalin, as Althusser contends, was a case in point. The managers of industry fetishized exorbitant levels of production, assuming that socialism and even a classless society had been realised. Reducing political and ideological developments to epiphenomenal expressions of economic process led to a theoretical erasure of persisting patterns of oppression and discrimination, and their resuscitation in a gradual process leading to the full-blown restoration of the free market. What both postmodern heterogeneity and determinist homogeneity lack, therefore, is an appreciation of history as a staggered, contradictory, yet explicable process. Here I theorise history as a process of transitions, without a singular organising mechanism. The Althusserian concept of the interrelated difference of all elements of the social formation serves as a promising theory for this enterprise, which shall be summarised below.

A gulf separates definitions of historical materialism between its adherents and critics of all stripes, thus a reiteration of an arguably orthodox view is pertinent. Here the initial axiom is that every society needs to secure their material reproduction. In the proceedings of a conference on Marxism and culture, Perry Anderson replied to a charge of 'economism' saying that Marxism is 'a kind of common sense' (Nelson and Grossberg, 1988: 337). The enterprise is constructed upon the verity of this 'common sense' premise. Historical materialism also posits that the inter-meshing of forces and relations of production – roughly speaking, the tools used for production and the organisation involved in putting them into use – shape and colour other areas of society, and finally, their workings are not immediately apparent to the actors involved, leaving room for ideological and political autonomy. The changes along these levels make up a historical succession, albeit one with temporal multiplicity. But the point that there is some directionality stands, accounted for by productive underpinnings.

Historical materialism helps to understand society in a way that illuminates historical specificities along with the universally applicable concept of the mode of production. As all societies are compelled to produce for subsistence, and develop the means for doing so, the construction of means of production for this purpose suggests a creative aspect to human societies, and its wide variation between societies reinforces the thesis of its ubiquity. My theoretical frame is thus a species of productive essentialism. This is not to say production is equally valorised in every society, as productivism, or the instrumentalization of wage-labour for profit, is actually a capitalist aberration. The mode of production covers the forces and relations of production, respectively referring to the manipulation of material found in nature into instruments of creating products, and the determinate relations in which these forces are used. These categories are relational as modes of organisation and technical know-how can be explained in terms of both. However, this does not sufficiently explain why the mode of production is key to understanding social change. Every moment of production is also one of reproduction. Similarly, productive activity and consumption can only be analytically separated but involve each other in their instantiations. Consequently, the mode of production casts a shadow over social life in varying degrees, and creates possibilities to cultivate new ones. Marx does not stop at these observations, which could, in themselves, be agreeable to the mainstream political economy of his time: he further argues that the capitalist mode of production is predicated on dispossessing labourers of the means and fruits of their labour, and turning the commodities into entities standing opposed to their makers. As productive activity is an immutable human quality, capitalist relations of production alienate their bearers from exercising this capacity. Contrarily, communism as a positive supersession of capitalism is the reappropriation of the means of production, and their utilisation for human self-actualisation.

2 Transition Problematised: Althusser, Balibar, and Gramsci

Marx's journalistic writings attest to a view of historical change more attuned to political vicissitudes beyond immediate economic developments. Subsequent inquiries of the relative autonomy of the political and the contingent can be found in Althusser and Balibar's Marxism. Targeting historicism, Althusser rejected the expressive totality of the 'essential section'. Instead, Althusser postulated a separation between the economic, political and the ideological as relatively discrete sites of social reproduction with internal tensions and temporal rhythms. This separation is not literal, as each moment is present at every step. Further, Althusser argued that the economy is determinant in the last instance, and manifests itself through the specific effectivities of the other levels. This means that the primacy of politics or law in a capitalist society is due to economic overdeterminations functioning in that way. The Althusserian theory of social reproduction provides a reasonable historical materialist outlook without slipping into either total contingency or determinism.

The immediate coexistence of these levels implies that all moments of social reproduction bear on subjective relations to the world, the nature of state power, and the mode of production. Unilateral determinations by an ensconced 'essence' are bound to misread the sociopolitical conjuncture. Balibar has developed this insight, maintaining that the difference between these levels is a temporal lag (*décalage*), a term that has remained in use in poststructural currents. This has utmost importance for transition, blurring the understanding of revolutions as clean cuts in historical progress. Using the example of economic downturns in crisis-prone capitalism, Balibar argues that revolutionary ruptures cannot take place unless downturns overlap with acute political struggle. As Althusser argued regarding the October Revolution, 'ruptural unity' can take place in moments of insoluble contradiction and temporal strain between different levels. The notion of multiple temporalities stands in stark contrast to theories that assume a self-identical present.

A confluence with Althusserian reflections can be found in Gramsci, who may strike the reader as an unlikely candidate for bolstering a structural view of historical change. However, Gramsci's comment on the October Revolution as a 'revolution against capital' is a telling example of how he also recognised a separation of the political and the economic. The Bolsheviks seized on the widespread disillusionment with the Tsarist autocracy to establish a state of Soviets, overriding stagist theses of a necessary phase of capitalist development. A socialist government, despite its later authoritarian turn, attested to the possibility of bridging temporal gaps between the *ancien régime* and the anticipations of egalitarian society in a context of minimal primitive accumulation and very recent abolition of serfdom. Gramsci witnessed this experience in his theoretical writings by emphasizing the 'historical' in historical materialism. He was thus held up as an exemplar of historicism, although his differentiation of the levels of social reproduction suggest that a compatibility with Althusserian approaches.

The inclusion of Gramsci serves to integrate temporal lag into transitional strategy. A term central to Gramsci's understanding of politics and society, hegemony has allowed us to envision the Althusserian separation of distinct levels with a view to chart socialist strategy. It encompasses the historically specific mixtures of consent and repression that help capitalism survive. Gramsci seizes on the observation that economic trauma is not always conducive to revolutionary upheaval, and he expands the narrow understanding of hegemony as political alliances, to argue that the stability of revolutionary regimes requires wide-reaching consensus.

Reaching for an emblematic moment of capitalist transition, the French Revolution, Gramsci elaborates how the bourgeoisie rallied the subjugated population to its side against the nobility and the clergy. This analysis takes account of the 'intellectual cells of a new type born with their economic counterparts', rather than assuming eventual capitalist supremacy (Gramsci, 1971: 18). While the political challenge was important for capitalist consolidation, the intellectual currents of liberty and equality also instilled hope among the downtrodden. Such prospects revealed the obsolescence of feudal ties and their pretensions to permanence. The Althusserian complex social formation, and its temporal lags, can be interpreted from a Gramscian lens as an injunction to recognize and activate non-contemporary social practices in their historical becoming. In other words, I have argued that *décalage* is translated into politics in Gramsci's work, which is fitting considering that he advocated translations, such as from philosophy to common sense, as a mode of political activity. Consequently, in spite of the alleged chasm between Althusser and Gramsci, these points of contact suggest a complementary relationship that could contribute to historical and political discussions of transition.

3 Post-Marxism: the Discursive Turn and the Disappearance of Transition

The final chapter of this part has followed the thread connecting Gramsci and Althusser to the post-Marxism of Laclau and Mouffe. The latter duo rejects closed social categories and historical materialist theses. Focusing on Laclau, I have discussed the evolution in his thought from the point of recognizing non-class interpellation as a way in which social subjects are identified. Building on this, Laclau argued that 'popular-democratic interpellations' operated above productive relations, and constituted a field of political conflict that Marxists should be involved in. The complete separation of the economy from the political in the early Laclau may be argued to be a continuation of the differentiation that Althusser and Balibar had suggested previously. However, the French authors had preserved a certain nuance and simultaneity to the separation. For Laclau, however, the economic field gives way to a political omnipresence, strongly expressed in his collaboration with Mouffe.

Mouffe has been a popular interlocutor of Gramscian theory, helping to bring hegemony to the centre of the post-Marxist political imaginary. HSS tells a story of Marxism as the continual expansion of contingency and a growing distance from essentialism and determinism. The theory of hegemony was a nodal point in this venture, as it recognised the autonomy of the political with a contingent attenuation, paving the way to open-ended articulation. Laclau and Mouffe contend that the economy has remained as the last bastion of endogenous dynamics, and so reformulate it as a site of politics, disposing of its privileged position. They go on to formulate a strategy of recognising 'collective wills', which arise from the increasingly fragmented new social movements. Yet, the practice of such discourse-based politics involves a highly subjective formulation by the analysts themselves. This theory is thus heavily skewed in favour of the constitutive role of discourse and the effacement of pre-discursive sites of determination.

Having denounced the 'ontological centrality of the working class, upon the role of Revolution, with a capital 'r', as the founding moment in the transition from one type of society to another' (HSS: 2), Laclau and Mouffe set about deconstructing the vocabulary of emancipation in the Marxist canon. I have in turn sought to deconstruct the discursive focus in HSS by drawing attention to its conformity with erstwhile postmodern and poststructural trends, and the concomitant loss of a postcapitalist horizon that I considered to be symptomatic of the domination of the right in the late twentieth century. The post-Marxist 'political imaginary' congeals temporal multiplicity by calling for an expansion of liberal democracy in favour of groups hitherto denied rights. While this is indeed a worthwhile effort, it is bereft of a postcapitalist vision and therefore leans towards accommodation with capitalism.

Chapter 3 concluded by contending that HSS is a forerunner of left melancholy, in the sense of downgrading revolutionary ambitions and acquiescing to the totality of capitalism. Post-Marxists have forfeited the critical ambition to discover underlying contradictions beneath the surface appearance, repeating the established pattern of postmodern relativism. This has also severed the link between economic interests and ideological expressions. Discursive analysis, while potentially useful in a complementary role, has become the single overweening explanatory model of society, making it unfeasible to conceptualise an overhaul of its political and economic structures. Consequently, the discursive turn reflects a demoralisation on the left, caught between Soviet authoritarianism and social democratic conformity, falling back on discursive manoeuvres. Thus, post-Marxism has a melancholic vision without an emancipatory horizon, or sense of a directionality to social change.

4   Temporality, Transition and Debates on the Left

Having set forth the historical epistemology underlying the problematic of transition and its neglect, it is pertinent to consider ongoing left debates to make a judgment on the utility of foregrounding transition. Part 2 will illustrate the utility of the notion of transition – and its expression along multiple temporalities – by bringing it to bear on a salient dichotomy in left theory. The dichotomy in question is between melancholy and utopia: two mutually constitutive yet attitudinally opposed dispositions, replete with implications for temporality and prospects of transition.

PART 2

Transition as Hermeneutic: the Dichotomy of Melancholy and Utopia

∴

Introduction to Part 2

A case to reactivate the transition debate initially requires an account of its ontology. In this sense, Part 1 has traced the concept in its implicit and explicit formulations within classical and Western Marxism, ending with a critical analysis of post-Marxism. To use a distinction invoked in Chapter 3, Part 2 sketches the ontic manifestations of ontological transitional tensions. In particular, melancholy and utopia are analysed as substantive frames. As undercurrents of alternative temporalities, these categories animate the temporal theory of transition as a hermeneutic of temporal lag.

Chapter 4 considers melancholy in general – and its 'left' variant in particular – as a mode of engagement with mainstream political life. The debilitating aspect of melancholy as a foreclosure of revolutionary ambitions, and concomitant calls for 'moderation', are contrasted with its potential as a political resource. On the latter notion, Walter Benjamin's approaches to left melancholy are discussed. For Benjamin, melancholy signifies a capitulation, seen in some of the art and literature that portray the working class as a pitiful group in need of bourgeois charity. While this is a compelling indictment of melancholy, Benjamin's poetic variety of historical materialism reveals a different picture. Referring to the 'tradition of the oppressed', Benjamin sees revolution as a redemption of past defeats and an incursion into the future. Melancholy can thus be a resource, as one sees in the swift remembrance of past events and figures in new cycles of social movements. However, melancholy is an inadequate analytic of the positive construction of alternatives, where the impulse behind it takes on a utopian character.

Chapter 5 thus formulates utopia as a positive complement to left melancholy. Utopia has been met with derision as a latently totalitarian tendency, substituting its blueprints of the ideal society for reality. Furthermore, anti-utopianism has also been a disposition within left theory, designating unattainable social arrangements that are ultimately detrimental to the socialist cause. This chapter seeks to rehabilitate the notion of utopia as a hermeneutic, taking a cue from the works of Ernst Bloch, Ruth Levitas, and David Harvey, and posits that utopianism is part and parcel of social life.

Both left melancholy and utopia are generated in temporal lags throughout the social formation, attesting to agents' visceral and preconscious resistance to being contained in the spatio-temporal moment. Left melancholy can engender a resignation as well as a redemptive ambition, while utopia is a conduit of this temporal discord, testifying to the subterranean pasts of a future.

CHAPTER 4

Left Melancholy: Obstacle or Resource?

In 2009, the 'Idea of Communism' conference was held in Birkbeck, London. The contributions were collected in a volume where the editors Costas Douzinas and Slavoj Žižek proclaimed: 'The long night of the left is drawing to a close' (2010: vii). The conference, where communism was explicitly named and discussed as a positive political project, received a level of attention beyond the expectations of its organizers. This suggests a shift in radical politics. As Alain Badiou (2010: 27) has remarked, this was a moment of shared enthusiasm over a term that was 'sentenced to death by public opinion 30 years ago'. The editors suggest that the rear-guard defence of the remnants of social democracy has given way to an eagerness towards new beginnings. Following the neoliberal triumphalism of the 1990s, they argue that this new order began to decline in 2001, and was shattered with the financial crisis of 2008. Exalting this 'return to full-blown history', they express their satisfaction that the 'period of guilt is over' (ibid: viii-ix). This reading of recent history has some traction in critical theory, in which a deradicalisation and inward looking diffidence has characterised the left until recently. Admittedly, this overstates the point as it ignores the diversification which occurred in left theory, and did not necessarily amount to submission. Even so, the discursive turn in social theory sharply focuses on the assertion of identities, rather than collective emancipation. Following Fraser (1995: 68), it can be argued that recognition as a paradigmatic form that also characterizes post-Marxism had supplanted the struggle for the redistribution of resources. As argued earlier, this approach unwittingly effaces the mortality of modes of production and makes the notion of transition untenable. Therefore, Žižek and Douzinas intimate a more profound transformation than a simple change in mood when they dispute the 'end of history' thesis.

The affective reference to a restored sense of capacity and self-confidence implies that there had been a melancholic attitude. It is possible to characterise this sentiment in the quotidian sense of a longing for a fictional orderliness. In theoretical terms, Laclau and Mouffe would claim that the classical Marxist attachment to a misleading neatness belies a displaced incapacity to deal with complexities. In contrast, melancholy can take on a cross-temporally mobilising function. For Benjamin, it is a manifestation of unsatisfied attempts to transform society. As I will explain, Benjamin ridicules the melancholy of the intelligentsia as cynical detachment, while expounding on the redemptive potential of the vanquished in history. This reformulation of melancholia can destabilise self-assured claims of an end to history as well as linear models of transition, and restate the temporal complexity undergirding the present.

This chapter considers the theoretical and political aspects of gloom and despair within the frame of 'left melancholy'. Beginning from the psychoanalytic roots of the concept of melancholy, I will broach 'left' melancholy through the works of Benjamin, Wendy Brown, and Jodi Dean. The chapter is analytically divided between conceptions of melancholy as a potential resource and inspiration for left practice on the one hand, and a debilitating after-effect of defeat and demoralisation on the other. By way of an analysis of the *Memorial to the Murdered Jews of Europe*, I seek to show how melancholy can be a provocative affective state, encouraging reflections on redemption. Underscoring the transhistorical temporality of redemption, I maintain that left melancholy aptly describes the contemporary aporias of the left, and acts as a resource for future imaginaries. By discussing the vexing memorialisation of trauma that concerned Benjamin, I conclude with an account of the non-linear temporality of melancholy, and turn to utopian studies as a resolution of this impasse.

1   Mourning and 'Left' Melancholy

While in colloquial language melancholy and mourning are used interchangeably with sadness and gloominess, Sigmund Freud (1957: 243–258) was the first to introduce a distinction in his essay *Mourning and Melancholia*. For Freud, despite the similar phenomenological manifestations of the two conditions – such as acute discomfort and lack of libidinal drive – melancholy plunges the ego in a wholly different process. Mourning is painted straightforwardly as the reconciliation with a lost object. It can result from bereavement, where a person that was invested with psychic attachment has been lost. This lost object can also be a thing or an idea, so political commitments or even one's vision of themselves in relation to the outside world can be at stake. Mourning, then, is a psychic response with a definite end, working through the ego when a loss occurs. This is a linear process with distinct states of intense grief and a recuperation from loss, whence the ego emerges intact. Robert Hertz, a contemporary of Freud, argued that this process cannot be conceived as a clean break from the object and the termination of its relationship with the mourner, arguing instead that a 'transformation' occurs in the nature of this relationship (1960).

The relation between the subject and the object of loss is complicated in melancholy. Freud rephrases the ancient understanding of melancholia in his explanation of mourning, giving it a psychoanalytic gloss. The word melancholia is a combination of the Greek words for 'black' (*melas*) and 'bile' (*kholé*), as it was believed to be caused by an excess of black bile, disrupting the balance of the humours (Traverso, 2016: 122). Similarly, Freud sees mourning as a disruption of equilibrium. While this attests to a process with clear demarcations, melancholia is more convoluted as the vantage point of the ego itself is obscured, making directionality harder to establish. The painful dejection and lack of interest towards the outside world can be observed with both mourning and melancholia, yet the ego at the centre of the psychoanalytic equilibrium undergoes a shock in the latter (Freud, 1957: 244). Melancholy is accompanied by a reduction in self-regard and desire, even a 'delusional expectation of punishment' (ibid: 244). On this note it could be said that mourning marks a withdrawal from external reality insofar as possible, yet the melancholic appears to carry expectations and a sense of responsibility towards it, maintaining a tenuous line of communication. This suggests that melancholia involves an element of unconsciousness. Self-flagellating behaviour and the disintegration of the ego sets melancholia apart from mourning, where despite the negative affective response, one's sense of self was not necessarily damaged. Freud maintains this is due to the lost object being consciously grasped in mourning, while this is not the case for the melancholic, for whom it remains unclear: one may know who or what has been lost but not be able to account for what has been lost about them (ibid: 245). This could even point to indecision as to *whether* the object has been lost at all. Conversely, the intense attachment to the lost object may maintain its psychic existence despite recognising its nonexistence, resulting in a turn away from reality.

The ambivalence towards the object, as indecision regarding what has been lost about it, even whether one should mourn this loss if indeed it has been lost, helps to analyse the contemporary aporia of the left: between the disintegration of past attempts at transition and uncertain prospects for future resilience. Since Benjamin's (1994: 304–306) polemical article of the same name, 'left-wing melancholy' has been discussed as a characterisation of the objective situation, and a factor to be considered in theories of transition. Benjamin targets the prominent poet Erich Kästner as the personification of a type of left publicist that markets revolutionary imagery and literature, in a literal sense, to bourgeois tastes and depoliticised consumption. Characterising this type of work in unflinchingly condemning terms as 'the decayed bourgeoisie's mimicry of the proletariat', Benjamin asserts (ibid: 305) that 'their function is to give rise, politically speaking, not to parties but to cliques; literarily speaking, not to schools but to fashions; economically speaking, not to producers but to agents'. This denunciation of the left intellectual lampoons the way they cater to the bourgeoisie with domesticated narratives of proletarian culture, commodifying its revolutionary content. This literary movement consists of the 'transposition of revolutionary reflexes – insofar as they arose in the bourgeoisie – into objects of distraction, of amusement, which can be supplied for consumption' (ibid: 305). Its political significance is exhausted to the extent that it actualises its aim of fostering an emotional yet distanced paternalism towards the exploited. Thus, the commodification of revolutionary literature saps the left intelligentsia's potential to radicalise, and mobilise with, working people, since its work has no underlying 'corresponding political action' (ibid, 305). Instead, Benjamin sees a left that propagates images of universal corruption and anonymised misery, equalising culpability across 'humanity', and a lifeless exhibition of working class stereotypes that turns sentiments into things.

Having chastised the melancholic attitude for depleting the subversive culture of resistance and revolution, Benjamin's approach to history nevertheless furnishes a transformative conception of melancholy. The enigmatic *Theses on the Philosophy of History* (1968: 253–264) is a posthumously published commentary on the notion of progress, and a statement of the redemptive side of revolution. The first thesis describes a mechanism dubbed 'The Turk', a chess-playing automaton that responds to the moves of its human rival and allegedly never loses. However, it has a secret compartment where a person who is adept at chess moves the pieces using a string mechanism. Benjamin (1968: 253) likens this to a habit of explaining anomalies away, and narrating history as a succession of events that are ultimately tied to a final, definitive victory: 'One can imagine a philosophical counterpart to this device. The puppet called 'historical materialism' is to win all the time'.

The density of Benjamin's writing needs some unpacking, although his intention is precisely to present a non-linear work. A continuum of progress can be summoned by appealing to 'objective forces' and a teleological, unalienated society. Conversely, Benjamin (1968: 260) states in the following thesis that assigning the working class the 'role of redeemer of future generations' stifles their militancy arising from accumulated grief, pain and ambition, 'nourished by the image of enslaved ancestors rather than that of liberated grandchildren'. This is a political outcome of social democratic stagism, counting on evolutionary progress. Considering that the essay was written in the 1930s, and that as Löwy (2005: 25) points out, 'historical materialism' is between an ironic set of inverted commas, it is plausible that Benjamin targeted the uninspiring doctrines of the Second International as well as Stalin's codified, cardboard historical materialism.[1]

---

1 It has been suggested that Benjamin was targeted by the Soviet secret police alongside the Gestapo, who collaborated when the Molotov-Ribbentrop pact, to his outrage, was still operational (Jeffries, 2011).

In the seventh thesis, Benjamin distinguishes historical materialism from prevalent currents of historiography and their political positions. Written in fleeting tracts while was fleeing Nazi persecution, alongside an ominous gas mask in the room, the thesis alludes to an 'indolence of the heart' among historians and Social Democrats (Benjamin, 1968: 256; Jameson, 1996: 95). Benjamin perceives a state of *acedia*, an attitude of listlessness, torpor, and lethargic disassociation from politics. Positivistic historians blotted what is known about later developments, to make observation more objective, but consequently empathised with the victor (ibid: 256). Benjamin (ibid: 256) writes: 'There is no document of civilization which is not at the same time a document of barbarism', arguing that the historical materialist – now without the inverted commas -, should 'brush history against the grain'. The silent vanquished remain to trespass historical confines, evincing a melancholia that can activate transition.

The melancholic attitude towards revolutionary politics fits Freud's conception of melancholia as a committed detachment, or as a despair that is incapable and unwilling to strive for transition. Affective displays of charity reinforce patterns of exploitation, satiating an appetite for flowery platitudes. Similarly, the absence of a line of action, or an agency primed to enact transformation, is both a cause and effect of melancholia, which would dissipate if the unconscious side of attachment to the lost object was dispelled. On that note, newer works on left melancholy consider the recent past along similar lines, diagnosing a draining debilitation, at the expense of transitional goals. That said, the refusal to mourn is a motif in the writings of Benjamin himself, which strongly suggests that he had a nuanced understanding of trauma and psychic reactions to it. It is possible to trace a view of melancholy as a positive resource that could aid in articulating and enacting paths of transition, such as by reactivating kernels of emancipation that have been dormant in the past. The following discussion will contrast these approaches.

2   Melancholy as Obstacle

Contemporary discussions of left melancholy engender conflicting formulations. The epithet is mutually directed amongst theorists from opposing standpoints. Hence, Wendy Brown (1999) and Jodi Dean (2012) reach the opposite conclusions as to the political consequences of melancholy. Brown's interpretation of Benjamin favours certain post-Marxist positions, insofar as she draws attention to new putative axes of struggle, and explains the left's reluctance to engage with them in terms of melancholy. There is common ground with Dean here, as she also sees melancholy as a retreat, but she also differs from Brown on this score. Dean charges Brown of neglecting Benjamin's commitment to working-class struggles, and his explanation of the left melancholic ineptitude as the result of market compromise. Both theorists thus view left melancholy as an obstacle, with marked differences in its content.

Brown's article 'Resisting Left Melancholy' (1999) has been the standard-bearer of the contemporary debate. Brown contends that an obstinate attachment to an ideal, and even its failure, holds back the left from seizing opportunities unfolding before its eyes. This alludes to the intelligentsia that Benjamin had disparaged for peddling proletarian struggle as a romanticism of abortive upheavals, which were abundant in the Weimar Republic. In fact, their enterprise depends on failures and melancholic responses, as a 'structure of desire' over a 'transient response to a death or a loss' (Brown, 1999: 20). The 'structure of desire' is the operative phrase in Brown's analysis, drawing parallels between Benjamin's 'hack' and contemporary left actors, both of whom idealise defeats and perpetuate cycles of demoralisation.

Brown argues that the contemporary left fails to account for its shortcomings, explaining that the concept of left melancholy can be transposed to the present and shed light on the reluctance to refine theoretical models and strategic assumptions. These 'formulations of another epoch', Brown (ibid: 25) explains, consists of defunct notions of 'unified movements, social totalities, and class-based politics'. Effectively, the left compensates for failures by subconsciously turning its gaze away from a historical reality that defies the models it takes for granted, manifesting as an ultimately conservative melancholic fixation that has calcified into a structure of desire. As the revolutionary hack would aestheticize a downtrodden proletariat, in the strong sense of blunting the resistant edge of exploitation in its depictions of poverty, the contemporary revolutionary would be equally distant from possibilities of radical change in the present, and plunged into an alchemy of esoteric quotations and historical reenactments.

In the face of this anxiety to revise anachronistic modes of thinking, Brown (1999: 22) asks 'What do we hate that we might preserve the idealization of that romantic left promise? What do we punish that we might save the old guarantees of the left from our wrathful disappointment?'. The answer is that the left heaps scorn on theoretical innovations in 'poststructuralism, discourse analysis, postmodernism, trendy literary theory' so it may remain attached to an orthodoxy. This is the displacement of a failure, and a search for culprits and their casualties within the established Marxist canon. Brown (ibid: 25) further maintains that this traditionalism at the heart of praxis urgently needs to be addressed; 'a clear and certain path toward the good, the right, and the true', if there ever was one, cannot remain foundational and untransformed.

While Brown appears to make a viable case for a brand of post-Marxism, Dean has challenged the Benjaminian foundations and psychoanalytic premises of her diagnosis of melancholy. In her book *The Communist Horizon*, Dean (2012) claims that Brown gets it backwards, since Benjamin's writings renounce the abandonment of principles rather than an obstinate allegiance to orthodoxy. Brown's formulation of melancholy is an evocative account, which could be used for 'reconceiving communist desire', if its faulty conclusions are rectified (Dean, 2012: 158). The left melancholic, Dean argues, relinquishes the analyses and strategies of proletarian revolution – and thereby the 'communist horizon – and accepts the bourgeois views of the world. For this reason, Brown's left melancholic does not do justice to the lack of a grip on politics that characterises Benjamin's target.

As a structure of desire, melancholy is less of a symptom of left defeat than of conciliation towards capitalism. The left, in this analysis, is not committed to radical social change, but instead invests its energy into a vision of totalised capitalism. The difference between the two protagonists is thus that Dean thinks the left has not held its nerve to come out of the other side, while for Brown the problem is that it has done so, missing present opportunities. To drive home her argument, Dean draws from 'The Author as Producer', an address Benjamin (1999) gave in 1934, where he maintains that the relationship between the writers of the 'new objectivity' movement was not a side-by-side alliance of fellow producers, but an oblique sort of paternal compassion towards the worker: '[new objectivity] actually functions in a counterrevolutionary manner as long as the writer experiences his solidarity with the proletariat only in his attitudes, not as a producer'. This text further testifies to the Marxism of Benjamin (ibid: 773), in that he criticizes the conception of the intellectual based on their thoughts and dispositions, stressing their position in the process of production.

Dean's appraisal of the left melancholic dovetails with her analysis of 'communicative capitalism' (2012: 119–156; see also Dean, 2005), wherein the contemporary, participatory forms of social media divert energies from organisation-building towards an image-obsessed perception management. This leads to the prioritisation of form over content, as political groups vie for attention in an increasingly chaotic milieu:

> Competition for attention – How do we get our message across? – in a rich, tumultuous media environment too often and easily means adapting

to this environment and making its dynamic our own, which can result in a shift in focus from doing to appearing, that is to say, a shift toward thinking in terms of getting attention in the 24/7 media cycle and away from larger questions of building a political apparatus with duration (Dean, 2012: 145).

Returning to Benjamin's criticism of the primacy of appearance, it can be gleaned from Dean's arguments that left melancholy amounts to a mechanism to cope with shirking responsibilities, rather than a historical refutation of orthodox positions. As Benjamin (1999: 777) contends regarding artistic creation, the 'exemplary character of production' is paramount for a left culture worthy of its name. Alluding to Brecht's epic theatre, Benjamin (ibid) argues that the 'author as producer' is tasked with involving their audience within a field of struggle and encouraging their transformation from consumers of their works to coproducers. Transposing Benjamin's view of the author to the recent melancholy controversy, Dean's characterisation of melancholy as obstacle appears more pertinent, as it carries a similar injunction to act rather than to revise long-standing principles. Dean's critique of communicative capitalism complements Benjamin's critique of the artistic movements of his time, both drawing attention to a conformism with the market. While Benjamin's left melancholic is ironically detached, presenting congealed images of poverty to bourgeois audiences, Dean's is too submerged in the social network of superficial appearances to exert effort for a lasting organisation.

The exchange between Brown and Dean shows that they agree on their conclusions yet find each other's rationales unconvincing. Relinquishing a melancholic attachment implies a preference for mourning in its stead, since it is a conscious coming to terms with the loss, and a clear process of leaving it behind. This begs the question of whether there could be a positive theoretical or political upshot to retaining melancholy and its convoluted temporality.

3   Melancholy as Resource

The comparative analysis above indicates how left melancholy can hinder left politics. To put it succinctly, both Brown and Dean believe that there is a condition holding back the left from putting down roots in wider society with a program of radical social change. The content and agency behind such a program is the point of separation. Although they arrive at different conclusions, they share the view that melancholy needs to be overcome. However, other conceptions of melancholy reveal an emancipatory dimension, particularly when its temporality is considered. This dimension can be seen across Benjamin's writings, with his refusal to mourn and his unique streak of 'messianic' historical materialism.

The discussion of Benjaminian melancholy suggests a political disadvantage along with a historical-epistemic gain. This gain is inscribed in the possibilities of redemption in the past. Stating that history is not a continuum of vacuous progress, Benjamin (1968: 253–254) vivifies the history of the present, appealing to a time both messianic and secular:

> There is a secret agreement between past generations and the present one. Our coming was expected on earth. Like every generation that preceded us, we have been endowed with a weak Messianic power, a power to which the past has a claim. That claim cannot be settled cheaply. Historical materialists are aware of that.

This contradiction can be reconciled by looking at the subject itself. Melancholy becomes a disarmed, hollow sentimentality in middle class poetry, but resentment and rage in the memory of the vanquished. This latter function leads Benjamin to oppose 'mourning' as a way of relinquishing the transformative potential of melancholia by ingraining it in a commemorative point in the past. This 'refusal to mourn', as Jay (1999: 235–236) explains, disavows a numbing of pain that prevents a visceral understanding of shocks, reducing them to a quantified historical positivism. Redemption is at the core of this intransigent rejection of the closure of mourning. In contrast, retaining the trauma enables what Mosès (1989: 31) has called 'unknotting the aporias of the present'. Melancholy cannot be abstracted from its temporality, as it enmeshes differential timelines including the volatile 'tradition of the oppressed' (Benjamin, 1968: 257).

Returning to the criticism of the left intellectual, the resource in melancholy can be further clarified. Benjamin had argued that these intellectuals portrayed a proletarian livelihood congealed in passive misery. This leads to a conceptualisation of proletarian demise as a component of its identity. Consequently, inscribing the traumatic experiences into a victimised identity prevents an understanding of the relation. Class is evoked in terms of a noun, which is reminiscent of Laclau and Mouffe's discursively constructed entities. The affective attachment to the identity is in turn reproductive of its exploitation. As Özselçuk (2006: 227) notes, 'self-absorption in injured identity' is a 'backward-looking politics', and relinquishes efforts to address the roots of injury. If exploitative social relations are transient and relational, then a reformulation of trauma as a continual imposition would encourage transformative practice. Therefore, it is necessary to distinguish the attachment to victimhood as identity from the retention of trauma as a lived relation in a society rife with oppression.

Benjamin's gestural and analogic prose deliberately stops short of advocating programmatic points, attenuating the reader to a stream of thought and privileging the affective connection. Accordingly, his subject matter concentrates on cultural relics of all sorts, ranging from the Parisian arcades to Paul Klee's *Angelus Novus*. By discussing human creations within their economic and cultural realities, Benjamin invokes a sociopolitical imaginary entrenched in communal memory. This tradition of the oppressed is as a secular conduit of the messianic intervention. Benjamin's historical materialism draws attention to an undercurrent of the flow of events. He privileges the epistemic gain of recognising potentials of redemption locked in this subterranean temporality, which intrudes on the present as a form of divine intervention. In Thesis v (1968: 255) on the philosophy of history Benjamin states:

> The true picture of the past flits by. The past can be seized only as an image which flashes up at the instant when it can be recognized and is never seen again ... For every image of the past that is not recognized by the present as one of its own concerns threatens to disappear irretrievably.

The past is thereby conceived as a fleeting, dynamic constituent of a present in flux. Its redemptive potential is a moving target of present political action, which Benjamin (1989: 281–291) surmises in the 'general strike' that would disaggregate the legal norms and political procedures enabling exploitation. The idea of such an intervention struck a chord with Benjamin: it represented an almost supra-historical break from capitalism, 'striking' into the heart of its logic, beyond the understanding of labour-power as bargaining chip. Rather than argue for mere concessions from the capitalists, the working class could obliterate the capital and wage-labour relation.

While Benjamin gropes for a political line imminent in his qualitative temporality, it is more instructive to follow his lines of reasoning. The picture of melancholy emerging from the revolution as redemption is patently distinct from the apoliticism of the intelligentsia. Rather, as Flatley (2008:65) explains, it is a 'politicizing, splenetic melancholy, where clinging to things from the past enables interest and action in the present world and is indeed the very mechanism for that interest'. This suggests a present riddled with the incompleteness of the past. Benjamin's historical landscape is a repository of ruins, and he identifies himself as a 'ragpicker', who solemnly inspects the anonymous pile for sake of posterity,

> [p]icking up rags of speech and verbal scraps with his stick and tossing them, grumbling and growling, a little drunk, into his cart, not without letting one or another of those faded cotton remnants – 'humanity', 'inwardness', or 'absorption' – flutter derisively in the wind. A ragpicker, early on, at the dawn of the day of the revolution (1999: 310)

Per the analogy, the bleakest periods can never totalise society and history. Such gaps marked by trauma can leverage change in the present.

The *Memorial to the Murdered Jews of Europe* (2018) in central Berlin is an installation with just such a Benjaminian incompleteness, and as a result is conducive to a positive construction of the future. The memorial itself is made of up over 2700 concrete slabs, or stelae, identical in length and width but varying from 0.2 to 2 meters in height over a large field, with an undulating surface. The differences in the height as one walks through the narrow grids create a sense of unease, as the monument has a dismal grey and austere façade. Although there is an information centre underneath, the stelae do not provide information, inviting the visitor to contemplate their significance uninterrupted. This has been criticised as a flaw, one critic arguing that 'The mollifying solemnity of pseudo-universal abstractions puts a great grey sentiment in the place of actual memory' (Brody, 2012). Accordingly, the memorial fails to fulfil its commemorative purpose as it relies too heavily on the symbolic representation of the Holocaust, and this is evident both in its uniform design and evasive name. It is unclear who the perpetrators were/are, and what the reasons behind this industrialised mass murder were.

However, the memorial's lack of closure also serves as a painful gap compelling the visitor to ponder on these questions, rather than presenting a pre-packaged set of facts. In this fashion, the architect of the monument, Peter Eisenman, has given it a visceral sentiment irreducible to simple cause-effect explanations, provoking reflection beyond a reiteration of the ravages of the past. As a design theorist well-versed in continental philosophy, Eisenman (2018) is likely to be aware of Benjamin, and his explanation of the design of the monument carries unmistakable undertones of imminent redemption and rejection of closure:

> In this monument there is no goal, no end, no working one's way in or out. The duration of an individual's experience of it grants no further understanding, since understanding is impossible. The time of the monument, its duration from top surface to ground, is disjoined from the time of experience. In this context, there is no nostalgia, no memory of the

past, only the living memory of the individual experience. Here, we can only know the past through its manifestation in the present.

The monument resembles a large, anonymous cemetery, and the neat alleyways between the concrete slabs invoke the rationally organised war machine that was the Nazi regime. Therefore, there is a clearly conveyed subject and mood, yet the viewer is thrust into the genocidal harshness of the twentieth century, encountering the melancholic processes still worked through into the present. The temporal inexactness of the monument, as seen in the way it could not be dated to a specific period, also taps into a subterranean, transhistorical temporality.

Disparate temporal rhythms, communicating sorrow and defeat, traverse the present and resist its containment. Regarding this traversal, Butler (2016: 276) has argued in her discussion of the *Theological-Political Fragment* that 'the hyphen that links the theological with the political in the title of this fragment names a way that the messianic operates as the flashing up of one time within another or, in this passage, a timelessness within the domain of time'. This may be referred to as a temporal overlap, where the messianic denotes the point of actualisation. As opposed to linear notions of history, which would paint ruptures as culminations of inevitable chain reactions, 'actualisation' refers to a level of temporality that transcends short-term developments, in the form of an almost extra-historic intervention.

Processes of mourning and melancholia play out through historical cycles of social struggle and defeat, and their interplay manifests a specific, psychoanalytic and political grasp of a different future. Melancholy enables agents to introspectively bolster their determination, and draw from the traumas of interrelated episodes, ranging from the Warsaw Ghetto Uprising to the Paris Commune, both of which suffered defeats. Challenges against established ways of doing things can spring from melancholy, as shown by its conception as a resource. However, melancholy ceases to be such when it is actualised, transforming into an assertive utopian drive, a persistent disposition that complements melancholy.

As an affective state, melancholy induces a disavowal of the state of affairs through its persistence and detachment from watertight explanations of causality, a potential which the *Memorial to the Murdered Jews of Europe* attests to. It can also be observed that this state has been dominant, at least within the Western left, but this is an inevitable and beneficial process of rejuvenation. In fact, it is hard to see how the connecting thread between a heroic early twentieth century of enthusiasm towards the future and impatient socialist construction, and the gloom of the close of the century, with increased introspection and turns away from revolutionary ambition, could have had a different colouring. Left parties and social movements have been compelled to a defensive position since the hegemonic takeover of neoliberalism. In this context, inward criticism and deconstruction, differentiating viable left visions from redundant models, has been the responsible path to renewal.

As the unexpected attendance for an unapologetically communist conference suggests, however, melancholy no longer functions as the main modality of left practice. Since then, the decade of post-crash austerity has further crippled welfare arrangements, exacerbated socioeconomic inequality, and deteriorated physical and mental health across wide swathes of society, to the point that even such an advocate of market liberalisation as the International Monetary Fund has questioned the idea of neoliberalism as 'oversold' (Ostry et al., 2016: 38).

Melancholia is now primed to play a temporal rather than simply affective role. Times of crisis, which compel decisive action, provide an auspicious backdrop for anti-capitalist movements. This is augmented by the melancholia of past defeats and their accumulated experience towards a possible redemption. However, once melancholia becomes a positive programme, it is not possible to analytically capture the emergent moment as melancholic, whereas utopia presents itself as a useful frame.

CHAPTER 5

Through the Melancholic Impasse: Utopia

The previous chapter has considered melancholy as the estrangement from revolutionary practice. As the perceived or real sense of a loss, melancholy can also be interpreted as an awareness of not being where one wants to be, or a manifestation of a visceral discomfort, of not being at home in the world. Through the lens of productive activity as a human capacity, melancholy can be construed as a reaction to alienation from the means to build a dignified and fulfilling livelihood. That is not to say that the possible resolution of alienation in terms of a reappropriation of productive activity would end all dissatisfaction, but that it would be of a different nature, corresponding to existential problems specific to postcapitalist societies. In the shorter term, this demonstrates a gap between what is, what has been lost, and what has not yet become.

This tension is pronounced across reactions to the decline in living standards and prospects following the 2008 financial crash. As economic doctrine, political project, and culturally perceived inevitability, neoliberalism has been a formidable success for its beneficiaries, and pushed the left further into disarray.[1] Now the present appears to stretch into a prolonged moment of 'crisis' without an end in sight, foreclosing visions of a different future (Toscano, 2014). The dismal recovery of the past decade, with austerity and increase in indebtedness, not to mention speculations of a 'next downturn', all contribute to the sense of an erasure of the future and attest to the nihilism of the financial-capital led political economy (Evans-Prichard, 2018; Roos, 2018). Policies are indexed to the needs of an unstable sector. The aimless fluctuations in stock markets show how the present period of capitalism lacks a 'prognostic structure', in Reinhart Koselleck's words (2004: 95). The present of the crisis subsumes the past and the future, and this calls for a restoration of futurity.

The lack of a guiding compass connecting solutions to an overarching vision of a different society is the residue of a left melancholy of adaptation. Žižek (2000: 661) argues that mourning what is not yet lost is a paramount melancholic

---

1 David Harvey (2005) has explained the perspective that beyond an economic doctrine, neoliberalism should be understood as a consciously implemented political project. A similar perspective is presented by Duménil and Lévy (2011), in terms of financial hegemony as a distinct phase of capitalism. For histories of neoliberalism that treat it along these lines, also see Peck (2010) and Mirowski (2013).

stratagem. In this vein, the left remained attached to idealised defeats and acted as though they were thoroughgoing losses. Past struggles are thereby mentioned to retroactively justify moderation, not for redemption. This compels a restoration of their inherent temporal complexity to future-oriented movements. Melancholy is an effective diagnostic frame, but deficient for addressing the form and content of contemporary social opposition. To illuminate how grievances are transformed into positive demands and programmes, it is necessary to consider how a utopian temporality, even if in muted form, traverses quotidian events. If melancholy was a product of an awareness of defeats and co-optation within the left, then the utopian drive for a different society is its positive complement.

This chapter will first elaborate on anti-utopian viewpoints, then differentiate the concept as a sociologically rigorous and anthropologically grounded tendency. In order to refute anti-utopianism, the views of Marx and Engels will be discussed, followed by Ernst Bloch's (1977; 1995) iconoclastic defence of utopia. Taking a cue from the formulations of Ruth Levitas (1990, 2013) and David Harvey (2000), it will be argued that utopian thinking is integral to the reproduction of human societies and attests to how, as Bloch (1977: 22) puts it, 'not all people exist in the same Now'.

1   Anti-utopianism and the Neoliberal Closure of the Future

The reduction of the communist vision to a fully resolved society was a fixture of Cold War conservatism and liberalism, where the terms Marxism, Leninism, Stalinism, utopianism, and totalitarianism were used almost interchangeably. A demonstrative example is the historian J.L. Talmon's (1952: 249) argument, claiming that Marxism furthered an eighteenth century current that exaggerated the application of the democratic ideals of the French Revolution, to the point of abandoning liberal tenets. Accordingly, this radicalisation of democracy was tantamount to an 'inverted totalitarianism' (ibid: 105). First published in 1951, this work prefigured much of the ensuing thought on utopia as an essentially dangerous and irresponsible project.

For Karl Popper (1948: 109–116; 1947), utopia represented an 'attractive and, indeed, all too attractive theory'. For Popper, utopianism lurked behind Nazism and Stalinism as a blueprint for holistic, violent change: the antithesis of the 'open society' he advocated. This was conditioned by a 'Platonic belief in one absolute and unchanging ideal' that a rational knowledge may be acquired, and the means to this end ruthlessly pursued (1947: 141–142). Popper would thus juxtapose his calls for restraint in redressing social problems with utopian social engineering that was oblivious to individual difference. Curiously, Laclau and Mouffe's (1985: 3, passim) critique of Marxism took a similar angle in that they accused its proponents of assuming a sutured society and reducing real complexity to theoretical simplicity. Their post-Marxist stance posited a totalitarian impulse at the centre of Marxism, which they accused of reifying categories and expecting conformity from conceptual social subjects. Accordingly, for Laclau and Mouffe, a revolutionary rupture was improbable and undesirable, and it was necessary to attenuate strategy to the concrete issues of heterogeneous social movements. This was perhaps a gateway to the resurgence of a liberal mode of politics, as the refusal of a coherent anti-capitalist vision implicitly affirmed neoliberalism as the only game in town (Scheppele, 2012: 45).

In his survey of the interrelations between utopia and Marxism, Vincent Geoghegan (2008: 111) notes that the crimes of Stalinism have deflected theoretical or political discussions of the elimination of unnecessary suffering. The quintessential anti-utopian argument, Geoghegan explains, acknowledges that hardships exist, followed by an assertion that those in the throes of such hardship are particularly susceptible to millenarian visions of a total overcoming of their problems. From this perspective, emancipatory politics is comparable, if not indistinguishable from, sinister far right visions of a – racially – homogenous society. Both sides of the spectrum present an idyllic vision of post-scarcity to the impoverished masses, and a dramatic, if not total, annihilation of work. However, once these movements capture power, not only are hardships not eradicated, but are multiplied. Thus, a prejudgment against utopianism has held that the existing state of affairs with its familiar problems was the tangible lesser of many abstract evils, implying that a responsible mindset should come terms with the world as it is.

The collapse of the Berlin Wall in 1989 compounded the understanding that extra-, post-, anti- or non-capitalist imaginaries were all but variations of an experiment foisted onto society and a predictable failure. In his essay 'The End of History?', Fukuyama (1989: 4) would claim:

> What we may be witnessing is not just the end of the Cold War, or the passing of a particular period of post-war history, but the end of history as such: that is, the end point of mankind's ideological evolution and the universalization of Western liberal democracy as the final form of human government.

Fukuyama (1992) reiterates this position in a book where the question mark is now absent, and argues that while liberal democracy may not be enacted in the same way across the world, the key values of liberalism such as individual rights and free market policies are set to be universally enshrined. Equally important, the goals of creating alternative societies and models of modernisation are increasingly cast aside for a pragmatic conciliation, as Fukuyama (1989: 280) says that 'it is not necessary that all societies become successful liberal societies, merely that they end their ideological pretensions of representing different and higher forms of human society'. The backlash against 'ideological pretensions' as a set of beliefs, or secular religion, mainly placed Marxism in its crosshairs. Daniel Bell's (2000) book *The End of Ideology* was published in 1962, and set the tone for a proliferation of denunciations of comprehensive, alternative visions of society, favouring a centrist sensibility. Its three sections were titled 'the ambiguities of theory', 'the complexities of life', and 'the exhaustion of utopia', cautioning against youthful exuberance and foreclosing considerations of ideas beyond what is currently politically acceptable.

There is reason to agree that and 'end' has been reached. As Žižek (2010) observed, even Fukuyama's trenchant left critics share a deep-set belief that the system is here to stay, which explains their distance from visions of alternative societies. Prior to the Occupy movement, mainstream political parties endorsed neoliberal tenets and offered hardly distinguishable remedial solutions. Occupy, with its grassroots nature and subversive rhetoric, indicated the gap between these parties and popular aspirations. Inverting Fukuyama's position, Badiou (2012: 15) argues that he was not wrong, as he had expressed a certain culmination of the established order. A sort of 'end' was in sight since the lull in social upheavals post-1968, yet this end is once again imperilled by a 'rebirth of history'. As opposed to Fukuyama's appropriation of the Hegelian end point, this end is a dialectical point of a sublimated beginning. For Badiou (2012: 1), the new forms of collective action embody a reinvigorated search, and shatter the illusion of an end to history through their sheer existence.

The closure of the future can also be traced across recent scholarly work on utopia. In the *Faber Book of Utopias*, written at the turn of the millennium, John Carey (1999: xii) forcefully reiterates the anti-utopian argument: 'The aim of all utopias, to a greater or lesser extent, is to eliminate real people. Even if it is not a conscious aim, it is an inevitable result of their good intentions'. For Carey, utopian projects implicate an arrogance that society can be manipulated to fit a preconceived mould. The brunt of this criticism is levelled towards Soviet communism, which he refers to as the 'greatest social experiment in human history' (ibid: xiii). A similar interpretation has been made by John Gray (2007: 86), who views utopia as inherently conducive to terror due to its emphasis on perfectibility and keenness on state-sponsored coercion to achieve it. For Gray (ibid: 26, 15–16), this impulse to modify human behaviour links Leninism and Nazism within the same totalitarian mould (Levitas, 2013: 9). Additionally, the forceful modification of society is also embedded in the American neo-conservative project, which Gray (ibid: 17, 53) believes lies in the past Trotskyism of some of its key proponents (such as its intellectual figurehead, Irving Kristol). Accordingly, Trotsky's (1969) theory of permanent revolution, which broadly argued for an internationally coordinated socialist transition, was appropriated in the combative post-9/11 American foreign policy. In a broad sweep, utopianism is thus attributed to a range of endeavours from the October Revolution to Operation Iraqi Freedom. Anti-utopianism equates all the efforts where the author detects a deviation from an organic development of liberal democracy and free markets. This stems from an assumption that the neoliberalism has been the dormant configuration of all societies, and utopianism is accused of imposing artificial fetters on their inevitable development.

The anti-utopian critique replicates what it claims to be the *modus operandi* of alternative social arrangements, since it assumes a suprahistorical command of the *telos* of human societies as a march towards Fukuyama's end of history. These critiques deploy a latent elitism, since their proponents claim a superior grasp of societies' needs, and upon consideration of alternatives, conclude that the existing state of affairs, *i.e.* a political-economic project of deregulation in the post-Keynesian context of the Global North, is the Panglossian 'best of all possible worlds'. Accordingly, defences of the *status quo* embody the very elitism that they reject in revolutionary vanguardism. The anti-utopianism is predicated on a fixed, cynical view of human nature. Ironically, this cynical denunciation of utopia is also glazed with a brand of optimism that having more of the same will fulfil the needs of those that are left behind.

Despite its detractors' hostility, utopian expressions go beyond an impossible and purely subjective blueprint. Anti-utopianism banks on utopia's externality to social life, and juxtaposes it to allegedly natural social flows. However, as Bourdieu (1998: 94) explains, neoliberalism conceives of itself as a science, whereas its premises evince utopianism. As an economic model, it posits a logic of individual rationality and perfected market conditions (ibid). The restructuring of states for this goal, and the repression of collective political advocacy, are justified by reference to the abstraction of *homo economicus*. Following this rearrangement, neoliberal reasoning presents itself as an impartial observer of this 'neutral' reality. *Pace* the anti-utopians, utopia is not strictly the domain of left and right wing extremisms. It also figures in the common sense around economic management. If utopia refers to state sanctioned efforts to intervene in the organic composition of society, as its opponents maintain, then neoliberalism should be seen as utopian *par excellence*.

Perry Anderson (2000: 17) maintains that due to the lack of systematic and global alternatives to neoliberalism, it is 'the most successful ideology in world history', to the extent that it is not even considered as ideological (Monbiot, 2016). Yet neoliberalism itself is a social experiment, with inimical results for people who sell their labour-power for a living. As an increasingly precarious mode of life, neoliberalism imposes a singular logic of futurity and dampens alternatives. According to Will Davies (2017), this regime of accumulation envisions the future as 'economic artefact', relying on its own terms of temporality to function. This is because capitalism, as an inherently dynamic system, requires actors to have faith in its prospects, and not just its present, to avoid stagnation (Beckert, 2016: 33). Thus, the closure of the future really refers to its reformulation as a monetary matrix, bringing to mind Koselleck's noted lack of prognostic structure. This can take the form of derivatives (and their derivatives) and sub-prime mortgages that draw economic actors into a monistic relation to the future (Davies, 2017: 11). The temporal logic of contemporary capitalism, while being future-oriented, considers its economic categories as objective representations, and the belief in its 'imaginary futures', as Jens Beckert calls them (2016), forecloses discussions of an alternative moral logic or a collectively defined social contract.

Based on these observations, it is tempting to draw the conclusion that neoliberalism is 'dead yet still dominant', as Neil Smith (2009: 56) argues. Operating as though by post-mortem spasms, its mechanisms self-replicate without democratic legitimacy. However, this reading of nihilistic self-immolation fails to capture the melancholic justification of a lack of alternatives, which has been sedimented over decades. The real collapse in the post-2008 period has also pushed neoliberalism on to the defensive. The gap between its goals, ideological legitimations, and lived circumstances reveals a vulnerability to new, positive challenges. As this discussion of the various dimensions of neoliberalism suggests, even at its most dominant phase, a hegemonic project that is at constant odds with its own temporality and professed aims, experiencing fractures as a symptom of its workings, and attempting to furnish a 'fullness'.

The trajectory of neoliberalism constitutes a political project, an economic doctrine, as well as what might be termed a utopian imaginary that took shape with the exigencies of its time. Based on assessments of the economic situation, neoliberal thinkers envisioned a capitalist futurity of unbridled accumulation. The future was projected as a market model, and the normative foundations of Chicago School economics were obscured in the language of amoral and dispassionate necessity. Despite its implementation at the cost of political repression and declines in living standards, neoliberalism has been able to convey itself as a future-oriented project of perfectibility, indexed to financial calculus. Employing the same yardstick of the anti-utopian thinkers, it appears that the sacrifice of living society to abstract historical projections is entirely consistent with the political-economic reasoning of our time.

2 Reformulating the Utopian

Considering neoliberalism as a utopian project yields insight into the sociological ontology of utopia. It is insufficient to conceive of utopia in general – nor neoliberalism in particular – as a timeless blueprint without geographical constraints. If neoliberalism has utopian traits, then it should be acknowledged that these have evolved in response to historical circumstances, in non-conformity with the social democratic consensus. This also reveals a limit to what might be labelled utopian. Historicising utopian thought and practice beyond the selective definitions of its detractors, it is possible to reappropriate the concept as a hermeneutic of transition. Taking a step back to consider the origins of utopia, the following discussion proposes an alternative mapping of the concept.

The confusion over the signifier of utopian is inscribed in its etymology. The term Utopia was coined by Thomas More (2016) in his eponymous work first published in 1516, *Concerning the Best State of a Commonwealth and the New Island of Utopia. A Truly Golden Handbook No Less Beneficial Than Entertaining*, now known simply as *Utopia* (Sargent, 2010: 2). Borrowed from Greek, utopia is a combination of *topos,* meaning place, and *ou-*, a prefix meaning 'no' or 'not'. As More's work is a description of an island, unmoored from specifiable coordinates, utopia has come to designate a figment of the imagination, a non-existent society. Additionally, More refers to the island also as 'Eutopia', this time using the *eu-* prefix denoting the 'good'. This gives the impression that utopias designate non-existent happy places (Levitas, 1990: 2–4). More's elision has vested the term with a troubled legacy. It is widely seen as a fidelity to unattainable goals of perfection. This has allowed it to be co-opted by the powerful, who can use the term as a charge against radical movements, while the target of the accusation has to plead their 'innocence' of utopianism. Avoidance of ambitious goals has been a feature of melancholy from the outset. Coupled with the pejorative connotations of utopianism, this has confined the term to a literary genre. The prevalence of this sense of utopia has forestalled its use in social theory.

On the left, the distinction between 'utopian' and 'scientific' socialism has informed a rejection of utopia, but a closer look at Marx and Engels' discussions of the subject reveals that they were attuned to the prefiguration of alternative futures. Thus, utopia can be reformulated and reclaimed as a sociological phenomenon intrinsic to the political and cultural imaginaries of all societies, and away from narratives of perfected, timeless fantasy. The following section follows this approach in the writings of Marx and Engels with reference to their interpretations of the connections between utopia and transition.

3   Marx, Engels and Utopia

Conservative critics had charged socialism as an untenable utopian project as early as the 1840s (Lovell, 2004: 632). The notion of utopia used in such criticisms, particularly against the French communist currents that had a formative influence on Marx, was appropriated by Marx and Engels themselves against rivals on the left, such as Louis Reybaud (Lovell, 2004: 639). However, they were also sympathetic to anti-capitalist communities and redistributive cooperatives. Their differences arose from a perceived underestimation of transitional necessities, while a shared horizon of communism provided points of contact. Following some the extensive primary-source studies of Geoghegan (2008) and Levitas (1990), this section argues that the founders of Marxism did not reject utopianism *per se*, but stressed an attenuation based on existing transitional tendencies such that it would have political leverage to bring about social revolution and coherently challenge capitalism.

An example of disdain towards utopia comes from the *Communist Manifesto* (henceforth cited as CM), where the writers describe their positions in opposition to other political currents. Surveying socialist and communist literature, Marx and Engels (CM: 71) discern a strain of 'Petty-Bourgeois Socialism'. Represented by Sismondi, these socialists correctly identified the destabilising effects of capitalist accumulation on established agricultural bonds and division of labour, yet their program was imbued with a nostalgic yearning for the pre-capitalist corporate guild structure in manufacture and its concomitant patriarchal relations in agriculture (CM: 72–73). Finding a base in the petty-bourgeoisie, which came into being as an intermediate class fluctuating between the proletariat and the bourgeoisie, this line of socialism was both 'reactionary and utopian' (CM: 74). As the medieval burgesses and proprietors of artisanal shops found themselves in a redundant position with the tide of industrialisation and the dissolution of traditional bonds, their hostility towards capitalism was rooted in these losses. They were thus not interested in using the capitalist forces of production to build a new society, as they were sidelined by their development. Where Marx and Engels attack petty-bourgeois socialism as a 'reactionary and utopian' enterprise, they draw attention to their uncritical rejection of capitalism, and longing for a glorified past.

The Manifesto goes further in denouncing utopianism in the section 'critical-utopian socialism and communism', now with a nuanced critique of neighbouring future-oriented doctrines (ibid: 79). Once again it traces the socioeconomic background and the political stances of this movement, followed by an explanation of its shortcomings. The critical-utopian socialists emerged on the scene with alternative social arrangements. However, as the proletarian class of wage-labourers had recently begun to expand, it remained a gelatinous group without a coherent program of its own, unlike its bourgeois, petty bourgeois and agricultural counterparts. As a result, these intellectuals and philanthropists thought of the working class as in need of their magnanimity (CM: 73). They would expect events to follow the trajectories that they plotted, and despite best intentions, these reflected a narrow class vision. Ironically, as they set up the entire capitalist society as their target, they ended up reproducing it by pretending to be impervious to class antagonisms and professing to have found the way to complete social harmony. For instance, Henri de Saint-Simon opined that the force of persuasion may unite the workers and bourgeoisie, between whom he did not see an antagonism, and opposed them to the truly 'parasitic' nobility and the clergy (Levitas, 1990: 43; Buber, 1949: 17). Ultimately, they were left with sectarian islands (CM: 75). Although their founders were revolutionary, their compliant followers turned conservative, failing to generate new challenges to the expansion of capitalism. These led to the disparaging conclusion that they were 'of a purely utopian character' (CM: 73), and their thoughts are met with an unsparing indictment (CM: 75): 'They still dream of experimental realization of their social utopias ... and to realize all these castles in the air, they are compelled to appeal to the feelings and purses of the bourgeois'.

The main theorists and practitioners of this type of socialism were the French communists Henri de Saint-Simon and Joseph Fourier, and the Welsh cooperative founder Robert Owen (ibid: 80). It is striking that Marx and Engels directed considerable vitriol towards these reformers, as this contradicts the commended 'concentrated brevity' of the Manifesto (Hobsbawm, 2012: 18). This was possibly due to the opportunity that these currents gave them to distinguish their 'scientific' socialism.

The hostility to utopia finds its apogee in Engels' (2012) work *Socialism: Utopian and Scientific*. Responding to a need for an accessible account of historical materialism, Engels' book encapsulates this perspective as its founders saw it, in contradistinction to the 'utopian' socialisms (Henderson, 1976: 406). Following a now familiar format of setting out the class background, then delving into the contents of utopian theories, Engels (2012: 62–63) contends that they represent an intellectual movement that demarcated reason from superstition, and presupposed a transparent access to the truth based on logical inquiry. The notion of a rationally mandated social arrangement belied the agenda of the ascendant bourgeoisie, at a time when the embryonic proletariat was not politically represented. This class rose to hegemony by denouncing the sectional interests of the powerful, and by portraying its programme as representative of the common interest. This impulse for a finally elucidated social vision contained the sectional interest of the bourgeoisie itself, even as its practitioners professed a belief in socialism. All things considered, they were lampooned as utopian thinkers as their standpoints derived from bourgeois premises, interpreting the hitherto historical development of society as their empirical verification.

Based on this observation, Engels (2012: 73) explains that Saint-Simon's credentials as an heir of the French revolution were both a hindrance and inspiration for his transitional proposals. Steeped in a struggle waged by the productive third estate of artisanal producers and workers against their idle priestly and aristocratic rivals, Saint-Simon articulated the interests of the 'working' population which, for him, corresponded to not only the wage-workers, but also the manufacturers, merchants and the bankers (ibid: 74–75). At a time when the chasm between the working class and the bourgeoisie was just becoming apparent, Saint-Simon considered the latter to be the intellectual and economic vanguard of the new society guided by science and industry (ibid: 75). Engels (ibid: 70–76) refers to the *Geneva Letters*, where Saint-Simon (1976) propounded on a worldview of fraternal harmony, governed by a scientific new religion (Meriç, 1995: 30). While Saint-Simon's ideas embodied the bold anti-clerical sentiments and scientific confidence of his time, his project remained utopian. Though he recognised the class struggle at the heart of the revolution, he did not consider the class of wage-labourers that was beginning to take shape. Nevertheless, Engels' critical remarks are less severe than they have been portrayed in posterity. While distinguishing the method of following the mode of production to shed light on political events, Engels (2012: 77) credits Saint-Simon for his 'comprehensive breadth of view' and capacity to keep a finger on the pulse of the ideological articulations of the shifts in ruling class structure, both of which have served as a catalyst for future socialist theory, including its 'scientific' type.

Similarly, Engels (ibid: 78) praises Fourier's satirical condemnations of the yawning gap between the promises of the revolution and the 'most pitiful reality'. He notes Fourier's witty observations of the conservativism of the bourgeoisie post-revolution, and view of the emancipation of women as a measure of human emancipation. Dialectically, Fourier argued that the immense precarity in capitalism was a direct outcome of prosperity at the other end. He would expand this key contradiction into a general historical observation that epochs are marked by 'vicious circles' which cannot be staved off, leading to their decline. Where Marx and Engels differ from Fourier, therefore, is not strictly on the point of analysis of an inherently unstable mode of production, nor the vision of communal, solidarity-based society. They diverge on the efficacy of establishing autonomous *phalansteries* (a portmanteau of phalanx and monastery), as a way to change global society towards a loosely connected federation. These utopian communities were designed to foster production for mutual benefit, and render work more enjoyable as a non-compulsory and variegated activity (Steadman Jones and Patterson, 1996: xviii; Beecher and Bienvenu, 1971: 4, 70; Fourier, 1971a: 240–242; Fourier, 1971b: 274–275).

Fourier's flaw, however, was in his total rejection of civilised society based on his vision of human nature. He sought to found a new 'science' based on universal laws of attraction and unity, purportedly on par with Newton's achievements (Fourier, 1996: 3; Beecher and Bienvenu, 1971: 1, 22–27). As Marx saw it, this amounted to making 'castles in the air' and had no correspondence in historical unfolding: 'Future history resolves itself, in their eyes, into the propaganda and the practical carrying out of their social plans' (CM: 73). Thus, Marxists after Marx emphasised a hard-headed pragmatism that would separate their political movement from the 'utopians' (Geoghegan, 2008: 55–79).

Also, Fourier had perceived that work had become drudgery under capitalism, as the sole means to make a living. He believed that it was a religious calling to turn labour into an enjoyable activity, as it was intended (Fourier, cited in Beecher and Bienvenu, 1971: 144). This message would resonate with Frankfurt School thinkers such as Marcuse (1974: 217), who were disillusioned with the productivism of the Soviet Union and sought to formulate a conception of work that was closer to creative play. The transformation of work has been a central debate from the outset, and it has come to the fore in recent times with 'postwork' literature, which will be explored in detail in the following part. Here, the focus shall remain on the tension between practicality and prefiguration central to the formulation of utopia.

Contrary to Fourier, Marx (1981: 959) insists that work, as an existentially 'necessary' activity, would persist after capitalism:

> Freedom in this field can only consist in socialized man, the associated producers, rationally regulating their interchange with nature, bringing it under their common control, instead of being ruled by it as by a blind power; and achieving this with the least expenditure of energy and under

conditions most favourable to, and worthy of, their human nature. But it nonetheless still remains a realm of necessity. Beyond it begins that development of human energy which is an end in itself, the true realm of freedom, which, however, can blossom forth only with this realm of necessity as its basis.

While the nature of work would undoubtedly transform in socialist conditions, granting workers control over their productivity, it would remain grounded in necessity, making it problematic to assert that it would become an end in itself. Consequently, Marx recognises a gradual side to transition, opposing this to utopian societies which claimed to do away with the categories of capitalist production.

Engels' critique of another formidable figure, Owen, is imbued with a similar disapproval. Perhaps due to his similar background as a Manchester manufacturer, however, Engels is notably charitable towards Owen. Beginning with a description of Owen's experimental cotton mill at New Lanark, Engels (2012: 82–85) explains how it afforded its 2500 workers advanced conditions, ranging from childcare when children were still coerced to work elsewhere, to a ten and a half-hour workday, where fourteen to sixteen hours was the norm. Owen's mill even paid wages in full when there was no production due to a crisis. That said, Owen remained a philanthropist, and his treatment of his workforce reproduced bourgeois domination over the working-class, though it was more generous. Owen recognised this as he said 'The people were slaves of [his] mercy' (ibid: 83). Thus, following a series of abortive attempts to establish communities in America, Owen would campaign with working class organisations to enact reforms. He fell out of favour with high society as he embraced socialism, yet persistently defended measures towards a socialist society, such as labour notes, whose unit was a single hour of work, and cooperative societies (Engels, 2012: 87). The former would inform Proudhon's blueprints for communal production, and the latter continues to demonstrate the redundancy of middlemen when workers run their companies cooperatively. Crucially, Owen did not consider his initiatives as panaceas, nor did he argue that they represented socialism in and of themselves. This contrasts with Proudhon and other utopian theorists, for whom socialism was an absolute, ahistorical truth waiting to be discovered and correctly applied by those with the requisite skill.

As his views on Owen suggests, Engels' approach to utopianism is not a blanket rejection of prefigurative attempts or palliative solutions. Rather, Engels highlights the need to set out from existing conditions, and of siding with those who have the most at stake from radical change through their own dissolution as a class. Following Dawson's (2016: 32) explanation of Engels' reaction to individual visionaries, it can be argued that Engels considers their socialisms to be *philosophical* rather than *sociological* alternatives: they have not created a strategy out of capitalism based on a study of its long-term trends, but arrived at their visions through their own imaginative volition. Thus, Marx and Engels were reticent to provide blueprints of the future society, as this would be consciously constructed by the working class, continually responding to the exigencies of their spatio-temporal context (ibid: 31–33).

Benjamin (1980: 99) attributes to Bertolt Brecht the maxim 'Don't start from the good old things but the bad new ones'. Marx and Engels' outlook resonates with this perspective. Their rejection of utopianism, always in adjective form as 'utopian socialism', is a denunciation of this distance from disheartening social realities. For their proponents, utopian schemes appeared to be self-evidently to the benefit of all. Their persuasive character would help to overthrow capitalism in a final triumph of reason. Consequently, while lacking a specific transitional, liminal phase, these projects portended a positivist complacency. In a preface to *Capital*, Marx (1990: 179) refers to a reproach to his method from a positivist journal, saying

> [T]he Paris Revue Positiviste reproaches me for, on the one hand, treating economics metaphysically, and, on the other hand – imagine this! – confining myself merely to the critical analysis of the actual facts, instead of writing recipes (Comtist ones?) for the cook-shops of the future.

Auguste Comte, a contemporary of Marx, believed that at the 'positive stage', the social scientists were closest to gaining a lucid view of society, seeing through religious and other metaphysical blinkers (Fay, 1981: 426; Allan, 2013: 11). While political philosophers had allowed their preconceptions to dilute the objective, verifiable realities of the social world, the positivist disposition towards neutrality made its practitioners ideally positioned to steer society (Fay: 426). In sum, the 'hard' view of social 'science' in a sense that emulated the Newtonian 'discovery' of underlying mainsprings of social life was a fixture of the positivist approach. Comte (2009: 43) would argue further that the role of social science was to uncover the laws governing social action and implement technocratic fixes in order to render it 'far more perfect'. The exaltation of perfection and discovery indicates an epistemological standpoint that knowledge is finite and absolute, disposing with historical anomaly and by extension, the notion of an alternative imaginary itself. This paradoxical pragmatism of the utopian socialists caused them to stray from galvanising creativity and led them towards a close-minded faith in their infallibility. Contrarily, the distance against regimented blueprints of the ideal society was a requisite for historical materialism, concerned with confronting evolving situations on their own terms, cutting through standard reproaches that Marxism is a totalising pseudoscience (*e.g.*, those of Popper, 2002: 49, and Russell, 1945: 788–789).

It is here that Marx's key divergence from the utopian socialism of his time arises. As Tucker (1972: 180–181) explains, Marx's view of science is derived from a materialist riposte to idealism, such that his emphasis on the scientific nature of his philosophy is predicated on a movement away from the latter and towards the former. Marx's use of the term *wissenschaft*, according to Tucker (1972: 181), designates the idea that the primary *explicanda* is social practice in its economic, political and ideological totality, rather than shifts in consciousness. While philosophers have taken their erstwhile intellectual environment as their referent, materialists look to social life to derive explanations (Marx, 1968: 12). Thus, philosophy *qua* philosophy is idealism, while a philosophy grounded in the creation of social life is a scientific inquiry going beyond the philosophical purview. Marx (1968: 12) does not claim that philosophy lacks a direct object, as the prevalent theoretical dispositions at any given space and time correspond to a 'conscious being' as a 'real life process'. This suggests that *wissenschaft* refers to a broader attitude towards the study of society, as a critique of practical social relations as they unfold, and against pure speculation. This also means that when using the term, Marx did not deploy the fetishized scientism of utopian socialists, which ultimately reproduced idealism. Historical materialism did not make a foundational claim to the underlying truth of social life, but indicated the sphere of production as an epistemologically superior vantage point to interpret it.

Notwithstanding the political rejection of utopian socialism, the work of Levitas and Geoghegan (2008: 39–54) has shown that Marx and Engels' interpretations of Saint-Simon, Owen and Fourier were not consistently frosty. Levitas (1990: 55) shows that the young Engels, prior to writing *The Condition of the Working Class in England*, had a high regard for Owen's projects and policy proposals, a standpoint he maintained throughout much of this period. Engels, like Owen and his followers, believed that gradual, peaceful transition to socialism was a possibility, and that Owen's proto-social democratic proposals were ahead of their time. In fact, Engels (cited in Levitas, 1990: 55) appears to have believed that communisation was underway in the manner of communities where the surplus was used for the benefit of all: 'Communism, social existence and activity based on community of goods, is not only possible but has actually already been realised in many communities in America and in one place in England, with the greatest success'. These communities were on track to supplant capitalism, and he anticipated that this would happen on a national scale in France while the process would be more voluntary and gradual in England (Engels, 1975a: 385–387).

Engels' position changes with the development of the Owenite groups as well as his own intellectual evolution, particularly following his collaboration with Marx. Claeys (1985: 472) makes the point that the Owenite settlements had increasingly become millenarian sects throughout the 1840s, becoming politically irrelevant and detached from the working-class movement. Marx and Engels, despite their appreciation of the prefigurative strengths of the utopian experiments, were henceforth exasperated with the refusal of the followers of Owen, and Fourier, to support ongoing mass movements such as the Chartists (CM: 75). Engels (1975b: 27), for instance, had considered Fourier's *phalansteries* to be intriguing innovations, suggesting translations of his books for a library of practically useful works ('omitting, of course, the cosmogenic nonsense'). Their alienation from social movements was more pronounced as they came to believe that a peaceful transition was unrealistic – a term that became synonymous with 'utopian' for future Marxists – as Engels (1987: 729) would write: 'If, indeed, it were possible to make the whole proletariat communistic before the war breaks out, the end would be very peaceful; but that is no longer possible, the time has gone by'.

Prefigurative societies, however, were still recognised as a mobilising force, as Marx and Engels would reiterate in the *Communist Manifesto* (op. cit., 74) that they had emancipatory potential, despite the idealism of their proponents: 'Such fantastic pictures of future society, painted at a time when the proletariat is still in a very undeveloped state and has but a fantastic conception of its own position, correspond with the first instinctive yearnings of that class for a general reconstruction of society'. The fact that utopian socialist projects resonated with the working class showed that despite their demise, they affirmed a longing that transcended the immediate historical context. Similarly, Engels' (1975c) appraisal of Thomas Müntzer, the radical German theologian that opposed both the Catholic Church and Lutherism, reveals an admiration of his capacity to channel the collective desire of a classless society. Engels considered Müntzer to be a visionary who had the correct criticism of his society and sought to achieve genuine social transformation. For Engels (1975c: 409–426), Müntzer's communism was transmitted through a theological language, yet struck a chord with a universal ambition to overthrow the expropriators, anticipating future social struggles before the time of industrial society.

Engels' resuscitation of a historical figure as a participant of a long-running struggle attests to the 'scientific' socialist view of history as a series of class contradictions across modes of production. This also marks the difference of historical materialism from other left currents, as a paradigm that can historicise itself and move through temporalities. A foundation in existing struggles allows this paradigm to look beyond transient considerations. The young Marx (cited in Bloch, 1995a: 155–156) reflects on this to his colleague Arnold Ruge in a letter:

> Our motto must ... be: reform of consciousness not through dogmas, but through analysis of mystical consciousness which is still unclear to itself. It will then become apparent that the world has long possessed the dream of a matter, of which it must only possess the consciousness in order to possess it in reality. It will become apparent that it is not a question of a great thought-dash between past and future, but of the carrying-through of the thoughts of the past.

This passage blurs linear notions of history, drawing attention to the qualitative temporality of subjective, conscious experience of social struggle. Consequently, one never literally starts from the beginning, but taps into existing political and theoretical rhythms (in Althusserian parlance, concepts cannot be isolated from their *problematique*). The dismissal of engagement in struggle as a 'thought-dash between past and future' is inscribed in the rejection of 'utopian' currents claiming to have discovered the formula that leads to transition. Therefore, Marx and Engels' cautiousness towards other currents is a call for humility before existing movements and the 'dream matter' that they give shape to. It follows from this that the distinction between 'scientific' and 'utopian' socialisms is not as watertight, or hostile to historical initiatives, as it has come to be seen. The quoted letter of Marx has been valuable to Bloch, the philosopher who integrated utopia as an anthropological reality into historical materialism, whence it was banished after being wrongly blamed for conceited retreat.

4   Bloch and the Not-Yet

According to Geoghegan (2008: 59), the Second International looked down on descriptions of postcapitalist society, an attitude implicit in Bernstein's notorious aphorism 'The Final goal, no matter what it is, is nothing; the movement is everything' (cited in Luxembourg, 2008: 41). While the left could produce cogent analyses of political economy, they were unwilling to describe how their resolutions would shape a new mode of life. Bloch (1885–1977), whose lifespan contained several permutations of German states, attacks this lack of imagination as the forfeiture of a field of struggle. Writing at the peak of Nazi consolidation, Bloch (1991) formulated a unique account of fascism in terms of an appropriation of the emancipatory impulses of the past in *Heritage of Our*

Times, published from exile in Zurich in 1935. The social memory of the struggles of the German peasantry and the *mittelstand* of small enterprise owners and artisanal producers was transmitted across centuries, colouring revolutionary discourse against feudal authorities. Yet in the twentieth century, this rhetoric figured in reactionary terms as a longing for a better future imbued with idealised images of the past (Rabinbach, 1977: 6–7). For Bloch, the victory of the far-right showed the incapacity of the left to reclaim these elements. Based on this, he integrates utopia as temporal conveyor of such expressions into Marxism.

Bloch locates utopia within historical materialism as a constituent, engendered in the 'warm stream' of social struggles. Their analysis, in turn, calls for the 'cold stream' of the critique of political economy. These streams are intertwined, as the matter taken up by the cold stream, identifying processes of exploitation, hinges on the understanding that capitalism is incapable of fully reducing productive activity to commodified wage-labour. Therefore Bloch (1995: 209) explains 'To the *warm stream* of Marxism, however, belong liberating intention and materialistically humane, humanely materialistic real tendency, towards whose goal all these disenchantments are undertaken'. It is noteworthy that Bloch deploys phrases such as 'materialistic' and 'disenchantment', indicating that he is not simply interested in a cultural analysis of utopia, but its tendency to materially move beyond the given circumstances. As Boer (2016: 14) maintains, the warm stream encompasses contemporary and historic struggles, which have not only furthered the contingent goals of left social movements and parties within their political situation, but, equally importantly, have introduced thematic issues to the cold stream.

Bloch's philosophy spans several decades and themes; *The Principle of Hope*, a systematic compendium of his key theories and stretching across 1600 pages, was written in the United States, edited in East Germany, and first published in Frankfurt, West Germany in 1959 (Habermas, 1970: 311). In this text, Bloch (1995: 343, 404, 1241, 1034–1051) develops his analysis of 'educated hope', unbound from convention yet grasped rationally, and demonstrates through myriad discussions ranging from the allure of advertising to Zoroaster, and Aztec symbols to Don Quixote, how the grasp of a better future, even though in embryonic and prelinguistic forms, attests to a 'preconsciousness' in human society. A common thread is temporal unease, accounting for prefigurative anticipations in cultural creation, particularly in utopias. This theory nevertheless has a decidedly Marxist inflection. Stating that 'the hinge in human history is its producer' (ibid: 249), Bloch (ibid: 12) articulates his view of human activity as partly composed of an expression of hope, which is to be 'understood not ... *only as emotion ... but more essentially as a directing act of a cognitive kind*'. In consequence, utopianism derives from and effects historical flows beyond mere wishful thinking. The temporal multiplicity of the present is an intersection of a variety of utopian assertions.

Theorising utopia beyond a literary genre covers a theoretical blind spot. As Bloch (ibid: 14–15) argues: '[T]o limit the utopian to the Thomas More variety, or simply to orientate it in that direction, would be like trying to reduce electricity to the amber from which it gets its Greek name and in which it was first noticed'. The common assumptions around utopia neglect that it consists of an essential tendency to visualise one's self as outside of the given. This is expressed in myriad forms such as day and night dreams, as well as more sustained meditations on different futures. The ubiquity of such thoughts raises the opposite question of whether Bloch is exceedingly inclusive and purposefully non-verifiable regarding the content of the utopian, as Levitas has pointed out (1990: 122). However, Levitas (ibid) also adds that a philosophical attention to wishful thinking and hope is needed against backward-looking materialism. This opposes the external unity in the Now, gaining sight of its temporal ruptures. The essential section, as we've seen with Althusser, obscures the real temporal contradictions of the moment.

In contexts where the hope for a different future is nullified in the grinding replication of the past, this imaginary does not dissipate, but conveys itself in subterranean forms. In this regard, Bloch radically democratises utopia, turning to unconventional sources and unofficial knowledges and teasing out their hopeful aspects. This does not mean that all cultural production has an emancipatory undergirding waiting to be identified. Bloch maintains that utopia can be palliative or inconsequential, as in the fleeting daydream or incoherent night dream. The appraisal of utopia is measured, considering how it can serve as a 'beautifying mirror which often only reflects how the ruling class wishes the wishes of the weak to be'. Here Bloch (op. cit., 13) alludes to the desire channelled towards the interests of the bourgeoisie, such as consumerism and nationalism (ibid: 13). Hope, in contrast, is postured towards the future, and draws its impetus from the Not-Yet. It sits uneasily at the present, reactivating the past and anticipating the future. It is thus an interlocutor between the present, and the futures in the process of becoming.

As Habermas (1970: 313) argues, Bloch diverges from Hegel, whose teleological sequence posits a mechanically expanding consciousness of freedom. The coexistence of temporal strains disrupts the understanding of compounding progress, proposing points of inflection where possibilities are unrealized, aspirations unfulfilled, and a nomadic search for a way out is disoriented. The task is to reclaim the future oriented thought suppressed in dominant ways of relating to the self and society. Bloch thereby politicises utopia beyond a figment of the imagination, conceptualising it as a field of struggle and the medium of its own expression. It is not a given that a different future is encoded in the human imagination, making a transition inevitable. A possibility, as amply demonstrated in history, is a regression to the 'devastatingly possible fascist Nothing' as well as 'finally feasible and overdue, socialism' (Bloch, 1995: 197).

Rather than a critique of political methods and discourse, Bloch's condemnation of abandoning the sphere of alternative imaginaries stems from his appraisal of temporal dislocation. This approaches the Althusserian theory of lag, even though the two outlooks may not appear as compatible. Bloch (1990: 97) states that 'Not all people exist in the same Now', explaining that while people cohabit a time interval externally, 'various years in general beat in the one which is just being counted and prevails'. As opposed to the line of the Communist International, there was more to the surge of fascism than the open dictatorship of capital (Rabinbach, 1977: 20). Undoubtedly, capital was the main beneficiary of fascism, which provided relief from working class militancy. However, this movement mobilised an array of symbols and concepts from folk culture, sprawled across the past and invoking worlds of classlessness and social peace. The 'Third Reich' itself was among these (Bloch, 1990: 57–60, passim). Noting that the term was used by the twelfth century theologian Joachim of Fiore, Bloch (ibid: 58) explains that it has persisted as a relic of collective memory. This indicates that there are untimely expressions that animate members of society in opposite directions. The 'Third Reich', like others, is tainted with an 'odour of blood', turned into a nationalism that numbs class consciousness (ibid: 59). That being the case, though these may seem clear now, Bloch had grasped in the 1930s the explosive potential of symbolism, and the importance of affect.

Bloch's analysis goes beyond a critique of left discourse, as he demonstrates that violent imperialism and the surge of romantic commitments to glory are related to the impoverishment of the lower-middle class. Now inhabiting a position that can be identified as proletarian, the German middle class further embraced Marx and Engels' derided 'petty-bourgeois socialism', longing for a glorified past, stripped of the rationalism that accompanied capitalist development. Bloch (ibid: 59) relates how a young Nazi exclaimed: 'You do not die for the programme you have understood, you die for a programme you love'. This dogmatism embraces ignorance, and the speaker is far from realising their material predicament. Echoing Žižek (2008: 138), there is no fascism *avant la lettre*, as one would not speak of a 'really existing fascism' and its relation to its theoretical underpinnings. Rather, various kinds of faith are conjoined to practically vent frustrations for reactionary ends. The blind faith of the Nazi supporter is also tenuously rooted in a deeper, 'primitive' discontent. Here Bloch (1990: 60) advances a bolder suggestion on the mobilising power of the myth:

> This streak could in fact, like every recollection of 'primitiveness', also have turned out differently, if it had been militarily occupied and dialectically transformed, on the 'enlightened' side, instead of merely being abstractly cordoned off. But since Marxist propaganda lacks any opposite land to myth, any transformation of mythical beginnings into real ones, of Dionysian dreams into revolutionary ones, an element of guilt also becomes apparent in the effect of National Socialism, namely a guilt on the part of the all too usual vulgar Marxism.

This insight sees fascism as one of the perverse, backward looking 'dreams of a better life', which was meant to be the original title of *The Principle of Hope* (Thompson, 2013). Left theory and practice needs to recognise the constructive potential of the myth to prevent its abhorrent actualisations. Yet, unlike Georges Sorel (1999), who had glorified the myth – in the form of an apocalyptic mass strike – for its destructiveness, Bloch is invested in building 'concrete utopias'.

Attacking perceptions of temporal and social stasis, Bloch (1995: 1375) maintains that 'the world is propensity towards something, tendency towards something, latency of something, and this intended something means fulfilment of the intending'. This encrypted statement contains the non-synchronous contradiction denoting a lack of continuity within and between classes, and their dissonant modes of being in the present. Opposing the preconscious to the subconscious, and privileging the former, Bloch locates latent futures unrealised in the present, in varying degrees of coherence. The tendency, complementing latency, refers to the *real* possibilities of what may become. Such a tendency towards an elusive 'something' links the cold and warm streams, remaining perennially as-yet-undefined. In turn, the possibilities borne by turns of social reproduction link Marxism and utopia, where utopia designates a mode of relating to the world. This is where 'concrete' utopia departs from mainstream receptions of the concept. As Thompson (2013) explains, the term concrete is used in its Hegelian sense as *con crescere*, or an intermeshed growing together of tendencies and latencies. The futures unrealised in the past and present, and the pressure of the repressed, objective possibility, are within the ambit of historical materialism. Bloch's enterprise is more programmatic than substantive, understanding historical change with a dimension of temporal instability, and suggesting an exploration of utopian routes to transition:

> History is no entity advancing along a single line, in which capitalism for instance, as the final stage, has resolved all the previous ones; but it is a polyrhythmic and multi-spatial entity, with enough unmastered and as yet by no means revealed and resolved corners. (Bloch, 1990: 62)

5 Spatio-temporal Utopianism as Method: Harvey and Levitas

In order to substantiate Bloch's performative reclamation of utopia, it is helpful to map its coordinates with a geographic perspective, as Harvey has done with the concept of 'spatio-temporal utopia'. Approvingly quoting Bloch's statement that 'possibility has had a bad press' and that 'there is a very clear interest that has prevented the world from being changed into the possible', Harvey sketches a historicist theory of utopia. This goes beyond the scale of the immediately present, and has a wide scope, but also addresses particularities (Bloch, cited in Harvey, 2000: 156). As indicated in the above discussion, utopia is intrinsic to social and political imaginaries, and activates within transitional moments. Levitas (2013) has made the case for the methodological utility of utopia, through the lens of the 'Imaginary Reconstitution of Society' (IROS). Combining Levitas' hermeneutic method with Harvey's discussion of the spatio-temporal ontology of utopia, this section argues that utopia can be prefigurative and descriptive at once, configuring the temporal tension between repressed futures and reproduced pasts.

Harvey (2000) grounds his theory of a 'dialectical utopianism' on a variety of sources, drawing from visual media, political literature, as well as bourgeois projections in urban planning, particularly in Baltimore since the late 1960s, when the author witnessed a decades long increase in social stratification and inequality. The unifying theme is a challenge against the infamous Thatcherite mantra 'There is no Alternative', to which even Gorbachev had subscribed (ibid: 53). Harvey argues that utopian thought follows purely spatial or temporal parameters. Broadening the scope of utopianism to political-economic doctrines, as I have also done above, Harvey explains that laissez-faire liberalism, with its emphasis on individual rights, free trade and equality of opportunity, comprises an example of the temporal utopia, or a utopianism of process. It is a theoretical construct, and indifferent to the shortcomings of its implementation (ibid.:173). Harvey describes the degeneration of the liberal-capitalist vision, and how despite having a few centuries to run its course and achieve its ends, it has failed by its own standards. Adam Smith's view of an ever-perfected market with rational individuals fails to account for drastic increases in inequality. This would contradict Smith's moral social vision of atomised individuals seeking benefit through the invisible hand of the market, delivering benefits for all.

The utopianism of process imminent in free-market fundamentalism is blind to the challenges in its spatial implementation. On the other hand, the utopianism of spatial play drafts the meticulously planned and regimented social relations of a fictional community, in a fictional space. Harvey (ibid: 160) refers to More's utopia as an example, characterising it as follows: 'Utopia is an artificially created island which functions as an isolated, coherently organized, and largely closed-space economy (though closely monitored relations with the outside world are posited)' (ibid: 159–160).[2] The enclosure of an island is convenient for devising the minutiae without external disturbances. Taking such a setting, utopian blueprints of this kind posit a mechanical and perpetual motion of a harmonised and sutured society. While More's work is also critical of its moment, Harvey points to an important omission in this utopia: it could be set in any geography and historical period. Practically, this would bring up concrete, specialised challenges and avenues of degeneration or improvement. Such a form – heaven being the obvious example – is noticeably static, and shorn of contact with the vicissitudes of the mundane, presenting examples of the wishful thinking often disparaged by Bloch.

Having discussed the spatially and temporally static modes of utopian thinking, Harvey proposes the spatio-temporal utopia and 'dialectical utopia' as alternatives. These terms combine spatial form and social process, incorporating an understanding of history and transition as inherently 'accidental' processes. Various Marxisms' suspicion of utopia is due to their acceptance that while utopias may be 'realised', they are ultimately subsumed by the historical process and allocated a temporal quality. This temporal attribute is not simply inscribed in their own merits, but also contingent on the aggregate relations and contextualisations they enter with the surrounding conjuncture.

Ursula Le Guin's (1999) novel *The Dispossessed* is an example of a utopia that is both critical of the society it is written from, and describes an alternative world. Subtitled in some editions as 'An Ambiguous Utopia', the science fiction novel takes place between the two worlds Urras and Anarres. While the former is a familiar capitalist landscape with a species of a 'Cold War' in its midst (the book was published in the 1970s), the latter is an anarchist society without a discernible state structure, and egalitarian customs. Le Guin's book tells the journey of Shevek, a physicist from Anarres who arrives in Urras to share his research. His observations of the capitalist setting provide an account of the

---

2 For a critique of Harvey's treatment of More's Utopia, see Johnson (2012: 12–15).

senselessness of some of its customs as well as shocking excesses and exploitative relations, defamiliarising the reader from the taken-for-granted absurdities of the everyday. In this way, the author speaks to the possibility of an alternative, as we see Shevek taking part in protests and becoming politicised. However, this work also includes descriptions of the troubling aspects of Anarres, Le Guin's fictional anarchic community. There are descriptions of a vast range of differences, such as a lack of law enforcement or any carceral apparatus, ambiguous parenthood and equality between the sexes, as well as more subtle changes like the generation of a unique and meaningless new name for every new-born. Yet, the people in this society have major conflicts and disappointments with their way of life, and a drought forces prolonged deliberations and poses morally challenging questions. Thus, Le Guin captures the reader's imagination without making a facile promise of an idealised, fully worked out society of unbounded happiness. Instead, fitting Harvey's 'dialectical utopia', *The Dispossessed* is a meditation on unforeseen outcomes and adaptation, which sways clear of pragmatic integration and palliative fantasy.

Maintaining the utopian mode at the expense of the blueprint is central to Levitas' (2005, 2013) sociological resuscitation of utopia. To substantiate the IROS, she sets out from this observation (ibid: 5):

> Utopia does not require the imaginative construction of whole other worlds. It occurs as an embedded element in a wide range of human practice and culture – in the individual and collective creative practices of art as well as in its reproduction and consumption. Utopian method here is primarily hermeneutic. If we start from here, it is evident that contemporary culture is saturated with utopianism, even (or especially) where there is no figurative representation of an alternative world.

While utopia may have fallen into disrepute in the social sciences, it was preserved in the 'critical utopianism' of literary works (ibid: 110–111). The works of writers such as Le Guin and China Miéville intermingle utopia with dystopia. For Levitas, this is also the case for social imaginaries of all hues, and rationalises her defence of utopia as an embedded desire.

Levitas contends that throughout cultural expressions such as art and music, as well as political movements demanding dignity and equality, one can discern a universal desire to lead a better life (ibid: 20–40; Levitas, 2007; Levitas, 2010). Like Bloch, Levitas rakes through popular culture and historical folklore to argue that this is a persistent impulse. Utopia has an intuitive shape in Levitas' (2013: 113) theory, because it does not necessarily refer to coherent projections of alternative societies. Rather, it conveys a libidinal energy to be outside of the quotidian reality, and may not be cognitively formulated. Unlike Bloch, Levitas does not privilege the subjective attitude and experience. Utopia is more useful as an analytic, helping to analyse the open-ended 'desire'. Being impulsive and emotional, the content of desire, in its cruder forms, may not be utopian, nor even progressive (there can be depictions of a better life that leave social structures intact while meeting physical needs). Based on this, utopia is a transhistorical tendency, arising from a longing to transcend the immediately given. Although, it still requires political initiative and the education of desire. Movements for radical social change should not posit utopianism where it is not, or introduce new desires, but situate themselves at moments where such desire is felt, and refine and sharpen it towards future goals, tightening the gap between needs and available means. Coupled with Harvey's spatio-temporal utopia, IROS situates utopia as a transitional impulse at the core of society; while the IROS accounts for the desire, the spatio-temporal utopia is a directly prefigurative project with a view to reaching the horizons with origins in the present.

6 Timelessness of Utopia

This chapter has evaluated approaches to utopianism, followed its Marxist treatments, and challenged some of the received wisdom around the concept. I have argued, drawing from Bloch, Harvey, and Levitas, that utopia is an imminent feature of social life and cultural production. From the cooperatives of Owen to the ambiguous fictional community of Le Guin's *The Dispossessed*, considerations of a different life are ubiquitous and immutable, illustrating how alternative temporalities in the shape of transformative imaginaries traverse the Now.

Following the discussion of the melancholic disposition, its utopian counterpart might suggest optimism. However, we have seen that utopia is a function of melancholy as much as hope, deriving inspiration from an uneasiness with the state of affairs. Melancholy persists as a residue of past defeats and initiatives, forming an impulse to act, even if within capitalist frames. On the other hand, utopia is angled towards different futures, and shapes human action with possibilities beyond presently existing means. In sum, melancholy attests to the futures in the past, while utopia, as a prefigurative not-yet, is the past of a future. There are transitional elements to both, including the melancholic sense of loss and its paths to redemption. In terms of the transitional elements of a positive, utopian programme, it is necessary to focus on contemporary policy proposals as potentially transitional steps to postcapitalism. This will be the task of Part 3.

SUMMARY

Melancholy, Utopia and Transition as a Hermeneutic

Part 2 has followed the arguments for the ontology of transition set out in Part 1. Moving from the theoretical underpinnings of transition as an outcome of the incarnations of productive activity, this part has explored its substantive manifestations in terms of two interconnected modalities of political engagement. Melancholy and utopia suggest that transition is imminent as a temporal lag, since they both indicate a sense of unease with the present, and a desire to move beyond it. Thus, a theory of societal transition, and political projects of bringing this about, would ignore these dispositions at their own peril.

We have seen that, in order to define melancholy, it is necessary to consider psychoanalytic theory, particularly Freud's work on mourning and melancholy. According to Freud, these are similar affective states, in which the mourner and melancholic may have identical experiences. Moreover, they are both responses to perceived or real loss. However, the subject's relationship with the object of the loss, be it a person or a concept, takes different forms depending on the state of the ego in the process. The ego, mediating between the unconscious and the conscious, may be immersed in mourning following a loss, but remains intact as the interlocutor of personal identity. On the other hand, melancholia endangers the ego, as the subject has an ambivalent attitude towards the loss, reconfiguring their sense of self and leading to a reassessment. In this process, the nature of the loss is questioned, along with the subject apportioning blame to themselves, and even expecting reprisals.

Benjamin's works on 'left' melancholy have provided a politicised interpretation of Freudian melancholia. Accordingly, the indecision regarding the loss, including as to whether it has occurred at all, or what aspect has been lost, addresses the aporia of the contemporary left, haunted by catastrophic failures and widespread adaptation to neoliberal normalcy, while attempting to chart a path forward. We saw how Benjamin uses the term in crosscutting ways, invoking its detrimental capacity at the hands of some intellectuals, who package the plight of the oppressed as a consumer good for the bourgeois conscience, and as a resource for a redemptive, messianic mode of revolutionary politics. I elaborated the latter function of left melancholy as a resource, to argue that past defeats and failures need not lead to disillusionment, since they attest to a subterranean temporality that traverses the quantitative time of capitalism. That is to say, transitional moments brought on by political action are rejuvenated with the memory of past defeats, placing contemporary political actors along a string of attempts to reclaim production for the benefit of the community. This political manifestation of a temporal discord with the state of affairs also prefigures the counterpart to the melancholic state, in the form of utopia.

Chapter 5 therefore turned to utopia as a purveyor of a positive program beyond the current predicament. The redemption of frustrated struggles is transfigured into a utopianism, informed by the sense of not being at home in the world. Even so, utopianism has been disparaged variously as totalitarian, or a waste of revolutionary energies into building 'castles in the air'. Here utopianism was reclaimed as a sociological reality, implicit in political thought across the spectrum, and as an organic secretion of social life. Anti-utopianism was explained here as a deliberate closure of the future, and presentation of the neoliberal moment as an embodiment of the perennial laws of human society. This necessitates the reconfiguration of the utopian to restore its explanatory power as a fount of political and cultural creativity. And upon a closer look, the standard Marxist rejection of utopia also appears to be misguided, since the works of the classical Marxists evince a sympathy for the prefigurative capacity of alternative societies, and recognise the broader temporal cycles intruding on the superficial one. I have excavated in detail how this point was forcefully made by Bloch, whose theory of utopia is bolstered with a vast range of discussions of its promise of a different future in cultural relics. Furthermore, a negligence of this has been calamitous for the left, whence it chose to abandon the 'warm stream' of symbolism and myths in favour of a positivistic 'cold stream' of political economic analysis.

Finally, we saw how Levitas and Harvey theorise a spatio-temporal utopia, both as a constituent of society, and a template for a politics of transition. In so doing, they elaborate a cogent account of utopianism as a domain of left politics. Issuing from the temporal lag between alienation and implicit potentials, utopianism can link quotidian politics with emancipatory horizons. Consequently, this formulation of utopia is predicated on its democratisation, emphasising its quality as a collective effort, and transitional *process* rather than end point. Correspondingly, the task of a left vision of transition has to be one of facilitating the emergence of, and helping to give coherence to, popular movements with a utopian edge. The following Part thus completes the theoretical to practical composition of this book, setting out a case study of such a substantive vision.

PART 3

Enacting Transition: Substantive Left Visions

Introduction to Part 3

This study has thus far advocated a historical materialist theory of transition, founded on productive activity as a parameter of temporal advancement. Every turn of social reproduction generates temporal lags with melancholic and utopian manifestations. While the initial Part grounded the social ontology of transition, Part 2 theorised the melancholy and utopia duality as a way of mapping alternate temporalities. What remains to show is the explanatory power of this theory *vis-à-vis* contemporary strands in left theory. This Part will concurrently subject existing transitional politics to a temporal analysis and seek to refine the theory of transition in the process.

Progressing from the theoretical discussion of transition, I turn to contemporary left visions. A series of worksites have emerged within the last few decades, reflecting wider political developments. Among these, one may count the nation-state and the question of its obsolescence, anti-fascist organisation that has acquired a new relevance, or theories of intersectionality. These examples can be multiplied, but probing into each and every one would hinder the depth they merit for a fair engagement. Rather, it is expedient to identify a single case within a comprehensive unity of its antecedents and political standpoints. This approach is theoretically fruitful due to its sustained engagement, and analytical openness to internal tensions and external critiques.

This Part considers the 'postwork' paradigm as an emerging left vision, relevant to transition with its evaluations of capitalist trends. As a nascent area of literature, postwork theory forms a nexus between the twentieth century and the present, transmitting the sensitivities and subject matters of earlier strands of left theory within its theoretical innovations that address new possibilities. Additionally, due to its popularity among left political actors, this paradigm has drawn a growing range of criticism and praise, provoking an insightful debate.

Since postwork has a rich grounding in theoretical currents with roots in the previous century, Chapter 6 identifies and critiques them on their own terms. Chapter 7 brings the discussion to the present, analysing salient postwork texts. A thematic exposition will be provided, outlining the theorists' solutions to the shortcomings of their predecessors. Finally, Chapter 8 departs from theory, drawing out political implications, and entertaining some criticisms based on an interpretation of Social Reproduction Theory. This then leads to an evaluation of the broader antinomies of left politics, and the book concludes with an analysis of socialist transition in particular, through the lens of a historical materialist theory of transition. Emulating the wider organising frame of the book, I set out an increasingly concretised discussion, coming to an end with an investigation of demands, agency, and strategy.

CHAPTER 6

Lineages of Postwork Theory

Postwork theory is a latticework of theoretical currents. This investigation provides a delineation of the family resemblances between the most salient postwork texts. For this purpose, the critique of productivism, Italian autonomist Marxism, and accelerationism are respectively discussed in detail, to put them in dialogue with leading thinkers of the paradigm. Postwork theory, despite internal differences in emphasis, provides a useful framework for a contemporary left vision, attesting to a viable techno-utopian standpoint. Through this discussion, I seek to show that at its best, postwork theory fulfils a utopian function by relating existing tendencies to the conception of a different society in the making, embodying a compelling vision of the future. However, if it falls back on the premises of its theoretical heritage, it also risks slippage into a techno-determinist program of transition through hierarchical reform.

The critique of productivism has been a connecting thread among these works, whether they seek to denaturalise conceptions about work, question the left's embrace of productivity and employment, or look for the causes of the anxiety around automation. Referring to Baudrillard's view that a valorisation of labour is intrinsic to Marxism, Kathi Weeks (2011) disentangles left productivism from historical materialism. Weeks' reformulation of productivism has helped to distinguish an ill-informed rejection of Marxism based on its political heritage, as seen in the cases of Soviet Taylorism and the social-democratic glorification of high levels of – white male – industrial employment. If reconsidered as a tendency to espouse work in its contemporary incarnation as alienated wage labour, the concept of productivism carries water as a charge against both left and right attitudes that maintain and reproduce capitalist categories. Such attitudes reduce postcapitalist visions to a negotiation of terms between wage-labour and capital. Postwork theory rejects taking this terrain for granted, removing the inviolable centralisation of work as a self-actualising activity or a prerequisite of survival and dignity.

Another corollary of postwork theory is autonomist Marxism, based on the observation that prevailing working class parties and unions are entrenched in the system, and act as productivist mouthpieces buttressing capitalist relations. However, there is a contextual gulf between postwork and autonomism. On the one hand, Italian autonomists sought to provide a realistic account of the prospects of revolution at a time of rosy expectations, as left parties dominated the official political scene and commanded high levels of mainstream support and respect. On the other hand, postwork has been voicing a left vision following decades of neoliberal social engineering, with inequality at unprecedented levels and public services ravaged, attempting to reinvigorate the same social democratic parties with solutions to the excesses of capitalism. Both standpoints thus highlight and realise the potentials of their own time, whether by building autonomous working class power outside of established channels, or calling for a four-day work week. Considering postwork and autonomism in continuity also helps to bring into focus the superfluity of the class and community divide. Additionally, autonomism defies academic boundaries, voicing working class concerns as a political and artistic movement. I shall therefore take up a novel and a film representative of this tradition to outline its features. In particular, I seek to underline the temporal complexity in the worldview of the 'mass worker', the typically southern migrant worker in the industrial north of Italy, as a remarkable contribution of autonomism to critiques of left politics.

A tertiary inspiration broadly sketched here is accelerationism, since Srnicek and Williams subscribe to what I term 'post-accelerationism'. This tendency has originated from the writings of Nick Land and the Cybernetic Culture Research Unit (CCRU), climaxing in the former's problematic embrace of 'speed' for its own sake. Srnicek and Williams are committed to a certain type of accelerationism, adding the crucial qualification that speed must be considered as a vector, with both quantity and direction. Thus, the modified accelerationism incorporates a political component, which reins back the nihilistic celebration of cybernetic proliferation with a much-needed attenuation for its social implications. In this sense, postwork theories gather their attention at the temporal disjuncture between forces of production and the ideological and political dimensions of social reproduction. This comes through in the example of Cybersyn, the short-lived Chilean apparatus for economic governance, which demonstrates how assemblages of the advanced technology can act in a prefigurative capacity.

This chapter critiques disparate components of postwork through drawing out implications for transition. This sets the scene for the following chapter, where I follow their repercussions in postwork perspectives.

1 Antiwork Politics: the Critique of Productivism

Work has a commanding position in the social psyche, and its critics target productivism as the culprit of the conflation of its current form with self-actualisation and identity. Here, this will be considered as it figures in

Baudrillard's critique of Marxism, with Weeks' (2011) formulation as the reference point for this theme within postwork. According to Weeks (ibid: 7), work has received scant attention as a subject of critique in political economy, a lacuna more bizarre due to the centrality of such a 'world-building practice'. Her book *The Problem with Work: Feminism, Marxism, Antiwork Politics, and Postwork Imaginaries* has been foundational. Mapping work as a regulative mechanism and ideological bulwark of capitalism, Weeks challenges assumptions of its indispensability, opposing its 'naturalisation' as a constant, neutral given (ibid: 7). Weeks outlines an antiwork politics grounded in the contemporary potential to marginalise the compulsory sale of labour-power (ibid: 102). While there are possibilities to drastically reduce work, ethical attitudes hold these back (ibid: 37–79). It is therefore necessary to problematise the steadfast link between work and survival.

Noting Max Weber's astute account of the unintended implications of the Protestant work ethic, Weeks argues that the secular work life is underpinned by the valorisation of hard and tedious labour for character and identity formation. This critique of the glorification of disciplined labour is also extended to the residual 'productivism' of the left, as evidenced by Lenin's fascination with Taylorist models of efficiency (ibid: 83–84). It is pertinent to concentrate on left productivism here, as it is subject to debate over later approaches to productivity and socialism. Lenin's earlier writings suggest a disdain towards the Taylorist management model. In an article written in 1914 and titled 'The Taylor System – Man's Enslavement by the Machine', Lenin (1972: 152–154) disparages the management of the workers' subtlest movements as a subjugating device. Saying that 'these vast improvements are introduced to *the detriment* of the workers, for they lead to their still greater oppression and exploitation', Lenin nevertheless qualifies his criticisms, and adds that 'this rational and efficient distribution of labour is confined to *each* factory' (ibid, italics in the original). The crux of the criticism is that the 'vast improvements' are in the service of the interests of individual capitalists, and not society as a whole. Accordingly, Lenin argues that these innovations can be repurposed to serve the working class, and he fails to question whether this process could be exploitative *per se*, regardless of whether it is overseen by the capitalist or the party supervisor. This position was further reiterated in post-1917 writings, where Lenin (1971: 417) defined Taylorism – the productivism of the time – as 'refined brutality', yet insisted on the need to build socialism using the 'up-to-date achievements of capitalism'.[1]

---

1 It would be academically irresponsible to present a one-sided picture of Soviet abuses without contextual qualifications. Notwithstanding its problematic approach to the relationship

The deterioration of the economy in the war-ravaged, lone socialist state compelled greater productivity, and it should be noted that the selective application of capitalist tools for modernisation was common currency in left debates at the time: even Gramsci (1971: 277–318), a thinker credited for his sensitivity to cultural issues, was sympathetic towards Taylorism.[2] Thus, the explication of socialist interpretations of industrial management herein is not a political judgment of Soviet economic development, as this would be anachronistic. Rather it is a statement on how productivity and its concomitant technological implements and management doctrines delayed a critique of their perception as 'neutral' devices. Also, the New Economic Plan was envisaged by Lenin as a strategic retreat where there would be wider scope for private initiative coupled with continued enthusiasm for factory discipline, though this was not tantamount to his vision of socialism *tout court* (Lenin, 1966: 204–207). Žižek (2009) argues that Lenin's ingenuity lay in his discernment of the particular and adaptivity to vicissitudes of socialist construction. Under different circumstances, he may have favoured more workers' control. Be that as it may, no matter how contingent and temporary Lenin may have considered this expansion of factory discipline in the fog of war and strife, the leaders of the Soviet Union adopted the same attitude in the ensuing decades. It must be noted here, however, that Weeks' depiction of the Soviet decisions to bolster productivity at all costs, and by any means necessary, is excessively voluntarist. Weeks creates the impression that this was a purely subjective choice over its alternatives, whereas it was actually conditioned, even dictated, by capitalist encirclement and the pressure to compensate for the lack of industrialisation. That said, the object of scrutiny here is the political and theoretical ramifications of productivisms, rather than the conditions of their emergence. All things considered, what once was a local decision to take a step back became an end in itself when, to return to Weeks' (ibid: 84) account, 'the utopia was either deferred into the ever-more-distant future or declared achieved'.

---

    between workers' control and central planning, the Soviet Union also made tremendous advances in basic economic security and all-round standard of living for its citizens (Pipes, 1990: 499; Service, 2000: 321). The welfare regimes of the more prosperous capitalist West were rivalled and spurred by the unprecedented extensions of the Soviet model, whether in terms of paid holidays, the provision of homes, or healthcare (Szymanski, 1984: 128–150). Whether, and to what extent, these achievements can be attributed to the productive discipline of the Soviet economic system far surpasses the parameters of our discussion, but this should be kept in mind when scrutinising its working regime.

2 To Gramsci's credit, he was fascinated with Fordism and Taylorism as *cultural* projects as well as economic ones, central to a mode of life populated by the industrial worker-citizen-consumer of modern America.

As Mason (2015: 60) has indicated, a notion of transition from the free market, to state monopolies, followed by socialism, or 'from Standard Oil to socialism', was common in the early twentieth century, with direct state involvement and control of certain sectors seen as necessary even in capitalist heartlands. The problem with this position, however, was that it is too seamless, as the process of production remained the same while property relations changed. The working class would be subjected to a factory discipline not unlike their counterparts in capitalist countries, which fell short of the transition envisioned in classical Marxism as a positive recovery of productive activity. Weeks (2011: 84) characterises this blind spot thus: 'The figures of Stakhanov and Oblomov offer an official Soviet version of the political economists' parable about the ethically deserving and undeserving, but with the class positions reversed: the worthy industrious worker and useless lazy nobleman'.

Stakhanov and Oblomov respectively refer to the Russian Soviet miner Alexey Stakhanov, who was hailed as a beacon of productivity in the 1930s, and the eponymous protagonist of Goncharov's 1859 novel, characterised by his indecision and laziness, epitomising the parasitic existence of the landed gentry. Weeks makes use of Baudrillard's (1975) provocative indictment of Marxism, *The Mirror of Production*, to inform a radical criticism of existing socialisms' valorisation of work as an end in itself. While Weeks does not agree with the conclusion that Marxism no longer provides an emancipatory horizon, she considers Baudrillard's work valuable as a criticism of the fetishisation of productivity that seeps into some accounts of Marxism. To draw out the transitional implications of 'productivism', it is worth examining Baudrillard's charges more closely.

According to Baudrillard, by maintaining the categories of classical political economy such as value and labour, Marx is tethered to the essentialism of productive activity implicit in his contemporaries' writings – after all, the LTV had also figured in Ricardo's work. By maintaining such categories, Marx simply inverts the signs to place emphasis on the role of labour-power as opposed to capital. Consequently the abstraction of the productive individual, and the communist vision of the disalienation of production, lend more credibility to the ideological underpinnings of bourgeois political economy. For Baudrillard (ibid: 30), this leaves untapped a source of subversion rooted in abandoning the idea of self-realisation in labour; he thus posits that 'Marxism assists the cunning of capital' as it 'convinces men that they are alienated by the sale of their labor power' while 'censoring the much more radical hypothesis that they might be alienated as labor power, as the 'inalienable' power of creating value by their labor'.

Considering the pivotal role of productive activity in historical materialism, its decentralisation and trivialisation would indeed threaten this pillar. As Baudrillard (1975, 1981, 1998) has argued, this would also indicate a lack of practical relevance since it relies on a circular argument, referring back to its own abstracted category of the labourer, whereas there is no reason to assume that this activity carried much weight at any given time. Accordingly, Baudrillard (1975: 49) claims that in primitive societies, such as the South American Bororo tribe studied by Lévi-Strauss, 'There is *neither a mode of production nor production* in primitive societies ... These concepts analyse only our own societies, which are ruled by political economy'. Furthermore, Marxism is inept even in the geography whence it emerged, compelling its revaluation according to new realities, and a conclusive break from the 'self-fetishisation of Western thought' (ibid: 49–50; Smith, 1990: 275–276). The critic of political economy mistakes her reflection for the reality in the eponymous 'mirror of production'. Baudrillard posits this narcissism, to then question the construct of the *homo faber*, a productivist inversion of the enterprising, proto-capitalist *homo economicus*, instead with a natural propensity to build tools. Moreover, this belies an enlightenment-style optimism, with the exaltation of improvement and belief in perfectibility (ibid: 32–33).

Baudrillard's criticism relies on the unsubstantiated presumption that Marx has not contributed anything of value to political economy, let alone providing an original philosophical anthropology that undermines its utilitarian premise of production and pursuit of profit as ends in themselves. It is pertinent to indicate in passing that – as Laclau and Mouffe have done to the detriment of the credibility of their post-Marxism – Baudrillard falls back on Marxian turns of phrase such as 'bourgeois thought', which would suggest some continuity between economic gain and political disposition. However, there is a still more fundamental flaw in this faulty depiction of Marxism. While productivity is lauded in some Marxist tracts, such as the discussion of the dynamism of capitalism in the *Communist Manifesto* (2012: 26), it is hard to see how the endeavour to transform working life to meet social needs and away from the profit motive could be construed as an injunction to carry out mindless and pointless tasks as a means of fulfilment, nor how that informs human nature in the minds of the writers. Furthermore, as Caffentzis (2013: 145–162) indicates, labour is a peculiar category in Marxist economics, as its remit lies beyond the purview of economics as such, finding expression in myriad culturally and historically special forms. For this reason, labour is neither a 'value', such as machines or other factors of production, nor solely a 'commodity' with use and exchange value. It is actually the sole creator of value as a function of its capacity to refuse work (ibid). Essentially, labour is external to political economy; it is the destabilising factor that makes the *critique* of political economy possible.

Marx's blueprint of historical materialism cannot be assimilated to classical British political economy, as he brings it into dialogue with German philosophy and French radicalism.[3] It is rather a supersession of the categories of political economy that puts them in motion with non-economic realities, which makes possible a critique of productivism as a drain on expressive vitality and as being a husk of what unalienated activity could be were it not hindered by the capital relation (Marx, 1968; 1959; Düzenli, 2016: 217). To borrow from Boots Riley (2016), 'Culture comes out of the way we survive', and if that mode of survival is one in which workers are bound to produce according to the whims of capital for their survival, then that condition shall inevitably play a central role in a critique of the relations of production. That does not mean that the productivism laid bare in this process is normatively shared by its practitioners. As all members of society are compelled to engage in relations of production – even in primitive communal tribes –, explaining the social organisation of production is also a step towards disenchanting the political and ideological layers, even though these also carry a relative weight of their own. Yet this weight is *relative*, as the productive underpinnings of social life give coloration to the ways in which its different aspects maintain or grate against the said compulsory productive relations. If Marx had stopped short at asserting this explanatory potential of productivity, his endeavour might have still been vulnerable to critiques of productivism, although the aforementioned French and German components of his philosophy of history introduce a dialectical movement which ensures the temporal differentiation of moments of social reproduction, and make visible the utopian radicalism that endangers established social relations. These bring into the equation a crucial instability that designates historical materialism as much of a study of temporal conflict embedded in social struggles as a cross-sectional analysis of class relations.

Additionally, those strands of thought that make up Marx's historical materialism have given it a political sting that denaturalises the transient mode of production and reveals its inherent tensions with an imminent resolution. More tangibly, as outlined in the theoretical premises above, the contradiction between the transhistorical character of productive activity and its stunted

---

3 Marx built his theories drawing from a very wide range of influences, encompassing Ancient Greek materialism, Italian political science, English biology, and American anthropology, among others. As his works carry elements of these constituents, it is further perplexing how he could be construed solely as a left-leaning political economist.

existence under alienating conditions compels a transition that either reproduces or unravels capitalism. While productivism criticises the focus on the production process and *a fortiori* the centrality of productive activity, historical materialism conversely foregrounds the latter precisely to critique producing for its own sake. In this sense, once mechanisms of alienation are removed, production is liberated from work as a pillar of surplus extraction, and restored to a self-actualising activity in a postcapitalist setting. The incapacity to turn human labour into another cost on the capitalist's balance sheet may transform how surplus-value is extracted – *e.g.*, from the Fordist factory to the networked late capitalist office -, or allow for an emancipatory exit from the yoke of wage-labour (Marx, 1959). Such an exit would further materialise as a self-erasure of the proletariat in terms of a class composed of the wage-labour relation.

As Weeks (2011: 107) and critics alike maintain, the struggle against work founded on transforming the process of production is also a struggle against mindless productivism and capital's pursuit of new sources of exploitation. This implies an undoing of capitalist relations, such that not only the conditions in which their actors operate is modified, but the social script that allocates such roles is discontinued. Mason (2015: 294–295), as a conclusive afterthought to his case for postcapitalism, adds that such a transformation will also liberate the one percent from the anxiety of supervising processes around market fluctuations, and their dependence on state bailouts to maintain their lifestyles. The expansion of disposable time resulting from the curtailment of work also calls 'leisure' into question. As Srnicek and Williams (2016: 85–86) mention, while it is currently associated with holidays and weekends, or idleness and catching up on sleep, leisure can denote strenuous effort applied freely in line with one's desires, such as exercising a sport or learning to play an instrument. Social theorist Bini Adamczak (2017: 88–89) argues that any critique treating circulation, production or consumption in isolation within capitalism, opposing it to the others – such as the productive Stakhanov against the idle Oblomov -, latently reproduces its vantage points. This echoes Marx's observation of these categories' copresence. Adamczak (ibid) further argues that 'leisure', equated with consumption and escape, is a by-product of the productivist strain of capital accumulation, stating that the goal is not simply its extension, but 'the collective transformation of all social spheres so that the need to escape – into 'leisure' time, the mall, or television – is overwhelmingly minimized'.

Class struggle founded on a critique of the work society contains the seeds of a future wherein the working class fades from the circuit of money-commodity-money'. This exit would remove a pillar of productivism as production is not simply negated, but transcended to serve increasingly refined human needs (Marx, 1990: 247–258). It is this misunderstanding that lies at the core of certain critiques of productivism, for they assume a teleology in which the endpoint of historical change is the perfection of the existing process of production, whereas it points to ways of decentring such alienating activity from social life altogether. In this sense, the critique of the production process is not solely, or even primarily, a critique of the conditions of work. The standpoint of this critique has reverberating implications for cultural norms of consumption and also a postwork vision of emancipation that makes use of advances in productive capacity.

To distinguish the biologically constant need from its socially determined fulfilment, Marx (1973: 85) uses an example of the culturally mediated satisfaction of hunger:

> Hunger is hunger, but the hunger gratified by cooked meat eaten with a knife and fork is a different hunger from that which bolts down raw meat with the aid of hand, nail and tooth. Production thus produces not only the object but also the manner of consumption, not only objectively but also subjectively. Production thus creates the consumer.

Expending effort to meet needs is an evolutionary imperative. But the ways in which these are met is imbricated with the dominant relations of production, and a production process that inheres in its consumer. Taking productive activity as one such imperative, this means that there can be myriad arrangements for its actualisation. Once baseline conditions of existence are met, it serves to explore a panoply of new needs – political, aesthetic, intellectual and so on. While work leads to an unsatisfying, alienated existence, its critique sheds light on a postcapitalist imaginary where it can satisfy more refined needs. For example, following a prospective liberation from work, someone may wish to explore a particular music genre, and progressively seek more specific products to further attune their senses, going from simply looking to seeing in an involved way as a producer. In short, the transformation of the production process sets in motion a deeper introspection. In Marx's (ibid: 680) words, while individuals are subordinated to the 'freedom' of capital, the erosion of this subordination can diminish the attitudes and patterns that characterise involuntary wage-labour for survival:

> The free development of individualities, and hence not the reduction of necessary labour time so as to posit surplus labour, but rather the general

reduction of the necessary labour of society to a minimum, which then corresponds to the artistic, scientific etc. development of the individuals in the time set free, and with the means created, for all of them.

Based on this review of productivism as a critique of Marxism as well as part of a Marxian critique of work, it is possible to distinguish valid points raised in the postwork paradigm, represented by Weeks, from the ill-informed blanket denunciation of Marxism in the postmodern thought of Baudrillard. Weeks correctly identifies a misplaced emphasis on work by way of valorised productivity within the organisational 'proletarian ideology', to put it in Althusserian terms. *Contra* Baudrillard, it is hard to detect an endorsement of bourgeois economic categories in Marx's work, yet across the palette of Marxian parties and movements, this may well be the case. When European social democracy and Soviet socialism lauded principals of full employment and productivity, they downplayed or ignored a deeper reality of the mode of production. The capitalist prefiguration of the process of production remained intact, fettering socialist transition. Changes in the economic level were confined to relations of ownership, and capitalist forces of production were uncritically repurposed to build the new mode of production. This predicament led to the 'left productivism' picked up by Weeks, but also earlier autonomist Marxism, which informed postwork approaches, and refuted productivism. Here it is apt to consider this theoretical-strategic arsenal to contextualise anti- and postwork literature.

2   The Autonomist Corollary

Informing her analysis with antiwork politics, Weeks criticises left productivism with the help of autonomist inquiries. Autonomism took a stance against the organisation of work, particularly in the large Fiat factories of northern Italy (Lotringer and Marazzi, 1980; Pansa, 1980). They recognised that the subjectivity of the working class was obfuscated in erstwhile Marxist orthodoxy; in so doing, they reformulated the primacy of class struggle for change, opposing self-appointed party vanguardism, and the objectivism of an impersonal development of the productive forces as the motor of socialist transition (Tosel, 2008: 56). Inaugurating a 'Copernican revolution', Panzieri (cited in Turchetto, 2008: 287), a foundational figure, asserts that the working class carves the path of capitalist development, and downgrades faith in the improvement of productive capacities:

Faced with the capitalist imbrication of technology and power, the perspective of an alternative (working-class) use of machinery obviously cannot be based on a pure and simple reversal of the relations of production (of property), conceived as an envelope which at a certain level of growth of the productive forces is supposedly destined to fall away, simply because it has become too narrow. The relations of production are internal to the forces of production and the latter are 'fashioned' by capital.

Capital is always on the back foot, pushing it to colonise every aspect of workers' lives, who resists conformity to its conventions in myriad ways, whether through absenteeism, sabotage or pilfering. Negri (cited in Weeks, 2011: 92), in a 1977 text, laments how the 'official socialist movement' mirrors the injunction on the workers to assimilate into the work ethic, decrying the imposition of work as a 'title of nobility'. Thus, autonomism envisions an alternative proletarian subjectivity, one that derives its power from antagonism to capital, rather than being a straightforward constituent of it.

Operaismo, as this tendency was also called, took a critical distance towards the popular-national reorganisation of the Italian state, at a time when the post-war settlement had paved the way for two electorally formidable working class parties, the socialists and the communists (Behan, 2009: 45–52). This had come at the cost of left commitment to capitalist normalcy, within the Western sphere of influence. As a reaction against this integration and moderation of revolutionary energy, *operaismo* was a historically apposite corrective. It was as much a cultural celebration of proletarian conviviality, a political project of grassroots action, and a theoretical frame questioning received wisdom. Working class insubordination to capital was the basis, setting forth demands to curtail work. Thus, the 'strategy of refusal', as Tronti (1980) calls it, carries relevance today, as the intensity of the working week increases alongside potentials to reduce work. Weeks also justifies postwork politics from this angle, exploring the social consequences of the refusal of work.

As *operaismo* was as much of a theoretical tendency as a political and artistic movement, this section shall illustrate its vision of transition using its artistic output. The refusal of work is depicted masterfully by Nanni Balestrini, an activist and novelist steeped in the convulsive 1960s. Balestrini's novel *We Want Everything* (2016), first published in 1971, reveals how refusal, which would appear insufficient against the rule of capital, can drive the system to occlusion. As a relation, capital includes wage-labour in congealed form. This interpellates workers as capitalist subjects, which suggests that the desanctification and refusal of work could seriously obstruct capital. Conversely, an abstract refusal can also provide an escapist vent for frustration. Capitalism can survive by marginalising this form of resistance, but even escapism contains utopian aspirations, spilling over from negative resistance to positive rebellion.

Balestrini dramatises the need for a political line autonomous from the disciplinarian Communist Party of the time, as well as the established unions. Constructed with a character ark resembling a *bildungsroman*, the novel is written from the perspective of a young worker arriving from the rural south to Fiat's Mirafiori factory in Turin. The protagonist is unnamed, reflecting the autonomist preference for collective subjectivities, as in the 'mass worker', a term used by Alquati (1962) for the new anonymous toiler yet to be broken into discipline. Likely modelled on someone known to the author, he despises all responsibilities. Even May Day is an event he attends out of boredom, where he reflects 'I didn't get what the festival of workers, or the festival of work, meant. I didn't get why work should be celebrated' (Balestrini, 2016: 50). This sentiment could be dismissed from an orthodox perspective as a lack of class consciousness. A closer consideration, however, reveals a precapitalist, meridional attitude of avoiding compulsory work that Gramsci would have celebrated. This intuitive resistance suggests a primordial sense of unease with the ability to apply productive capacities in voluntary directions. In this sense, the glorification of idleness here is more than a knee-jerk reaction to wage-labour, suggesting a deeper revulsion from alienated work. Romanticising an idyllic retreat is questionable, but in line with the theory of multiple temporalities, the mass worker's attitude has a postcapitalist aspect once the precapitalist impulse is actualised in factory militancy.

While Balestrini's worker is initially interested in shirking responsibility in favour of hedonistic pursuits, he becomes a hardened activist, revealing the grating political and ideological temporalities within his psyche. The novel recounts a breathless struggle, with vivid descriptions of rallies, repression, tactics to dissuade rebellion, heated debates in smoke-covered rooms, and reflections on revolution, where the protagonist conceives of his role in transition (ibid: 115): 'It's logical that we need to take one step at a time, but ultimately, when there's the base, when there's the mass pushing from below, that says everything is a mess, in a disruptive manner, the Party keeps holding back, and the union too'.

The political and economic organs of the left trail behind the fervour, inverting the temporal 'backwardness' of the migrant, unorganised worker in relation to these institutions. The refusal of work comes into fruition as worker's self-exploration through conflict with the state and the ruling class. The scattered folk wisdom of inconsistent, abstract refusal is systematised into a more coherent philosophy after going through these tribulations. In Gramscian parlance, this is a translation between levels of common sense, rather than a simple removal of the blindfold of false consciousness. Also, postwork possibilities organically arise from working class participation in work society, or lack thereof. However, there is a conspicuous absence of other facets of social life such as the invisible domestic labour of women and the family. Without feminist contributions, autonomy and the postwork cases for the reduction of work can fall flat or even deepen traditional roles. This has led to a critique of postwork, to be discussed in the following chapter. In sum, Balestrini presents a gripping account of the discrepancy between the construct of the dutiful worker and the rejection of work as the path to self-realisation.

The tension between antiwork activism and the sobering day after is illustrated in another work from 1971, the film *The Working Class Goes to Heaven*, directed by Elio Petri. Unlike Balestrini's anonymous hedonistic and insouciant mass worker, the protagonist in this film, Lulù takes pride in his productivity as a machine operator. This makes him unpopular among his colleagues and the student and union activists railing against the working conditions. He is an efficient worker favoured by management, and dislikes those trying to disrupt the working day. His devotion to work almost sounds like a parody of Stakhanovism, with sense of duty to the state replaced by pointless obligation, hard work being carried out for lack of any meaningful alternative, as he describes it thus (Petri, 1971):

> I'm a little champion. Then you find the southerners, like him, from east Sicily, tired since the first morning. So, I beat'em on the rate! … But running, running… Because I can concentrate myself, I keep my mind busy. I've a method to keep me busy. Here, there's nothing to think, what do I have to say? We must work, so do it. With no excuse.

Lulù is somewhat aware of the mindless drudgery. But he identifies himself through his participation in it (making him a 'little champion'), and condescends upon his colleagues, one of whom could have been Balestrini's worker, for not having the same perverse ethic. However, he has an accident caused by the pressure of piecework, whence he becomes agonisingly cognisant that process only values the worker as a tool (the US release is titled *Lulu the Tool*). He then sympathises with left movements, especially against piecework, to the point that he reiterates his superior efficiency, but now in a contrary light, and disparages those making a virtue out of this. Now, the work is seen as dehumanising, showing how exploitation generates resistance. The capitalist may simply want a pair of hands to put in the labour, but they end up with a fully formed person. While this complicates the extraction of surplus-value, it is also its source. As Caffentzis (2013: 162), a theorist with autonomist inspiration, maintains, other factors of production cannot create value because they *are* value, necessitating living wage-labour, and implanting a contradiction at the centre of capitalist (re)production. Lulù, now mindful that he is vital for the factory, cooperates with activists and union workers, disseminating their views. Only he goes further than the union, which sought to renegotiate piecework rates rather than demand compensation based on time.

Both works portray workers who, despite their diametrically opposite initial approaches, resist reduction to mere cogs as multidimensional human beings. Balestrini's narrates an ideological transformation in the subject's resistance against interpellation into a wage-labourer, contorting that subjectivity. Reiterating Althusser's (1971) theory, ideology 'hails' individuals into subjectivities, such as the worker responsive to the exigencies of production. The migrant worker experiences interpellation as pressure from the factory management directly, and official working class representation indirectly, to shed those aspects of their biography that are incompatible with discipline. Althusser's depiction may be flawed in that while it captures a process, it appears as though interpellation appears in a vacuum and the individual is a blank slate prior to it, giving the descriptive device a mechanical feel. However, the outline helps to describe subjectivities within working class struggle. Drawing from fellow workers and the surrounding community, both fictional workers build alternative subjectivities through a reconstruction of existing ones. This reactivates precapitalist impulses in postcapitalist directions.

With its attentiveness to the sociological composition of the Italian working class, autonomism identifies Gramsci's scattered 'good sense', transmitted from the still mainly agrarian Italian south to the northern metropolis as a rejection of ungratifying and precarious work. This rejection goes beyond a preference for idleness. It is radicalised in a direction where the workers, precisely due their insight that they have to work to live and not *vice versa*, can withhold work without an attachment to its supposed merits. Autonomism thereby restores the class capacity of the mass workers who palpably make sense of the world through conflicting temporalities, aiding in their disinvestment from capitalist relations. This disenchantment from dutiful work has also informed postwork.

3 Accelerationism

Postwork politics emphasises the liberating potential of automation and technology, with Srnicek and Williams as key proponents. Their interest in the role of technology can be traced back to their 'accelerationism', a heterogeneous current worth considering due to its implications for transition and temporality. Coined by Noys (2010: 5) as a term of disparagement, accelerationism broadly refers to an intellectual and artistic movement that diagnoses an unprecedented speed up of technological trends and a heightening of contradictions in globally connected capitalist societies, with the prognosis being an encouragement, or at least a lack discouragement, for these processes. As Shaviro (2015: 8) sums it up: 'accelerationism is best defined – in political, aesthetic, and philosophical terms – as the argument that the only way out is the way through'. This also denotes the nihilistic culmination of Land's (2018) enthusiasm for all-round speed up and intensification. Land expresses a morbid fascination with the pervasive expansion of capital, which contains the seeds of its own demise (ibid: 338). For Land (2010), acceleration has found its apex point in China, where an unbridled economic liberalism proliferates under authoritarian state tutelage (Beckett, 2017). Not unlike left productivism, innovations in productivity are seen by accelerationists as part of a welcome procession towards technological 'singularity', and capitalism's eventual incapacity to contain such advances (Mackay, 2012; CCRU, 2015: 6).

Through an ostensibly techno-futuristic aesthetic and prose, accelerationists identify an ever-increasing 'flatness' where processes and products, the future and past coincide in singularity, styling their works as rogue communiques from a nondescript temporality. Accelerationism simultaneously stretches the present towards teleological endpoints, and announces an intrusion of the future back into the moment. This celebration of futurism ironically obliterates temporalities, since difference and temporal lags are sacrificed at the altar of singularity, whose encroachment is announced in millenarian fashion. It would be hasty to conflate the views of the CCRU with the later writings of Land, in that the latter expends more effort to underline the temporality-speed relationship. This is important to bear in mind as it is such a conflation that Srnicek and Williams avoid in their critical defence of accelerationism. Yet Land's accounts have been the most forthcoming elucidations of the perception of the time-speed continuity. Also, not least because the authors of *Inventing the Future* build on a brand of accelerationism defined against that of Land, it is useful to entertain his description as a stand-in for this endeavour. Thus, the novelties of Srnicek and Williams' postwork departure can be appreciated more fully.

For Land (1992: 112), we are enmeshed in the 'real-time' that civilisational notions of progress make futile attempts to temporally colonise, always to be vanquished with the eventual re-emergence of this transcendent, asynchronous time that cannot be confined to anthropomorphic frames. Land (2014) accordingly sees a complacency in the assumption that there is time to consider and apply solutions. Appealing to the rapid developments in cybernetics and artificial intelligence technology, Land (2017) thus maintains that there was never such 'time', which is only an artificial relic, or to put it in different terms, 'real-time' has a characteristic of being always-already: 'No contemporary dilemma is being entertained realistically until it is also acknowledged that the opportunity for doing so is fast collapsing'.

The transcendent time is a process and its critique, and the crux of accelerationist thought. For Land, theories of human cognitive-creative sovereignty are hopelessly outdated, and opposition to cybernetic 'positive feedback loops' that increasingly take over aspects of production verge on Luddism. Going further, Land (2018: 294) announces the obsolescence of traditional philosophical models, and possibly even philosophy itself, because of a totalising technological super-intelligence:

> Traditional schemas which oppose technics to nature, to literate culture, or to social relations, are all dominated by a phobic resistance to the sidelining of human intelligence by the coming techno sapiens. Thus one sees the decaying Hegelian socialist heritage clinging with increasing desperation to the theological sentimentalities of praxis, reification, alienation, ethics, autonomy, and other such themes of human creative sovereignty.

Here the self-replicating mechanisms of cybernetics become autonomous, in a way that is analogous to the market and Marx's schema of Money – Commodity – Money'. The market is indifferent to normative conceptions of value, and perpetuates itself according to its own logic. Hence, the spatio-temporal expansion of capital – *e.g.*, imperialism, stock trade in futures – nullifies human agency more than ever, and this occurs together with the development of singularity (MacDougald, 2016).

This notion of capital's pervasive figuration of the social and beyond is reminiscent of some of the Italian autonomists' diagnosis of the 'social factory' (Wright, 2002: 34–35; Turchetto, 2008). However, while autonomists allowed for ample prefigurative space for the insubordination of labour to capital, accelerationism, at least in the variant that epitomised Land's journey, denies an 'outside' to capitalism, remaining confined to a fetishism of the development of productive forces. Taking a cue from Land's fascination with capitalism, particularly in the booming Chinese economy, it is tempting to conclude that accelerationism amounts to a call for heightening contradictions to the point where revolt is inevitable, as captured in the phrase 'the worse, the better'

(Noys, 2010). This is enticing for people on the left side of the spectrum, with financial and political crises threatening the whole edifice. For Land, however, it is difficult to make this attribution based on what he has said about capitalism, even though such a catastrophic narrative is often associated with him. Typically, Land (2018: 626) exalts the deterritorialising aspect, affirming its acceleration not necessarily towards destruction, but an endless self-replicating flux.

Mainly writing in the 1990s, Land's account may have been a convincing embrace of the all-encompassing potential of capital, such that it renders politics as an arcane anachronism. This coincided with the *End of History* and the closure of alternatives, with Land's neoliberal turn to 'right-accelerationism' being excoriated by his detractors. Criticising Land, Williams (2013: 4) argues that the notion of neoliberal perpetuity is outdated, and reintroduces politics:

> The very agent which Land identified as the engine of untold innovation has run dry. This is alienation of an all-too familiar, ennui-inducing kind, rather than a coldly thrilling succession of future-shocks. All of this opens up a space for the political again: if we desire a radically innovative social formation, capital alone will not deliver.

Williams maintains that acceleration is not speed, adding that Land only fixates on the latter. The continuation of the state of affairs, no matter the speed, has an acceleration of zero. For Williams (ibid), this insight merits an appropriation of accelerationism, challenging the parameters that may permit speed but themselves remain stationary. Even if there is a speed up, this would remain as a quantitative change rather than qualitative break, discrediting the accelerationists' futuristic register. Despite the self-conscious bricolage and non-linear tones of their writings, they are objectively grounded in a cultural context, the eccentricity itself signalling the bounds of the literary and aesthetic currents of its time. Despite its ruminations on the philosophy of what it means to be human in an age of ever increasing AI devolution of tasks, and substantial output in terms of non-European and feminist futurisms, with reverberating consequences for the arts, accelerationism has little to contribute to the question of transition itself. To clarify the postwork interpretation, society and politics need to be reintroduced, even though they are sentimental residues for Land. This way, implications of cogent observations on speed and capitalism can be drawn out with reference to the work society.

Accelerationism does not go further than projecting existing trends indefinitely towards the future. The project assumes a continuity between cyber age technology and postcapitalist imaginaries, if it can even conceptualise a *post*-capitalism. Therefore, while suffused with references to ancient civilisations and artefacts alongside contemporary technological advances, accelerationism unduly universalises cybernetics, subsuming temporal complexity into a misleadingly smoothened temporality. This is symptomatic of the evacuation of the social from their expressions of new models of production, still only partially constituting social relations. Another outcome of this is an erasure of the left-right distinction as a redundancy of a yet unachieved singularity, echoing a Silicon Valley-type optimism for the eventual relegation of the profane tasks of administration to technology (Turner, 2018). Thus, the praised Chinese model, as an engine of development that tears apart existing social bonds and creates widespread precarity (let alone being based on violent state repression), is only appreciated as an atemporal representation of a futurism voided of politics. The celebration of dizzying transformation lacks a vector. Contrary to speed, vectors also express direction. Added to Williams' qualifications, Srnicek and Williams also identify this missing factor, without naming it as such. Thus, their outlook is 'post-accelerationist', qualitatively and navigationally revised. Meanwhile, they maintain the universal scope formally present in accelerationism.

Based on this incorporation of the strengths of accelerationist theory, Srnicek and Williams (2014: 354) hypothesise two models of left-wing political action: the 'folk politics' of localism, direct action, and relentless horizontalism'; and 'an accelerationist politics at ease with a modernity of abstraction, complexity, globality, and technology'. In this appropriation of accelerationism with a positive connotation, the faith in endless technological progress is jettisoned in favour of an approach that is attentive to its social impact. Clearly, there are points where such progress can be detrimental, as nuclear proliferation or enhanced surveillance. In sum, the concern is not with the pace of change, but of setting standards of its direction. After all, as Theodor Adorno (1973: 320) once poignantly observed: 'No universal history leads from savagery to humanitarianism, but there is one leading from the slingshot to the megaton bomb'. This is a discernible break from the neoliberalism of some strands of accelerationism, which wishes to see existing trends expanded to the utmost.

4 Postwork Departures

The critique of productivism has been a necessary corrective to a dominant left tendency, with its social democratic and socialist variants exalting productivity and employment. However, as discussed, the problem was not unnoticed, provoking contributions from Italian autonomism to Baudrillard's postmodernism-inflected gauntlet. The former approach aimed to cultivate the organic working class consciousness, at a remove from party and state diktats, and the latter problematised the centrality of productive changes for the creation of a different society. In particular, autonomism has carried Gramsci's enterprise forward, with a fresh perspective on the mass worker and their discordant attitude to the industrialised way of life. Not without their shortcomings, these critiques reveal a misplaced prioritisation of alienated work. They compel a reappraisal of productive activity within historical materialism, and a refined account of this axial point of transition. On the other hand, accelerationism provided a late capitalist snapshot of cybernetic singularity, experimentally forcing the logic of endless accumulation to its conclusions, some more disconcerting than others. This current has had a lasting legacy, with the embrace of its universalising ambitions with crucial qualifications in Srnicek and Williams' work. As the following chapter will discuss, postwork theory and politics embody iterations of these currents, as well as others beyond what has been discussed thus far. While making key departures in the light of twenty-first century realities, postwork also reproduces the dynamics of the tendencies scrutinised here.

CHAPTER 7

Postwork: a Contemporary Left Vision

This chapter turns towards a discussion of what Erik Olin Wright (2010, 2012) termed 'Real Utopias', *i.e.* proposals and projects that resonate with the vision of futurity. If the past dominates and subsumes the discussion of alternatives, a positive project beyond capitalism must be future-oriented so it may expose the artificiality of capitalism (Fisher, 2009). Utopianism as such does not lead to the construction of alternative societies; it can encourage cynical detachment rather than political engagement, a point made by Lewis Mumford (1922: 15) who distinguished 'utopias of escape' from those of 'reconstruction'. According to Wright (2012), the 'real' in 'real utopias' is a necessary corrective to the abstraction of the pure utopia.

Following Wright's injunctions, the postwork paradigm will be discussed as a candidate for a real utopia. Postwork can be called a theory or political movement, as it embodies a philosophical lineage with explicit policy output. Here, the theoretical side is considered in more detail, indicating the continuities and ruptures with the tendencies identified in the previous chapter. Salient works are discussed, with the themes of postcapitalism, techno-determinism, and techno-utopianism as organising frames. In particular, I argue that postcapitalist theses are predicated on a problematic reading of the labour theory of value (LTV), synthesising Dean's critique of communicative capitalism with Marx's revisions to this theory. Considering Srnicek and Williams' influential work, I further argue that they avoid the determinism of technological and networked development that is implicit in Mason's work. This leads to what I identify as a utopian strain within postwork theory, culminating with the argument that this is necessary for a future oriented left politics, linking present potentials with their eventual actualisation.

1   The Postwork Agenda

Productive activity was outlined as a universal feature of human societies at the outset of this book, in that the prevalent mode of interaction with the environment is to mix one's labour with it in a productive synthesis. The alienation of productive activity under a commodified labour-power form is its specific manifestation under capitalism. Today, it is hard to envision labour as a fulfilling activity *per se*, rather than an ungratifying imperative of sustenance. Since the post-war 'Golden Age' of rapid growth and employment, the nature of work has undergone dramatic changes. Stable jobs with predictable paths of advancement and reliable salaries are less common, and recent decades have seen a deterioration in workers' rights (ITUC, 2019). According to a report published in 2017, the wealthiest one percent have more than recovered lost gains since the recession, yet typical real incomes of working families in the bottom half of the income distribution are still lower than they were during the years of 2003–2004 (Corlett et al., 2017: 6). In 2019, the outlook for typical real incomes for low to middle-income households including families with children, single adults, and social renters, forecasts 'zero growth' until the 2023–2024 period (Corlett, 2019). More than a decade on from the crash of 2008, living standards for those in the bottom and middle income percentiles have not only stalled, but regressed, meriting a designation of depression rather than a minor downturn (Davis et al., 2018). This dip in prospects is accompanied by a rise in people taking multiple jobs to complement their incomes, incorporating 'crowd work' found mainly through online platforms by carrying out extra work in evenings, weekends, and even lunch hours (Huws et al., 2018; Gallagher, 2019). This is partially due to the stark difference between the high union density and labour militancy of the post-war welfare states, with an unprecedentedly high share of labour in the national income, and the contemporary precarity under financialised capitalism that has taken shape since the 1980s (Kristal, 2010). Social democratic hegemony had given the left a clear advantage in the post-war period, with booming economies and rising incomes in the capitalist Global North, to the extent that right-wing parties had to endorse popular welfare measures (Wallerstein, 2011). The high rate of (male) employment, a less fragmented model of production, powerful unions and governing social democratic parties, ensured that precarity was not a pressing question.

In this context, the New Left and Italian autonomism formed the backdrop to an eventual debate on postwork futures, each taking a critical distance from social democracy and Marxism-Leninism. This distancing was not a result of economic conditions as much as political and cultural developments. The welfare states' outlook of class collaboration rather than struggle was seen to dull working class militancy, while social movements without explicit class politics were gathering momentum. Autonomism made inroads into a critique of the production process by exploring ways to resist the sale of labour-power, and the New Left explored the neglected cultural and aesthetic aspects of social struggles. André Gorz (1982), who corresponded with both currents, would develop a unique ecosocialism that rejected the unnecessary drudgery of work, and aimed to expose the environmental blindness of existing capitalism and socialism, concluding with a disqualification of the proletariat from revolutionary agency altogether.

The conditions in which the critique of work took shape were thus removed from those that contemporary postwork theories bring under the spotlight. While building on these commentaries of alienation in the context of the welfare consensus, postwork addresses work at a pressing point where there is a visible lack of correspondence between educational and occupational qualifications on the one hand, and the proliferation of short term, precarious jobs on the other (Standing, 2011). Over much of the latter half of the twentieth century, workers could secure long-term jobs with benefits and state pensions. Involvement in left politics during these decades could have implied taking one of two paths: integration with state apparatuses through parties and affiliated unions; or a voluntary boycott of the world of work and official politics: to 'turn on, tune in, drop out', as the countercultural slogan went. Clark Kerr et al.'s (1970) benchmark study of global industrialisation argued that working class militancy had dissipated into the administrative bargaining of working conditions, with protests increasingly taking place outside of work. Inquiries into left alternatives to the realpolitik of social democracy emphasised revaluations of work. This has been more pronounced as welfare regimes disintegrate, leaving fewer prospects to 'drop out' of. Postwork theory takes this casualisation and immiseration of the neoliberal moment as its basis.

In the United Kingdom, the fifth wealthiest country in the world by net worth, two-thirds of families living in poverty are also in work, while nearly one million people work precarious zero-hour contracts (Armstrong, 2017; Credit Suisse, 2018). Additionally, a recent study has found that 4.5 million UK children live in poverty because of cuts to welfare measures and a dearth of career opportunities, a number that is projected to increase to a record level of 5.2 million by 2024 (Butler, 2018).

The fact that work has become more precarious and incapable of providing a dignified livelihood, coupled with the number of children exposed to poverty before having a chance to enter the workforce, flies in the face of any justification of economic inequality based on 'hard work'. The work ethic should be regarded here as an embodied ideology. As Althusser had argued, ideology was not simply, or even primarily, a matter of subjective conviction, but a material practice. The spontaneous actions of individuals interpellated as market actors selling their labour-power, for instance, directly instantiates the work ethic. This is not to say that ideology operates on an ideal level beyond the grasp of agents, but that it is precisely the observance of such actions that make up ideology. Therefore, regardless of the discrepancy between work and its remuneration, ideological mores have a materiality that maintain and reproduce themselves insofar as the social pattern, *i.e.* the need for surplus-value and its appropriation, is implanted in the overdeterminant economic sphere. In other words, the appropriation of surplus-value *is* the work ethic to an extent. Furthermore, as David Graeber (2018) argues, the work ethic that equates work with self-worth both maintains the stigma of not working and leads to a proliferation of 'bullshit jobs' solely serving to entitle people to a means of existence, and a meagre one at that. The fact that people in many fields think that their jobs are socially unnecessary, if not also detrimental, does not directly threaten the proliferation of said jobs, as they emanate from capitalist imperatives.

The theorisation of, and resistance against, obsolete work helps to relativise it as an historical anomaly, which could lead to jobholders refusing their interpellation. There is evidence that while precarity is on the rise, the rectification of working conditions has been central to many instances of collective struggle in the 'gig economy' where jobs are fleeting, multiple and often beneath the educational level attained by workers (Standing, 2011: 10). This is visible in recent cases of unrest and organisation among workers on zero-hours contracts. Such cases are more notable considering the atomising nature of casualised work in companies such as Uber, Deliveroo, and McDonalds – as well as the University of Birmingham – that contract large numbers of employees on individual, short-term bases (Chakelian, 2018; Syal, 2018; Chakrabortty and Weale, 2016). Job precarity and temporary work are not new, yet their proliferation to current levels is. And crucially, that the workers in precarious situations do not feel a sense of attachment to their occupation, and that they conversely lack the socioeconomic benefits of a community built around the occupation, have also been comparatively recent trends (Standing, 2011: 12–13; 2018: 5–6; see also Sennett, 2006).

In a situation where workers are working more hours for less pay in more degrading terms, it is fair to say that 'work isn't working', as Stronge (2019) remarks. Seizing on the insight that an activity so central to people's lives fails to meet basic needs, the contemporary social research agenda focuses on 'work', and explores ways to transform it. This 'postwork' literature has certain theoretical and political antecedents that problematised the glorification of work as personal actualisation, and wrote on liberation *from* work (Virno and Hardt, 1996: 263). Taking some of these cues and further elaborating on contemporary possibilities, postwork proposals have also been influential in recent policy debates; notably, the neo-Keynesian economics of the Jeremy Corbyn-led Labour Party, with the Green Party and several unions backing the call for a four-day work week (Stronge, 2019; Eaton, 2018; Sabbagh, 2018, see also *Economics for the Many*, edited by Labour Shadow Chancellor John McDonnell (2018)).

On the surface, this literature overlaps with the abstract utopianism of the abolition of work in favour of endless leisure. However, the transformation of work poses new questions regarding leisure time. Since the limitation of work and its removal as a prerequisite for social inclusion would create a space to build alternative arrangements and discover new needs, leisure would also be relativized. Thus, the critique of work problematises the many aspects of social life organised around it. In the following discussion, I will map postwork theory, to be followed by an analysis of its political proposals.

2   Postcapitalism: Mason on the Information Economy

Paul Mason's book *Postcapitalism: A Guide to our Future* is a widely-read account of the journalist's conviction that developments in digital capitalism pose a mortal danger to capitalist dynamics. However, Mason's account is telling not only for its merits, but also its faults. Within the corpus of postwork, this work is distinguished by a journalistic, policy-based approach that presents certain trends of capitalism as mechanisms of its demise. Here I maintain that Mason's account involves a political deficit that can threaten postwork. Even though Mason underlines the necessity of political action, the premises of his theses belie a determinism. Amplifying certain processes that compel a transition, Mason reduces the temporally layered transition advocated here to more of a transmission from one trajectory of production to another. Examining this book is instructive as a culprit of techno-determinism within postwork, in terms of delegating social transformation to automation and networked production.

Mason's argument utilises a briefly sketched idea in Marx's *Grundrisse* (1973: 678–681), known as 'The Fragment on Machines'. According to Mason (2015: 146–148), and before him to Negri (1991) and Virno (2001), this passage carries a ground-breaking suggestion that knowledge may replace labour as the driving force of production, if the worker's input is infinitesimal when their role is reduced to setting in motion processes that can replicate themselves. As Marx did not have reason to suspect that this would happen imminently, he may not have integrated this insight into *Capital*, and as Mason recounts (2015: 146), it would take until the late 1960s for these fragments to be available in Western Europe (Brewster, 1972). In autonomist analyses, these sketches towards the more unified theory of value in *Capital* had encouraged the conclusion that value creation was severed from traditional working routines, leading to formulations that firstly, the 'end of work' was in sight but capitalism impeded it, and secondly that 'cognitive labour-power' encompassed workers across all levels of production and management, and was increasingly removed from material production and the factory (Turchetto, 2008: 296–297; Virno, 1990).

Similarly, Mason presupposes a transition to a post-industrial economy where digital codes are infinitely more capable of communalising production, given that even though they may be privatised within legal patents, the knowledge itself cannot be fully fitted into the same straitjacket (Mason, 2015: 147–148). Furthermore, signs of this already abound in the proliferation of open-source platforms such as Linux and Android, the latter utilised by Google and Samsung to undercut competition from Apple, who prefers to fence in their products with exclusionary compatibility and legal safeguards (ibid: 135–136, 155). The showpiece of this networked model of content creation is Wikipedia, which operates on a collaborative basis where users create sophisticated and peer-reviewed entries for the encyclopaedia through cooperation and debate (ibid: 141–144). It is widely used to the point that it has single-handedly contributed to the extinction of the physical encyclopaedia, and is accessible to all with an internet connection. The work of crafting articles is carried out on a voluntary basis, often involving people who hold professional and academic qualifications in the field. Moreover, this takes place beyond the purview of the market, incalculable by the standards of economic orthodoxy.

Based on the potential of networks, Mason (ibid: 144) suggests that there are vestiges of a postcapitalist future in the present, asserting its destructive potential: 'Info-capitalism is real, but if we analyse the whole thing – the collision of neoliberal economics with network technology – we must conclude it is in crisis'. This position is informed by a literalist reading of Marx's (1973: 679) hypothetical meditation on a potential outcome of the development of productive forces:

> [T]o the degree that large industry develops, the creation of real wealth comes to depend less on labour time and on the amount of labour employed than on the power of the agencies set in motion during labour time, whose 'powerful effectiveness' is itself in turn out of all proportion to the direct labour time spent on their production, but depends rather on the general state of science and on the progress of technology, or the application of this science to production.

Once information can be copied at virtually zero cost, price setting is increasingly difficult, before anything else because the scarcity requisite to the valuation of goods is redundant. Further, according to Mason's (2015: 117, 136) reading, socialised knowledge production has a disruptive capacity. That said, he finds the commonplace prioritisation of central planning in left approaches to be insufficient as well, since a proper allocation of resources cannot be preconceived by planners; the network functions better than the hierarchy (ibid: 266). Thus, the conflict between networks and hierarchies is central to the contemporary discussion of transition, beyond considerations of planned or market economies, and the task is to show how a system without markets and finance-driven decisions could work (ibid: 227–228).

Mason believes transition is imminent in the mismatch between new technologies and the form of society. The 'information economy', where corralled data is worth more than the physical goods firms produce, may not be compatible with the market if it ceases to produce value. Giving the example of the Nike+ campaign strategy, Mason (ibid: 152) argues that the US-based company's expenditure on marketing and the information side of production is several times higher than on producing physical goods, which is outsourced to the Global South. Nike was among the first global brands to adopt a model of cognitive capitalism, where access to vast swathes of data generates more revenue than the sale of industrial products: people are more driven to access to a pool of digital resources – and the social signifier of the brand logo -, than they are to the sportswear itself. Since the introduction of its digital products in 2006, where individual sessions of activity can be recorded and tracked by compatible devices, Nike has been more of a business of 'information plus things' (ibid). That said, Mason qualifies the reach of this new model, referring to the prevalence of industrial production among the BRIC (Brazil, Russia, India, China) countries, and dismisses the notion of the totalising 'social factory' so dominant in autonomism. Rather, Mason is concerned with networks as revenue-generating assets within hierarchical corporate decision-making. According to Mason, the consumers' role as 'producers' of a commodity when they partake in networked production sits uneasily with the extraction of value, and such networks could be directed to serve the public good rather than private interest, hence the imminence of postcapitalism.

Here it is pertinent to heed Dean's (2005, 2012) theory of 'communicative capitalism' as a corrective to Mason's purported ruptural undercurrent embodied by networks. For Dean (2012: 119–156), the convergence between neoliberalism and networked communications is not antagonistic but mutually supportive. Contrary to Mason, Dean (2012) sees 'communicative capitalism' as a pervasive privatisation of a commons, not as an unintended consequence, but as part and parcel of it. Approaching the late-autonomist positions of Negri and Hardt, Dean (ibid: 137) posits that the unremunerated labour of content production for platforms such as Facebook and Amazon complements the extraction of value, rather than driving it into crisis. The 'newness' of such industries is also overstated at the expense of the modes of management and ownership in these sectors, leading to a misplaced celebration of the potentials of new technology and peer-to-peer networks. Writing in 2005, Dean (62–63) argues:

> Worries about the loss of the beloved paperback book to unwieldy e-books weren't presented as dooming the publishing industry or assaulting the very regime of private property. Why should sharing music files be any different? It shouldn't – and that is my point; Napster is a technological fetish onto which all sorts of fantasies of political action are projected.

As Dean maintains, it is apparent that networked circulation of data does not inherently pose a threat to the regime of private property, especially insofar as it sustains an illusion of being a non-capitalist space. This misconception is also symptomatic of the melancholic apprehension around the left's usual templates of class-based organisation. Dean examines the political ramifications of the accentuation of knowledge as a factor of production, but this theorisation of the networked commons also reveals a flaw in Mason's idea of a gradual transition towards postcapitalism, emerging once networks are freed from hierarchy. Beyond Dean's objection that networks enhance rather than hinder communicative capitalism, the position that Mason accords them invokes a classical, and controversial, Marxist theory.

Deploying the LTV, Mason (ibid: 159) posits that since value is created by labour, its redundancy with respect to the sheer increase in production drives capitalism to constantly reach for fresh sources of unexploited labour. The continuation of the passage from the Fragment above lends some credence to this affirmation of postcapitalism (Marx, 1973: 680):

> As soon as labour in the direct form has ceased to be the great wellspring of wealth, labour time ceases and must cease to be its measure, and hence exchange value must cease to be the measure of use value. The surplus labour of the mass has ceased to be the condition for the development of general wealth, just as the non-labour of the few, for the development of the general powers of the human head. With that, production based on exchange value breaks down, and the direct, material production process is stripped of the form of penury and antithesis.

The Fragment and Mason's account both indicate that the site of value-creation is labour-power, that is to say the exchange values of goods and services springs forth from the 'zero-point' of the sale of the capacity to work. Accordingly, the capacity to work – and that of its refusal -, is the sole generator of exchange-value, as use-value can readily be taken from nature. So argues Marx (1990: 131) in *Capital,* saying that the value-form is acquired through the expenditure of labour and circulation. When people meet in the market to obtain products, they are making decisions based on valuations indexed to their embedded labour. In networked capitalism, however, this point of valuation cannot be reliably located as the circuit of production covers many nodal points, virtual or otherwise. For Mason (ibid: 181), this has caused a current crisis in measurability once labour is no longer commensurate with value: 'monopolies are arising to prevent software or information goods becoming free; accounting standards are becoming garbled as companies resort to valuation guesswork'.

However, as *Capital* is the still-incomplete working out of preliminary ideas in the *Grundrisse,* it does not directly translate into the latter. Instead, Marx (1990: 131) notes 'social use-values' that appear to be distinct from use-value as such. The air we breathe has a use-value prior to the 'social' use value invoked here. But this value and the exchange-value would be instantiated at the point where clean air is only available to those willing and able to pay for it in gated communities. In this example, once the allocation of air requires labour to be expended, it is commodified. That said, Marx's demarcation of the modalities of value is obscure, and also suggests some continuity among the variations of the value-form. As Spivak (2000, 2) maintains, simply contrasting use value against exchange value is 'far too Luddite a binary opposition' to account for Marx's argument. This is partly because value, as with the other categories of *Capital,* is an abstraction that cannot be neatly discerned in lived social relations; it is impossible to take a commodity, say a book, and point to where the use-value ends and the exchange-value begins. In addition, exchange-value is neither instantiated at the moment of its production, nor that of its sale. Since Marx's own thoughts were in motion at the time of his writing, the account of the LTV is open to an undue emphasis on the value-creating productivity of labour, resulting in a reductive reading. As commodities contain a *social* value, Marx implies that value is obtained not solely at the moment of production, but also circulation.

A counterfactual example against the notion that classical Marxism reduced value-formation to the moment of labour can be found in the *Critique of the Gotha Programme* (Marx, 1972). Commenting on a proposed social democratic party programme, Marx (ibid: 8) immediately denounces the opening statement that 'Labour is the source of all wealth and all culture', arguing that human labour-power is one manifestation of nature, which is at least as much of a source of value. The Gotha Programme had called for a fair distribution of all fruits of labour, which is commonsensical enough from a socialist perspective (Vasina and Vasin, 1988: 5–22). However, Marx drew attention to how this argument vests labour with a supernatural capacity, assuming that its fruits can be distributed equally without a concomitant change in the mode of production. This also speaks to the postcapitalism thesis; while the emphasis may have shifted from the industrial to the service sector, and currently to the information economy, these changes do not presuppose an overthrow of the mode of production.

Bonefeld (2001: 5) states that the central question to critical social theory is why this content takes this form. It is necessary to examine the transforming modes of value-creation, rather than prematurely assuming its implosion with the shift towards immaterial production. Thus, instead of an emergent postcapitalism, it appears more realistic that capitalism runs into obstacles in generating the forms that sustain it, but also assimilates them under its categories in renewed forms (Pilling, 1972: 283–284). The overwhelmingly capitalist nature of the social formation continues to reproduce value, money, and with these, capital. Once this is established, the prevalent temporality of capitalism in the abstract can be described with reference to the specific moment in the social formation. While this moment will have unique features, its reproduction is overdetermined by capitalist relations, a point downplayed in the postcapitalism thesis. As Pitts (2017: 18) argues: 'Capitalism is characterised by categories of social mediation and antagonistic social relations of production. They persist regardless of whether a worker uses a keyboard or a hammer, ideas or nuts and bolts'.

The LTV, in this variation, does not consider the social determination of value, as a function of the exchange of commodities. While it should not be discarded, it should be considered with its contextual surrounding in Marx's oeuvre. Otherwise, the theory constitutes a straw man to which an otherwise nuanced account of the unique role of labour in social relations can be reduced to, paving the way for an ill-informed post-Marxism. Rather than springing forth from labour expenditure alone, a commodity gains value throughout its journey along historically specific circuits of exchange. To recall Balibar's distinction, there is a temporal gap between the formal subsumption of labour under surplus-extraction, and its real subsumption, which sees its completed in a historically located manner. The transformation of manufacture attested to this process in the transition from feudalism to capitalism, and we are currently in the midst of a subsumption of knowledge-based production as the transit between disparate regimes of surplus-extraction.

The amount of labour as such cannot be used to measure value, a notion that Mason and the autonomists incorrectly impute to Marx. As Pitts (2018: 12) has also noted, there is an inverted productivism at work here, transposing earlier emphases on industrial productivity to the sphere of information. Accordingly, older, vulgar accounts of the centrality of the physical work process and the postcapitalism argument converge: both hold that the knot of value-creation needs to be cut at the source where the worker applies their labour to the raw material, missing sight of a process in which labour is necessary but not sufficient.

In contradistinction to the earlier iterations of LTV, Marx alludes to the 'socially necessary labour-time' that is prefigured beyond the confines of the production locale, and untethered from the exact time the worker has spent. Marx (ibid) explains that it may seem that the work of the 'unskilful and lazy worker' should be costlier, as they will spend more time producing the same output as their more skilled counterparts. However, a closer examination shows that each unit produced 'has the character of a *socially average unit of labour-power* and acts as such' (my emphasis). This being the case, value does not depend on the characteristics of an individual worker, but on the 'socially necessary labour-time', which Marx (ibid) goes on to define as 'the labour-time required to produce any use-value under the conditions of production normal for a given society and with the average degree of skill and intensity of labour prevalent in that society'.

Be that as it may, the untethering of value from its former, narrow source may still be compatible with the thesis of postcapitalism in the contemporary economy. Instead of the clearly demarcated workplaces of the twentieth century, the site of social struggle is the networked economy that can potentiate non-market production, and private and public hierarchies that seek to rein in this creativity. Thus, Mason's argument for postcapitalism could be qualified such that it takes a reorganisation of production to overcome capitalism. In its current form, *post*-capitalism solely implies a distinct phase of capitalism, rather than a socialist transition, which would be a positive project rather than a networked rearrangement of production. Nick Srnicek (2017: 128; 2018: 162), a prominent voice in the postwork debate, provides an example of harnessing the potential of networks, calling for 'platform cooperatives' along with the state-led creation of public platforms. For Srnicek, this could help to construct democratic ownership over these twenty-first century necessities. They are currently monopolised, providing owners with an intense concentration of capital and political leverage. Srnicek's proposal goes beyond the hierarchy and network dichotomy and implies a degree of state planning in order to counteract private competitors. This involves reconfigurations of political power and, in a postcapitalist setting, would also allow for a networked mode of planning the economy. The difference from Mason's proposals is Srnicek's recognition of the substantial political shifts they necessitate.

Posing the question in this way, the notion that the hierarchical chaff can be split from the networked wheat appears too facile a transition. Furthermore, Mason's (2015: 14) agents of the postcapitalist transition are ensconced at the core of information-based production: 'By creating millions of networked people, financially exploited but with the whole of human intelligence one thumb-swipe away, info-capitalism has created a new agent of change in history: the educated and connected human being'. Surveying contemporary anti-capitalist movements, it is indeed possible to glimpse the young, urban, technologically literate activists of the last decade as agents of a transformation. These effervescent movements have also shown – their contribution to toppling authoritarian regimes notwithstanding – that social media use does not directly threaten capitalist exchange.

The fault in Mason's analysis is not that such agents' capacities are exaggerated, but that, as with other autonomists, he takes for granted the hypothetical breakdown of value in Marx's Fragment. In this way, Mason takes a literal reading of a postcapitalist scenario and overlooks how the same networks that the 'educated and connected' human beings rely on are also complicit in not only the production of value, but also in the exploitation of cognitive labour-power. These new sites of production usher in 'new forms of exploitation that are often not just precarious, but also unseen and hidden', as Fuchs (2016: 237) maintains. Fuchs (2016: 236) illustrates how capital institutes new norms of labour-time, referring to the staggering increase in the information technology sector in Germany, which saw a rise from 765 million annual hours in 2000 to 1.069 billion in 2010 due to the auxiliary service work, patches and updates associated with information goods. Adding that there is a globally uneven division of labour in the digital sector, encompassing mines in the Congo and assembly plants in China, Fuchs further argues that global online connectivity does not manifest itself on a frictionless, egalitarian surface where all can make an impact, as has been the vision of Silicon Valley. Furthermore, the time spent using such products by the consumers is productive work, yet their communication and generation of knowledge is utilised as unpaid labour then used to attract advertisements; Google and Facebook are not communications companies, but the world's largest advertising companies (Fuchs, 2016; 2014).

Based on Fuchs' charges, it can be argued that although Mason is careful about sweeping assertions about the reach of the information economy, he is mistaken in taking 'capitalism' and 'postcapitalism' as monolithic categories with the latter folding over the former with the passage of time. According to this narrative, the information economy is growing in the interstices of industrial capitalism, leading to a quantitative transition to postcapitalism. However, as even Mason's example of Nike shows, production based on the networked generation of data is grafted onto a global division of labour, where the old-style sweatshop labour of industrial capitalism proliferates in tandem in the networks. Marx (1972: 12–15) had argued that 'fair' distribution that leaves the mode of production intact is illusory, and at best a palliative measure. This was not because the current allocation of resources was 'unfair'. On the contrary, the trends of capitalism at Marx's time and ours precisely create the 'optimal' results according to its own criteria of productivity and revenue. Mason (2015: 277) suggests that planning to a high degree of precision exists in capitalism, but it is not accountable. Creating an open-source simulation of the economy, open to democratic input and transparent to the community, Mason argues, could reveal that the Nike shoes that cost $190 can be reduced to a price lower than $20 once the marketing expenditure is foregone. While this form of planning could be feasible in postcapitalism, it seems doubtful that a multinational corporation could be brought under public scrutiny by educated and connected actors, without working class confrontation in the peripheries.

Herein lies the main problem that while the socialisation of knowledge may engender a postcapitalist temporality, in a context where capitalism prefigures the conditions and ends of production, it can also strengthen the hand of capital. Reconceptualising Nike in a postcapitalist setting would be putting the information-based cart before the horse of capital accumulation. The company's internal planning and production necessitate the branding expenditure, without which it would be unnecessary to consider bringing it under public ownership. According to the prevalent mode of production, the allocation of a large budget to advertising is already 'optimal'. Tampering with these decisions does not address the problem at the root, since the production process in itself implicates the consumers' decisions, rendering Mason's argument a sophisticated case for proactive consumer sovereignty.

Referring to the misplaced faith in the emancipatory role of information technology, Fuchs (2016: 233) charges Mason with determinism. Even though Mason had criticised the early twentieth century assumption that a complete state takeover of the economy would be tantamount to socialism, he comes full circle when he assumes that its eventual networked takeover will amount to postcapitalism. Even so, Mason (2015: 271–276) provides a useful map of the recent trends in global capitalism, and does not shirk from suggesting ways forward, or acknowledging the possibility that his blueprint may be brushed aside in ensuing waves of social opposition. This picture of transition also rests on the observation that the left has been accustomed to opposing bad things, but not to promoting good ones: 'Today we have to relearn to do positive things:

to build alternatives within the system; to use governmental power in a radical and disruptive way; and to focus all our actions towards the transition path – not the piecemeal defence of random elements of the old system' (ibid: 249). In this sense, there is a utopian streak, even though it envisages a simplistic transition, conjoined more to late-phase capitalism than its overthrow.

3 Inventing the Future: the Post-accelerationist Techno-utopian Strain

In their criticism of postcapitalism, not just that of Mason but also in Srnicek and Williams' (2015) postwork future, Pitts and Dinerstein (2017) maintain that a 'techno-utopian' fault line runs through their arguments at the expense of sociocultural possibilities for non-market production. While this is meant as a serious omission, the 'utopian' label is problematically applied denoting an unfounded optimism of enhanced technical productivity. It is necessary to distinguish utopianism from techno-determinism, which was shown to carry water as a criticism of Mason. Nevertheless, Srnicek and Williams' volume *Inventing the Future: Postcapitalism and a World Without Work* (2015), widely received as a postwork manifesto, evinces a utopianism that can be extricated from determinism. Here I consider Srnicek and Williams' contribution, noting their critical reformulation of accelerationism, leading to a discussion of postwork demands in the following chapter.

This book, published around the same time as Mason's, is a theoretically oriented defence of a postwork future. Unlike Mason, however, its writers deftly situate their analysis within a string of left social movements, and more clearly predicate the realisation of their proposals to the transformation of common-sense, in Gramscian manner. They thereby address the political deficit that leads to techno-determinism. For this reason, the better part of the book reflects on why neoliberalism has been so dominant, while the left has been mired in what they call 'folk politics' (2015: 5–25).

According to this narrative, once a fringe group in economic circles, neoliberal thinkers had a long-term, universal vision for their doctrine. They incrementally influenced the common sense, and while they were doubtless helped by the crises of the post-war Keynesian consensus, they did not take their proposed path to be inevitable, but gained governmental and academic positions where they could shape the agenda (ibid: 66). Conversely, the left, particularly in the post-crash Occupy movements, has made a virtue out of horizontal and heterogeneous congregations at the expense of a concerted reach for power with clear demands. Added to this was an unfounded prioritisation of the local scale, emphasising the particular over the universal. Totalising goals of global emancipation and radical change that once figured prominently in left discourse were thus rejected (ibid: 11). Arguably, Srnicek and Williams detect a residual post-Marxism prioritising identity formation and unmediated political action. Contrarily, they argue that this is a historically constructed political common sense, and 'out of joint with the actual mechanisms of power' (ibid: 10). While direct action and disruptions at the spatio-temporally immediate level can effectively counteract local grievances, they cannot dent the capitalist structure, as a 'globally dispersed abstraction' (ibid: 36). To challenge capitalism in its totality, it is necessary to build a movement at a correspondingly radical scale.[1]

The argument for the direction of the state towards social needs alludes to the abundance of technological innovations that can be implemented at the national level and beyond. For Srnicek and Williams, technology must be a factor in left ambitions, who need to reclaim the future as their 'natural habitat' (ibid: 141). Technology is used in a broader sense than the digital economy or improvements in machinery. It is rather part of daily life as a 'politicised infrastructure' (ibid: 145). The social fabric is saturated with the outcomes of conscious decisions, made by capital and the state, to shape the working day and social life. The development of the forces of production is not an automatic process humming in the background, but directly implicated in social reproduction. The intertwinement of technology with capitalism can be seen in the Amazon employees' subjection to surveillance and pressure to meet quotas (Bloodworth, 2018). Concurrently, Germany's ongoing adoption of renewable energy attests to alternative directions towards which technology can be used (Srnicek and Williams, 2016: 231).

Considering technology as adaptably socially ingrained raises the prospect of its modification as part of a transitional agenda. On this point, Srnicek and Williams (ibid: 231) indicate that technology is created with existing materials, which may transmit an already repurposed older technology, thus the difference between modification and repurposing is one of emphasis rather than opposition. This invokes Marx's (1972; 1993: 123–124) dialectical argument that the production process inherently involves that of consumption; thus labour and technology are nature recycled and repurposed in productive activity. This view of technological development and labour allows for more nuanced assessments, compared to the crude application of the LTV that isolates labour from cycles of capitalist social reproduction. Also, departing from Mason's

---

1   This use of radical denotes its etymological Latin sense, of the 'root' (*radix*) rather than the extremities. In Marx's (1975b: 251) words: 'To be radical is to grasp things by the root'.

determinism, Srnicek and Williams apply the notion of multiple temporal directions to the case of technological development, citing the historian Melvin Kranzberg: 'Technology is neither good nor bad; nor is it neutral' (ibid: 152).

Having argued that the function of technology is secondary to the social context, Srnicek and Williams maintain that the rate and direction of its development emerge from the interplay of the state, capital, and the working class. The state often undertakes longer-term projects without guarantees of success – *e.g.* space exploration -, as an overlooked force behind much of the technology that private monoliths capitalise on, from the touchscreen to the hard drive (Mazzucato, 2013). In contrast, capital is likely to invest in short-term profit, based on productivity enhancement and piecemeal amendments for quick returns. Also, some of this investment translates into intensified exploitation of the working class. The workers, on the other hand, can use their leverage to shape the specific ways in which new technologies are implemented, which could mean resistance against piece-work enforced by impersonal AI technology, or even a complete boycott of automation, described in Mason's (2015: 196–197) account of the skilled Toronto work-force in the 1890s. This leverage could also divert development towards 'socially useful goods' (Srnicek and Williams, 2016: 147–148), as seen in the UK company Lucas Airspace, whose workers made plans to use their capacities to develop medical technology and renewable energy rather than high-tech military equipment.

Srnicek and Williams (2015: 189) explain that they abide by some tenets of accelerationism, as they have an appetite for wide reaching changes in production and working patterns, finding 'folk-politics' insufficient. Their qualified approach incorporates contradictory temporalities alongside acceleration, dispensing with the notion of speed as a unilinear, monolithic arrow of time. Instead, a positive account of 'left modernity' is presented, involving the possibilities of utilising technology and global interconnectedness to build a new mode of life. They would appreciate the pessimism of the likes of Adorno, who link modernity to concentration camps. Srnicek and Williams would concede that though there is a history leading from the slingshot to the megaton bomb, there are also others leading to double bypass heart surgery and space travel.

Here Srnicek and Williams (ibid: 148–150) refer to Project Cybersyn – a portmanteau of 'Cybernetic Synthesis' – to illustrate the point that the left needs to think beyond the immediate. Inaugurated by the socialist government of Allende in Chile, this project included a proto-internet horizontally connecting factories, an economic simulator and statistical forecaster to streamline planning, and an operations room that would not look amiss in a space opera. Rather than an all-knowing and omnipotent cybernetic entity, Cybersyn was meant to modulate economic flows, facilitating self-management while allowing for an overall supervision and direction of the national economy (Medina, 2011: 26). Due to US hostility, it was impossible to obtain new computers, so existing tools were combined to fulfil their functions (ibid: 64). In its short lifespan, Cybersyn allowed the government and producers to coordinate production, building vestiges of democratic socialism, and using real-time information to bypass sabotage from the property-owning classes.

As Srnicek and Williams (2016: 150) explain, this showed the potential of technology when its use was not limited to capitalist ends: 'In the end ... the experiment provides an imaginative and utopian example of the repurposing of cybernetic principles, existing Chilean technology and cutting-edge software'. Following the CIA-backed coup led by General Pinochet, the physical infrastructure was destroyed with particular brutality, to an extent that is laid bare in this episode from the day: 'One member of the military took a knife and stabbed each slide the graphic designers had made to project in the operations room' (Medina, 2011: 2015).

The short-lived Cybersyn project showcases that advanced tools available could be pieced together to create a postcapitalist infrastructure that is more than the sum of its parts. However, contrary to Mason's belief, such an infrastructure does not lie dormant in the womb of the old. It is rather a product of conscious deliberation, requiring state-level administration and local self-management. Restructuring the economy with technological means can therefore take place insofar as the lag between a future mode of production and an increasingly outdated political mechanism can be addressed.

4   Techno-utopian Futurity

In temporal terms, a possible conclusion to draw from Cybersyn is that the gradualism of the Allende government, as well as the formidable imperialist threat from the north, were impediments to the 'catching up' of the political with the economic. The cybernetic networks horizontally connecting the capillaries of production, and enabling informed decisions, could also be said to surpass our time, embody an unrealised future in the past. On the economic side, the development of the forces of production can be conceptualised along a linear path. The means required to transform the nature and quantity of production evolve in discernible ways, from the windmill to the steam engine, or the telex machine to the supercomputer. From this angle, using the most advanced technology available could have been a transitional step towards a popular reappropriation of the means of production, if only the government could have resisted deposition. The allocation of resources at the point of production, with updates on shortages and demands, would have helped to avoid the inefficiencies associated with Soviet socialism (Srnicek and Williams, 2015: 151). The overdetermined political life, however, is relatively autonomous from these subterranean advances. While there is ample opportunity to produce quantity and quality for all, or make ever-shorter working days possible, the political structure and its ideological scaffold can fetter such goals. This also invokes a postwork argument that technological capacity has temporally surpassed the political arrangements and work ethic, once justified by alluding to scarcity.

This temporal 'backwardness' of the sociopolitical surrounding needs to be qualified since the means of production are not solely maintained, but also shaped by the political and ideological levels of social reproduction. For this reason, the relations of production are imbued with the results of political struggle and ideological interpellation, implying that they do not necessarily go in lockstep formation with advances in the forces of production. This insight complicates a conception of the linear development of such forces, since this process does not take place in a meta-social vacuum, making it more difficult to discern a direction. Advances in the forces of production, necessitated by capitalist rivalry, can be adapted and purposed for contradictory interests. To account for this, it is necessary to consider political events outside of the immediate economic sphere.

Althusser (2014: 174–176) had proclaimed 'ideology has no history of its own', referring in part to the non-ideological loci of its development and its 'eternity' as an organic part of social life. Taking up the template of ideological, political and economic axes of social reproduction, it can be argued that none of these spheres have histories of their own. Even the seemingly objective forces of production are subject to obsolescence or flourishing depending on political will. This means that if it had been inaugurated as planned, Cybersyn may have exerted a temporal pull on the social formation. But we have also seen that its emergence was not only fraught with antagonism, but made possible primarily due to shifts in the political and ideological domains towards an associational, voluntary mode of production, embodying this articulation as a makeshift, futuristic apparatus in embryonic form. It can only be speculated what a twenty-first century Cybersyn, with the cybernetic capacities of the day, could achieve to complement these political and ideological shifts. But it is apparent that the bricolage that made up this technology was assembled through political initiative, and maintained by social participation. Consequently, Cybersyn was arguably behind the times in the sense that the result fell short of surrounding expectations. A socialist political will was the driving force behind its assembly, and due to a lack of such a will at the heights of governing power in the ensuing decades, with Chile being turned into a neoliberal laboratory, a new initiative for it is yet to be made. Once the temporal positioning of the forces of production and their political support is thus rearranged, it is more accurate to conclude that these forces, and the economic level of social reproduction, can remain tied down to the interests of capital, hence Cybersyn remains a historical curiosity today.

Srnicek and Williams (2015: 148ff) also seize on this insight to promote a hegemonic program, in order to develop the forward-facing tendencies of the present, rather than projecting the process backwards. The prioritisation of the political helps to situate the 'advanced elements of the present' within a context where their repurposing and proliferation are contested. This prioritisation is qualified, however, in that it needs to avoid overcorrecting the techno-determinism present in their intellectual heritage. Thus, a contrasting techno-*utopianism* remains anchored in the material prospects of a universal program of alternative modernisation.

Finally, this techno-utopianism needs to be demarcated from techno-determinism, which is the faith in an inevitability at the heart of contemporary trends. Even though Mason calls for political action to realise networked potentials, the assumption that postcapitalism has germinated within the capitalist economy is a rushed conclusion that does not stand up to scrutiny in light of the exploitative aspects of networked production. Similar to the accelerationist erasure of temporality, this attests to an inverse end of history, one where a new historical beginning is immediately present, regardless of its recognition. Here my argument diverges on the fundamental point that contrary to an inevitability, postcapitalism is one of many potential outcomes, which include a reinvigoration of the past with a vengeance – of which the Chilean experience, and many others, are poignantly reminiscent -. This is different from immediate actuality. The futures in the past and present are not undifferentiated realities. As in the case of Cybersyn, they are indeed composed of contemporary elements – none of which literally comes from the future – but their emergence is conditioned through the nexus of temporal lag. Their characteristics are shaped by a historical becoming, as opposed to supplanting current ways of doing things as a monolithic bloc.

Having set out the theoretical premises of postwork as a case of a left vision imbued with utopian temporality, this investigation now turns to a substantive discussion of strategy.

CHAPTER 8

Demands, Agency and Strategy

Concluding the third part of this book on enacting transitions, this chapter considers concrete demands in contemporary left visions, particularly those of the postwork tendency. These demands serve as transitional reforms and organising frames, rather than silver bullet remedies to capitalism. In fact, some of the proposals have already been implemented to a certain degree, such as the Alaskan variant of Universal Basic Income (UBI) (Feinberg and Kuehn, 2018). This policy features in mainstream debates with advocates from across the political spectrum, and continues to amass a growing repository of pilot studies from Kuwait to Canada, and Finland to Kenya (Widerquist, 2018: 57–70). The demands considered here are not particularly unique or novel since, for instance, the call for a four-day work week can be traced to earlier movements for the eight-hour work day, and the legal recognition of the weekend. However, they are part of a broader transitional programme that incorporates certain twenty-first century realities such as the prospect of far-reaching automation, and are presented as part of a series of reforms. This indicates a tension at the heart of the postwork paradigm, since it can be variously construed as a retrogressive defence of a defunct social democratic model, or a series of feasible demands that hold the potential for emancipatory rupture. The argument here is that there is a grain of truth to both positions: the postwork paradigm embodies both a melancholic, negative reaction carried over to the neoliberal present, while creating a potential for transition through a positive articulation of this reaction. More specifically, postwork politics inherits a contradictory heritage between the horizontal focus of the Occupy movement and its global iterations, as well as a long-term socialist agenda bent on the capture of state power and its wielding for egalitarian ends.

In analysing left demands as transitional stepping stones, it is necessary to consider the agencies that might bring them about and maintain their viability. Weeks (2011: 222–223) has drawn attention to this in her discussion of the manifesto as an agitative text. Performatively, the demands of the manifesto aim to mobilise a subjectivity, as much as to be met. This subjectivity (such as the proletariat) pre-exists the manifesto, but in an amorphous form, and the text highlights their shared interest in heeding its call. In this way, a manifesto invites the masses to make history. Conversely, a lack of agency in this capacity may take the form of a policy paper addressing those in power without necessarily enacting a transitional process. For this reason, an examination of substantive left visions must go beyond the feasibility of reforms, and make a judgment on the audience that they position themselves towards. This allows a deeper understanding of how reforms can serve ameliorative or transformative ends, depending on the direction in which they are inserted. Regarding postwork, some critics have asserted that it reduces political struggle to the realm of direct wage-labour and capital relations, contrasting this with a framework inspired by Social Reproduction Theory (SRT) that considers capitalism as a conjunction of relations that encompass the entire society (Pitts and Dinerstein, 2018: 474). Their critique thus attacks postwork for narrowing down the plausible agents of social change. While its conclusion will be disputed here, this method of agency-based criticism is valuable.

Following the analysis of demands and agency, or the questions of 'what' and 'who', it is also necessary to discuss the question of 'how', or the strategic-organisational dimension. These questions are implied in each other; as shown, postwork demands indicate assumptions about agency and ways to organise. Contemporary waves of struggle carry over some of the melancholic baggage of the previous century, while making remarkable utopian forays into the political scene at the level of prefigurative action. The global iterations of Occupy have not fulfilled transitional expectations in terms of socialist seizures of political power. However, as their afterlives in institutional politics suggest, they also have not only dissipated following a haphazard uprising. They have also integrated themselves in established and newly-emergent left parties to various extents, resisting neoliberal economic governance (Della Porta, 2017; Brand, 2012). Thus, emulating the structure of this book that moves from theoretical to concrete manifestations of transition, this chapter begins with a consideration of demands and the agencies of transition, ending with an appraisal of the network/hierarchy dichotomy traversing debates on organisation.

The following discussion is organised in three sections. The first, considering demands, focuses on what left theory strives for in terms of policy. The overarching argument is that the melancholy and utopia dichotomy is a useful template for discerning the transitional implications of making political demands, going beyond the presumed watertight distinction between revolution and reform. A utopian angle can transform what would be otherwise considered as modest reform into a revolutionary prospect, depending on the context. Crucial to this is the agency implicit in the form in which a demand is pursued, which leads to the second section. The theme of agency is explored through the actors invoked in postwork, and a salient criticism that it has too narrow a basis in the process of production. Additionally, this section refers to the discussion of Laclau and Mouffe's controversial injunction to build political agency beyond, and in spite of, preconceived notions of class. While this appears to be compatible with the inclusivity of postwork demands such as Universal Basic Income, it is argued here that this approach eschews class altogether, consequently jettisoning the objective material bases of transition. Finally, the third section turns to the question of organisation, or 'what is to be done?', central to left politics since Lenin's (1960) notorious pamphlet. This section explores the contradictory heritage of horizontal and vertical organisation, arguing that a temporally differentiated theory of prefigurative politics is needed to illuminate contemporary strategic debates.

1   Postwork Demands: Non-reformist Reforms

The policy-based output of postwork includes various propositions, but converge on the aim to shorten the working week. The authors argue that this is not only possible, but also an imperative for left and working class demands. These policies can be most accurately construed as transitional arrangements to realise the overarching goal of a drastic reduction in involuntary wage-labour, which would then transform the capital-wage labour relation and leverage further gains (Hester and Stronge, forthcoming: 5). In this way, the demands are advocated for as 'non-reformist reforms' (Srnicek and Williams, 2015: 108), or 'directional demands' (Weeks, 2011: 221). The writers discussed here, except for Mason whose account is laden with determinism, and others who have not been included such as Frayne (2015) and Bregman (2017), look to the near future rather than an abstract utopian end-goal. The emphasis is thus on the vectors on which such gains will position political actors, hence the 'non-reformism' of the demands for automation investment, UBI, and the reduction of work as part of an updated welfare state. Notwithstanding the internal discrepancies in the approaches to policy within postwork, these are taken as representatives here, with the intention of tracing this reform/revolution dichotomy across their discussions.

Despite some of its proponents' partiality to the futuristic, postwork has been criticised for a slippage into mainstream social democracy (Brown, 2016: 169–170). Accordingly, 'postcapitalism' is evasive and shy of confronting capitalism by naming its alternative, socialism (Brown, 2016; Hatherley, 2016). There is merit to these arguments, as the discourse of postwork, with its emphasis on services and welfare, is reminiscent of a bygone social democracy. Additionally, transition appears as a delayed prospect, following a consolidated neo-Keynesian arrangement. However, the utopian edge of this project is reiterated across postwork accounts, such as Weeks' arguments in the key of Blochian hope (2011: 175–226). Also, while not explicitly central to this paradigm, Levitas (2013: 202–206) makes use of postwork demands as harbingers of concrete utopia. This is a novelty to postwork, since the traditional anti-utopianism – and anti-communism – of social democracy does not register in this tendency. Yet, this programme may be appropriated for non-utopian reformist goals, as measures to restore profitability. The articulation of postwork demands may risk retreating to a melancholic self-limitation of negating capitalist excesses. But, this section seeks to show that these demands' utopian function enables a disinvestment from the state of affairs, encouraging a positive construction of alternatives.

The Universal Basic Income has appealed to an unlikely array of political positions, from the right-wing think-tank Adam Smith Institute (Kilcoyne, 2018) to the left-wing economist Guy Standing (2011: 171–178; 2014). Recently, the latter (2019) was commissioned by the British Labour Party to compose a report where he urges its trial, and Labour Shadow Chancellor John McDonnell has confirmed that it would be piloted in three cities if the Party were to come to power. In the past, a base-line, unconditional income for all citizens was supported by Bertrand Russell (1918) as well as the Nixon administration in the US, where the bill failed due to Democrats believing it did not go far enough (Bregman, 2017: 40–41). Thus, UBI is not a new idea, nor one purely of the left. However, its postwork revivification frames it within a larger socialist program. Also, left advocacy of the measure has been more vocal, from the Fabian socialist G.D.H. Cole (1935: 253) to the ecosocialist André Gorz (1999), as well as Erik Olin Wright who construes it as a 'real utopia' (2010: 5; see also Wright, 2004). When the right favours this measure, it is because it would accompany further sweeping privatisations and dismantling of the welfare state, where the provision of a base-line income would allow its recipients to remain afloat while employers can retrench their responsibilities (Lewis and Stronge, 2018). In this scenario, UBI could revamp neoliberalism as a corporate handout, and deprive beneficiaries of an argument for an increased wage. Consequently, as Srnicek (2017a) maintains, the question of UBI should not be seen in the blinkered terms of an explicitly transitional or restorative step:

> As with any other policy (such as healthcare or childcare), a basic income can be implemented in ways that push beyond the limits of social democracy, and it can be implemented in ways that consolidate the present neoliberal order. The question of whether we want a UBI or not turns out to be secondary to the question of 'which UBI?'

The reform itself is secondary to the direction of it implementation, and it should be considered within a set of surrounding demands and assumptions.

For instance, a left case for UBI should include not only the maintenance of existing social services, but an extension of Universal Basic Services (UBS) *as well as* a basic income that is enough to lead a dignified existence above the poverty line. Otherwise, the proposal on its own falls short. As people have various needs due to disability, family and caring responsibilities, debt, region, and countless other variables, an additional income will mean more or less to different people (Dawson, 2016: 176). Considering that there is also a pressing issue of socioeconomic inequality, this relativity would be even more pronounced as a provision of a basic income would not be meaningful to a landowner who makes many times more than this amount from rent alone, for instance. Questions of how much and for whom are therefore transitional insofar as they are complemented with UBS. This more expansive view is in line with the recommendation in a report by the Institute for Global Prosperity (2017), who define UBS as crucial for securing equal access to the social product, consisting of shelter, food, local transport, legal services, and access to means of information and communication.

Once these needs are met as part of an expanded welfare state, UBI would enhance personal autonomy, allowing people to take up the kinds of work or study that they aspire to. UBI could enhance gender equality by providing house workers and those with caring responsibilities, most of whom are women, to seek additional, more fulfilling activities, without the threat of precarity (Pateman, 2004). This would not necessarily supplant domestic and care work, although with a revised net of UBS, child-rearing and day-care may become socialised and less gendered, dislodging patterns that narrow down women's career options. Keeping in mind that UBI would be financed by transferring some of the social surplus in terms of a progressive tax, it has an equalising effect, with the potential to foster social solidarity. It could be objected that this creates an illusory sense of unity, as the homeless person and the member of the 'one percent' are entitled to the same basic income. Such an objection is valid if UBI is introduced exogenously as a singular measure into the economy, without a redistributive angle. Mason (2015: 285–286) views the policy 'as a postcapitalist measure', which he explains as 'the first benefit in history whose success measure is that it shrinks to zero'. For Mason, this is due to the redistributive aspect of a UBI that targets the market sector. As a basic income provides sustenance without having to take up 'bullshit jobs', the position of labour is strengthened, pushing employment standards higher (Graeber, 2018). This simultaneously contracts the market-based tax pool by curtailing the gap between the sheer amount of productivity and the skewed distribution of its proceeds. According to this economic account, redistribution through UBI approximates a socialised wage in the form of collectively provided services.

For Weeks (2011: 113), this universalism is politically expedient; like the Wages for Housework campaign, the introduction of a basic income is empowering not as a panacea for social problems, but a way to blur the arbitrary distinction between remunerated and unremunerated work on the one hand, and forming bonds among its advocates that is instrumental towards a popular hegemony on the other. Offering a genealogy rooted in feminist politics, Weeks (ibid) considers UBI to be a 'working demand', where the journey prefigures the destination. The unconditionality of UBI transforms the expectations between state and citizen, as well as worker and employer, reconfiguring assumptions of reciprocity by enabling a reduction of working time. Wright (2010: 220), while not directly associated with postwork theory, broadens this argument, saying that the implicit redistribution can help to erode the capitalist determination of production; returning more value to workers and their communities, it forms a 'mechanism to transfer part of the social surplus from the capitalist market sector to the social economy'.

Wright's statement that UBI would return more of the socially created wealth to its creators should be further underlined, since with the rise in automation, the question of its beneficiaries is coming into sharper focus. A report from the pressure group Compass (Lansley and Reed, 2019) maintains that UBI is both desirable and feasible as more menial jobs are automated. It is desirable since the increased proceeds of automated productivity need to be allocated justly for a sustainable future, and it is feasible for the same reason in ways that it has not been before. As Aaron Bastani (2015, 2019) warns, automation can have a paradoxical outcome of jobless growth, where products are made more efficiently and in higher quantities, but this is accompanied by falling real wages and stagnant living standards. To avoid such caveats of technological and cybernetic progress, it is apt to emphasize a political program that embraces the techno-utopian strain in postwork theory. As discussed earlier in Chapter 7, Cybersyn was a seemingly anachronistic embodiment of this utopian tendency. Here, a Blochian striving for equality and common ownership converged with technological innovation to create an instrument for a socialist reconfiguration of not only the means, but also the process of production. With time, the benefits of a horizontally organised allocation of resources would have created a commonality that would even benefit the wealthiest. Similarly, automation and a combination of UBS and UBI can open a transitional space atemporal with capitalist logics. At its best, postwork theory can be conceptualised in a similar way, not only demanding the reduction of toil, but also posing a philosophical question of how to build the good life, unhindered by market forces. As Dawson (2016: 177, 200) maintains, getting lost in the practicalities of UBI is not a useful exercise, since its implementation will inevitably vary and may be delayed based on local considerations. However, this does not compromise the fact that UBI inspires the imagination, a key ingredient of the utopian politics advocated here (ibid).

The left melancholy and utopia dialectic examined in Part 2 is a central tension in postwork. Highlighting the imbrication of left melancholy with utopia, I have argued that while left melancholy has denoted a negative refusal of the symptoms, utopian searches beyond the system were of a positive nature. These are not mutually exclusive, but expressions of unmaterialised temporalities, as in the remembrance of past defeats in new waves of political contestation. Benjamin's counterintuitive refusal to give closure to trauma is therefore a call against the memorialisation of defeats, and for their subterranean capacity to refresh collective movements for alternative futures. Turning to the substantive accounts of postwork, this tension manifests itself as a negative refusal of neoliberal nihilism, irrational even by capitalist standards. Considered through the lens of melancholy, postwork may appear as nostalgia for twentieth century social democracy, albeit one equipped with contemporary potential. However, its reliance on a more minimal framework of key political proposals does not mean that it is a longing gaze into the past since, as its advocates rely on these measures as a transition towards positive socialist construction, postwork is more of a techno-*utopian* viewpoint that invites political agents to grasp the reins of their own temporality.

Weeks (2011: 169) beckons the masses to give content to their historical existence beyond the work society by alluding to the famous slogan of the movement for the eight-hour work day: 'eight hours labour, eight hours rest, eight hours for what we will'. This last open-ended demand of a space of autonomy 'for what we will' gets to the essence of the utopian side of the positive construction of postcapitalism as a mode of life. Refraining from detailing a blueprint for such an existence, this iteration of postwork politics is a '*keeping open*', as Bloch (1995b: 622) had characterised Marx's endeavours. The reduction of work, eponymous to postwork politics, finds expression most resolutely in the call for reduced working hours (Srnicek and Williams 2015: 127). These calls for a reduction of the work week expand on the older struggles to wrest life away from capital, shifting the window of possibility to points once thought to be unfeasible. In keeping with the focus on temporal lag here, such demands invoke an alternative temporality within the interstices of the totalising capitalist temporality. Besides their immediate contents, postwork and Marxist theory have a performative side that conspicuously avoids ready-made templates, contented by exposing the historical artificiality of systems otherwise taken for granted. This invites new popular interpretations of ways to organise work and production, bringing with it the possibility of new anticapitalist interpellations.

Out of joint subjectivities within capitalist temporal rhythms subvert the false sense of temporal 'cohesion' that structures in dominance seek to gloss over. To recall from Althusserian theory, ideology presents a sense of 'fullness' to cover the void where levels of social reproduction do not align. Depending on historical particularities, the economy overdetermines the structure in dominance, such as the legal ideology that raised the bourgeoisie to power. Having repudiated the inherited privilege of the aristocracy, this class instituted property laws and abstract legal personalities. They thereby weaved a texture of universal right, where all can raise themselves by their bootstraps, and engage in the market place as voluntary agents. In this way, the non-contemporaneous aspects of the refusal of labour, or the historical individuality of the worker, were formally subsumed under their capitalist logic. Accordingly, the role of left politics is to reinforce these temporal rifts, and devise alternative interpellations to shine a light on them. Insofar as its postwork proposals point to an alternative future, they empower interpellations outside the wage-labour rubric. As Gramsci (1919) argued, proletarian political power can only arise from 'a type of organisation which is specific to the activity of producers and not of wage-earners', and postwork may serve to construct this organisation. In short, regardless of how ambitious or modest the proposed reforms appear, their importance as mobilising poles of attraction takes precedence over their immediate feasibility. In fact, while the specific demands merit examination on their own terms, their transitional impact lies beyond these intrinsic qualities, taking on a level of significance in condensation with surrounding social and political factors.

The travails of the phrase 'Fully Automated Luxury Communism' (FALC for short), coined by Novara Media (2014), is an instructive example of how demands can gesture towards wider alternatives. The term is deliberately appealing, provocative and catchy. At the same time, most recently formulated by Bastani (2019) in a book of the same name, it provides a roadmap out of capitalism based on technological development and a state-sponsored array of reforms. A critic notes that Bastani's (ibid: 233) proposals are similar to those in Mason's *Postcapitalism*, or the Labour Party manifesto of 2017 (Jefferies, 2019). Accordingly, Bastani makes the same mistake as Mason where he effaces class struggle in favour of a technocratic arrangement, where the working class only appears as a voter base. This charge, however, undervalues the performative function of FALC, as a canvas on which to project a plurality of postcapitalist visions. This is evidenced by the widespread social media embrace of the slogan, with new qualifiers added behind the signifier 'communism'. Currently, the favoured version in social media is 'Fully Automated Luxury Queer Space Communism' (FALQSC), a tongue-in-cheek expansion of a utopian demand surpassing terrestrial and heteronormative barriers. A cursory web search of the phrase brings up posters of Soviet space programs, digitally manipulated to include rainbows and other symbols of the LGBTQ+ movement. Concurrently, there is a striking lack of academic uses of the term, which further attests to this performativity spurring the imagination of open-ended, alternative futures, decidedly removed from the realities of neoliberal precarity and resurgent social conservatism. In this sense, the anonymous, internet-based appropriation of the phrase is a cultural expression of the desire to break from abstract, neoliberal temporality. Even though the phrase belies a hyperbolic techno-optimism, the technological argument is relegated to the background in a utopian subversion of the hegemonic common sense, propagated through virtual circuits of communication.

Bastani's vision of the future as already here, due to the proliferation of technology and artificial intelligence, risks the same determinism found in Mason. Moreover, both writers draw from a problematic reading of *Grundrisse*, interpreting Marx's musings as prophecy, and downplaying the capitalist capacity to exploit technical innovations. This also indicates an essential caveat that the aforementioned proliferation of online images is still enmeshed in the networks of communicative capitalism. Yet, the transfiguration of this vision into a canvas of creative temporalities also evinces the prefigurative potential of postwork. Beyond specific demands and their academic justifications, the notion of a society significantly less burdened by toil can mobilise radical political imaginaries.

Considering the broader range of postwork theory, its advocates also emphasise this utopianism that finds its realisation as its cascades through popular culture. There are varying levels of emphases and even divergence between which reforms to pursue. Weeks' (2011: 113–175) political proposals rely more on the feminist heritage of the Wages for Housework campaign, while Lewis (2019), another feminist author, focuses on the socialisation of child raising as a way to erode familial patterns that act as confines of invisible domestic labour. Neither Weeks nor Lewis rely on the automation and UBI frame reductively attributed to the entirety of postwork theorising, although these are admittedly key points of concern (Pitts and Dinerstein, 2018). Postwork theory is rich in detail about the means to reduce work's significance. As its 'post' label implies, there is a normative paucity regarding the contents of a postcapitalist society. Despite objections based on this lacuna (Pitts and Dinerstein, 2017), this reticence is a strength. Since postwork clears the ground for cogitation on the good society, its corpus can include voices from communist, anarchist, feminist, and social democratic leanings. These can be at odds as to the meaning and intended aims of the reforms, and express their advocacy in terms compatible with the eventual society they envision.

The afterlives of autonomism, accelerationism, and feminism in postwork theory all contribute to the postwork consideration of work within the totality of social reproduction beyond the workplace. Bringing these influences out of their twentieth century habitats helps the postwork theoretical formulation of transition, recognising vestiges of the future in the advanced elements of the present. Stuart Hall (1988: 157) observed that the welfare state 'both achieved something in a reformist direction for the working class and became an instrument in disciplining it'. Postwork politics rejuvenates the welfare state to construct a social architecture that can *complete* it to the point of its own redundancy, as achieving more equality would make measures such as UBI less urgent. In this sense, postwork can be as utopian as it is pragmatic, with policies that are modest as well as radical. In Weeks' (2011: 228) words, these are 'reformist projects with revolutionary aspirations', amendments to the system that can open vistas of postcapitalist imaginaries.

2   Social Reproduction and the Agency of Transition

If postwork policies are not a body of measures to optimise capitalism, but non-reformist reforms, then this can be judged by the agencies they invoke. As mentioned, right-wing defences of UBI appeal to the ruling class, claiming that this measure will enable a confiscation of rights obtained in the last century. Furthermore, the World Economic Forum (Dadwal, 2018) extols basic income in explicitly restorative terms, soberly underscoring the need for concessions to counteract injustices:

> We have already seen civic unrest in cities where rates of poverty and inequality are rising. In addition to reimagining the culture of work, cities must look to adopt UBI as a preventative strategy to assuage existing mass frustrations resulting from skills shortages, unemployment and systemic inequalities.

Aside from this justification of UBI as a band-aid solution against social unrest, it is telling that it addresses the political and economic decision-makers, taking them as their interlocutors over and against the affected populations. Contrarily, postwork positions itself as an instigator of unrest among those that have most to gain from a socialist transition. Political agency is not assumed to take the form of a sutured group, to invoke a phrase from Laclau and Mouffe's contingency-oriented theories. Rather, it is envisioned as a result of the struggles to bring demands into realisation, and a function of their dissipation among groups recognising their interests in them. That said, some proponents of Social Reproduction Theory (SRT) argue that postwork has an outdated and misplaced focus on the wage-labour and capital relation, fixating on this at the expense of the wider societal bulwarks of reproduction. What follows builds on the argument that postwork theory can play a prefigurative role in transitional searches, through its positive proposals as well as its silences on the description of the good life. I will then show that this critique is unfair, and that SRT and postwork have more commonalities than divergences.

An exception to postwork's self-positioning within the subaltern can be seen in Mason's work. While internally consistent as a case to facilitate the eventual predominance of networked postcapitalism, one is nevertheless left to wonder who would be its midwife. It appears that minimal – if any – agency is needed for this transition, since Mason identifies an undifferentiated postcapitalist economy that is eclipsing capitalist confines through its own mechanisms. Mason is then guilty of a type of techno-elitism – evidenced in his reverence for the founders and editors for Wikipedia – that dovetails with his determinism: if networked production with the aid of technological innovations is the order of the day, this suggests that an educated, technocratic elite could best arrange it. This iteration of postwork invokes a linear notion of progress, of the networked Reason bringing itself about in a monolithic whole, whereas most accounts retain some form of class struggle as the precondition of the project.

Mason updates the interpretation of the *Fragment* based on more recent trends, but its unfolding was more central to the *postoperaismo* in Hardt and Negri's (2004) concept of the 'multitude'. Similarly to Mason, Hardt and Negri posit a crisis in value-formation because of the knowledge-based shift in the production process. Here the 'general intellect' that Marx had identified as the instigator of the breakdown in the spontaneous generation of value is the contemporary bearer of communism. Now unbound from the superintendence of capital, the multitude's 'creativity of desire' places an imminent transition front and centre (Hardt and Negri, 2000: 51–52). This has significant implications for agency where society as a whole generates value in a unity of 'singularities' (ibid: 53). Such singularities make up the 'human faculties, competences, and knowledge' that are 'directly productive of value' (Hardt and Negri, 2009: 132–133). Here, the paradigmatic image of the industrial worker is dissolved in the multitude producing in an already communalised manner, forcing capital to find new ways to reintroduce its yoke on the process. At face value, this suggests a wider agency of transition, as capital is on the back foot and communism is imminent. However, although this would be at odds with Mason's techno-elitism, it also effaces class struggle, and severely downplays capitalism as a still-dominant mode of production. While Mason's technologically literate bearers of transition can be discerned from his account of postcapitalism, agency disappears from Hardt and Negri's account altogether once they eschew the antagonism at the heart of capitalist relations of production. And once this conflictual core is supplanted by a *sui generis* communist transition, then, as Barron (2013: 609) contends, it is no longer possible to 'distinguish evidence of co-optation from evidence of contestation – or a resurgent capitalism from an emergent communism'. In sum, both Mason and Hardt and Negri rely on an emphasis on the *Fragment* and the LTV to argue that postcapitalism – or communism – has significantly replaced capitalism. Both contributions fail to capture the relevance of class struggle to transition, falling short of adequately addressing the question of agency.

Having addressed the deficit of agency in certain tracts of postwork theory, it is pertinent to heed a criticism based on the charge of a narrow focus on the productive process. Making use of SRT, Pitts and Dinerstein (2017b) argue that postwork loses sight of the multifarious sites of activity making up capitalist society, and thus limits itself to policy proposals solely bent on reforming the wage labour and capital relation. Before elaborating on this critique, this section will provide a snapshot of SRT. Subsequently, the criticism will be explored, followed by an alternative argument that postwork and SRT are compatible, and separating them misrepresents the agencies implicated in postwork.

The fundamental stance of SRT, according to Tithi Bhattacharya (2017: 2), is that 'human labour is at the heart of creating or reproducing society as a whole'. Consequently, SRT expands the purview of Marxist analysis to those areas of social reproduction taken to be 'neutral', such as the family. This sheds light on the invisible, unremunerated gendered division of labour in the household, paving the way for a feminist critique of surplus extraction. Looking beyond the immediate relation between the male industrial worker and the employer, Hartsock (1983: 234) identifies an equally crucial third party:

> He who before followed behind as the worker, timid and holding back, with nothing to expect but a hiding, now strides in front, while a third person, not specifically present in Marx's account of the transactions between capitalist and worker (both of whom are male) follows timidly behind, carrying groceries, baby, and diapers.

Seizing on this, Bhattacharya (2017: 2) argues that only an understanding of class as a conjuncture of an array of social relations, encompassing the communities and the families of the workers, can maintain this category's explanatory power. Consequently, a worker is not simply someone with a job, as would infer apprehending class as a static socioeconomic position. They are rather someone who enters relations of production selling labour-power as a function of the societal relations they are enmeshed in (Bhattacharya, 2015). The supports of the class struggle are thus incorporated into the 'economy' (ibid).

While wage-labour directly produces value, the lifeblood of capital accumulation, it is itself dependent on other overlooked forms of labour. Bhattacharya (2017: 3) maintains exploitation front and centre in her arguments, echoing Caffentzis' point that labour is exploited precisely because it resists assimilation into an economic category. This singularity of labour power is due to the fact that it is not produced *capitalistically*, that is, its (re)production takes place outside of circuits of capital accumulation. This is significant, since while the critique of exploitation uses the category of wage-labour, or the abstract character of labour within capitalism, SRT expands the scope of analysis to the pre-mediated point where the wage-labourer prepares for their shift. Even in circumstances where capitalist social relations prefigure access to life's necessities, this sphere of social reproduction remains a site of contention, since the capitalist and the worker are both aware that value-formation depends on the *voluntary* attendance of the worker to the needs of the former. Following Marx's diatribes against the illusionary division of the political and economic, they are taken up in unity. In Bhattacharya's view (2015), this introduces to the economic process its 'messy, sensuous, gendered, raced, and unruly component: living human beings capable of following orders – as well as of flouting them'.

This expansion towards social reproduction is analogous with the Althusserian analytics of ideological and political sites of the social formation. These are not ontologically separate. The blind spots of domestic and racialized labour, and the critique of the oppressions that take shape on the turning lathe of capitalism, require sustained attention without reducing them to an abstract logic of exploitation. Equally, removing exploitation from the equation goes against SRT's avoidance of the fallacious, liberal separation of gender and racial discrimination from economic processes, or the intersectional theories that separate vectors of oppression (McNally, 2017). Such an outlook also helps to dispel vulgar Marxist approaches to oppression inclined to see these struggles as divisive, secondary distractions to 'class struggle'.

According to Pitts and Dinerstein (2017a, 2017b), SRT is a superior alternative to postwork. The latter takes the narrow understanding of the 'economy' as a site of market exchange, falling behind the more comprehensive coverage of SRT. Taking aim at UBI as a demonstrative example, they argue that even if it were enacted, it would simply 'defer this contradiction to a higher level of monetary abstraction' (ibid: 428). Against postwork, they maintain that the view of social reproduction reveals possibilities for prefigurative activity, including 'Community-Supported Agriculture schemes, food and housing co-ops, a 'return to the land' and a creation of new commons around life's necessities' (ibid). Considering that this vision now constitutes a pillar of Corbynism in the UK, Pitts and Dinerstein lament that it has led to a focus away from the 'Green Surge' of early 2015, particularly since the leader of Labour Party, himself famously an allotment holder, was poised to be its spokesperson. Such prefigurative practices address the ties between wages and sustenance directly, embodying an alternative mode of politics. Instead, postwork takes a more palatable path for the ruling class, lacking a strategy to section off market exchange from social reproduction through direct action. Accordingly, this accounts for the popularity of a basic income, because it packages the strenuous necessities of social transformation within the logic of capitalism (ibid: 439): 'Land ownership, care of loved ones, labour relations, decommodified access to food and the means of living: all go unquestioned, the mess and mud and struggle they imply elided. You can have the world on a plate, this says, but nothing else. Free money, but no free lunch'. The provision of 'free lunch' would be a more profoundly transitional step since it dispenses with the cash nexus. As the critics see it (ibid: 5), postwork theory amounts to a blind belief in the liberating potential of technology, testifying to a techno-promethean impulse, indifferent to the array of prefigurative practices that are not reliant on this.

Returning to the case of UBI, this criticism contrasts decommodifying practices with state-sponsored programs, implying that they confiscate popular agency and channel energies towards top-down measures. Accordingly, Pitts and Dinerstein (2017b: 3–4) assert that postwork falls victim to a type of workerism, in the Francophone pejorative sense of *ouvriérisme*. It retains money, commodities and the rule of value due to its insistence that work is the defining social relationship under capitalism. This myopic focus displaces the defining bind of capitalism in the form of value-creation, pushing postwork politics to effectively argue for a tepid social democracy. The workerism is a gateway to the elision of class struggle, since postwork theorists falsely believe that ensuring state provision of the means of sustenance can resolve class contradictions. Going further, Pitt and Dinerstein (ibid: 13) suggest that UBI 'harkens back to fascism', as it is compatible with ethnic-nationalist projects, as seen in the Modi government's consideration of the measure for India.[1]

---

1 The reference to the Indian interest in UBI is slightly misleading. According to the article in *The Economist* (2017) used by Pitts and Dinerstein, while the measure was 'floated' following

Accordingly, UBI can be a sinister tool of entrenching nationalism through selectively distributed citizenship. The SRT perspective is useful in that it provides a wider picture of social reproduction as the site of struggle against capitalist domination, while postwork has reified the solution of such conflicts with a vision of state dependence. This state may be more or less generous, but it remains at a remove from class struggle, at once its superintendent and participant. Therefore, these critics contend that transitional politics needs to prefiguratively create fissures along the social formation, rather than consecrate an updated welfare state.

While this criticism draws attention to the problematic versatility of UBI, it misrepresents postwork and does violence to the basics of SRT. The allegation of an uncritical belief in technological progress also belies a superficial reading. While certain accounts – *e.g.,* Mason's postcapitalism and possibly Bastani's (2019) enthusiasm about the probability of space mining -, may be vulnerable to such a charge, there are as many, if not more, discussions of technology that explore the limits of its repurposing for social benefit, as Srnicek and Williams elaborate. As explained above, postwork is at its best when it reflects a techno-*utopian* temporality, provoking an imaginary of social life with work dislodged from its commanding position. Contrary to some proponents of these measures, this utopianism can only be maintained by asking 'which UBI', with a combined UBS and UBI as the answer. Scrutinising its focus on work, Pitts and Dinerstein eschew the more crucial silences of postwork on the contours of postwork society, which they construe as an amenability to liberal and nationalist appropriations. Yet, this reticence to provide the blueprint can help give it a creative openness. This being the case, the postwork programme is dialectically utopian, as it wishes for its demands to become redundant as its vision unfolds, leading to new questions of a *post*-postwork nature. The seemingly minimal focus on the provision of automation, and the means to design of a sustainable life for all members of society, maintains an agential flexibility – but not erasure -. These measures therefore underpin a more profound transformation. In sum, Pitts and Dinerstein read the postwork agenda as an end in itself, with predefined political actors, while it is a means to the end of realising the not-yet.

---

an economic survey, it has had a long history with advocates on both sides, as well as a 2015 pilot study conducted by Standing and colleagues, which the writers do acknowledge (Dawala et al. 2015). Presenting the measure as a categorically right-wing proposal eschews this nuance, raising the suspicion that the example is used for its disconcerting effect.

SRT interrogates the scaffolds of exploitation, and opposes partitioning employment relations as the sole site of domination. This does not quarantine the working day as an overly theorised area, but brings it into sharper relief by showing how it intrudes into wider social life, indexing all kinds of life-sustaining and nourishing activity to capital accumulation. Therefore, it is bizarre that Pitts and Dinerstein have opted to cordon off labour relations while celebrating the sites of social reproduction outside of them. For instance, they place a heavy emphasis on community gardens as a site of non-capitalist social reproduction, since, with the appropriate level of support, they can form an alternative social economy. However, as Bhattacharya (2017: 10) maintains, alienation is not specific to one form of productive activity. Bhattacharya argues that there are indeed 'abstract' and 'concrete' variations of work. The former pertains to the kind of work performed directly for the capitalist. In physical terms, it is also 'concrete', the abstraction referring to its alienated character. In social life, commodities are encountered as 'social crystals' of alienated wage-labour (Diefenbach, 2006). 'Concrete' labour refers to activities carried out voluntarily. It corresponds to use-value as opposed to exchange-value, since these activities are not directly instrumental to commodity production. Tending to one's garden could be seen as such an activity. Also, there is the thorny issue of care-work and affective labour that are socially considered to be concrete labour, while SRT draws attention to its intertwinement with abstract labour. Pitts and Dinerstein's proposal to expand concrete labour outside of the formal subsumption of capital is thus erroneous, since they ignore how SRT reveals that even pastime hobbies or leisure are imbricated with the schedules of work society, an issue that postwork theory also cogitates.

As Bhattacharya (2017: 10) maintains, these activities are not less alienated than the sale of labour power. Extending the example of gardening, it may enhance self-sustenance and environmental consciousness. Upon closer inspection, however, we see that the questions of when, where, and what to cultivate are all prefigured elsewhere, in the 'structuring impulses in the time of production' (ibid). In fact, studying the modalities of this structuration is a central concern of SRT. As alienation is imbued in the social formation, its influence cannot be localised to a specific point, notwithstanding temporally discordant practices. Pitts and Dinerstein (2017b: 15) approvingly cite Bhattacharya's (2015) inference that there is no singular point of domination, yet they see this as a reason to oppose policies for the betterment of working conditions. This has led them to prioritise non-market activities, relying on the problematic reading of SRT that the moment of production is secondary, and even irrelevant, to social reproduction. Contrarily, SRT begins precisely from the moment of production, but emphatically rejects stopping there, tracing its ripple effects along neglected areas.

Rather than positioning SRT in opposition to postwork, it is more theoretically and politically expedient to synthesise them, as Weeks has done. According to Weeks (2011: 28), this can inform strategic decisions. Social reproduction sheds light on the practices and agencies that grate against the contemporary working regime, and 'pose the full measure of its antagonism with the exigencies of capital accumulation, a biopolitical model of social reproduction less readily transformed into new forms of work and thus less easily recuperated within the present terms of the work society'. This approach accentuates the importance of alleviating the problems of work by contextualising them within social reproduction, in a 'struggle to wrest more of life from the encroachments of work' (ibid: 30). As Bhattacharya (2015: 5–6) also notes, Weeks underlines the 'most common articulation of labour under capitalism, namely, work', and 'points to the fundamental incommensurability of capitalism with any productive or creative sense of work'. SRT reveals the arbitrariness of the remuneration of work, examining of the suffusion of capital into areas beyond its direct control, while postwork, making a case to marginalise work in social life, brings numerous agents who would benefit from this to the limelight. This perspective therefore articulates new agencies under the sign of anticapitalism, remaining cognisant of the producers' position of destructive refusal.

In keeping with the favoured techno-utopianism here, it is important to underline the sensitivity to the utopian in Weeks' and Srnicek and Williams' accounts, as well as Bastani's (2019) manifesto for FAL(QS)C. The 'postcapitalist' corollary of postwork downplays the arduous work of enacting transitions, but much of postwork theory is animated by a desire to rekindle futurity. The utopian attenuation evinces the temporal openness of the present without facile presumptions of existing postcapitalism, due to the gap between the practical suggestions and the scarce elaboration on how to use the time gained from drudgery. Postwork theory furnishes reasoned justifications for reforms that hold open a door of possibility for creative energies. These address people directly involved in the official workforce, as well as the mass of society that undertake unrecognised work. In this light, it is more helpful to make judgments on the agential implications of theoretical tendencies by considering how much of its normative positions on future societies is left uncharted, to be realised by social and political actors that emerge in its construction. This is not to suggest that any form of agency has equal weight. While the producers of the social product have a unique leverage over capitalist mechanisms, this group is more numerous than often portrayed. Different perspectives will suggest certain socioeconomic strata, or political groups, as agents of postcapitalist transition, but it is more revealing to ask of them how much autonomy they allow their agents.

Marx, Gramsci and Althusser intimate the tasks that a transitional politics would have to engage in, whether in terms of creating a post-revolutionary socialist economy, achieving cultural and political hegemony, or reinstating class struggle. These lend themselves to detailed and possibly contradictory inferences around political goals and methods. However, they are at a remove from the immediate arena of social struggle, rather participating and gaining insights from praxis to inform and modify their theoretical output. In doing so, these works are positioned at a temporal dislocation between the political and ideological levels of social reproduction, with lapses in relevance followed by periods of intense interest (*e.g.*, the sales of *Capital* are inversely correlated with capitalist cycles of growth, soaring at times of economic downturn, and *vice versa*). Conversely, overtly political writings taking positions in their historical milieu can have short-sighted judgments, such as Marx's initial refusal to endorse the Paris Communards that sits uneasily with his own philosophy of the self-emancipation of the exploited. Even though such writings are instructive because they document the theoretical turns over their authors' lives, it would be a misrepresentation to deduce a singular political line or agency based on these alone – after all, many of the demands concluding the *Communist Manifesto* have already been met. This would make Marx redundant, belonging to nineteenth century thought 'like a fish in water', as Foucault had opined (2005: 285). However, as Weeks (2011: 216) has observed regarding manifestoes in general, they serve a utopian function that calls on a political subject to rely on its own strength, only positing action items as stepping stones in the process of their historical becoming. For this reason, Weeks' (ibid) thoroughgoing account of the agencies in autonomist and feminist political theory rightly focuses on slogans, demands and policy proposals before setting out their agents.

The invocation of the process of identity-formation as a function of articulating political demands finds its apogee in Laclau and Mouffe's post-Marxist theories. It is thereby necessary to briefly reiterate this perspective, to introduce limitations to open-ended notions of agency. Post-Marxists argued that rather than presupposing social fragmentations, left theory needs to build analytical tools from the ground up, devising strategies based on contingent articulations. Rather than socialism, Laclau and Mouffe (1985) advocated 'radical democracy' that is inclusive of these articulations. The working class, for its part, was discarded as a revolutionary agent. In an era of myriad social movements, it could at most integrate itself into a 'chain of equivalence' of shared grievances, without an independent weight of its own.

It is possible to deploy this theory to the postwork agenda. As indicated, many adherents of UBI defend it for cross-cutting purposes. A post-Marxist politics would mobilise a campaign for UBI discursively welded to the movements of downtrodden groups. In fact, Mouffe (2018) has recently lauded the rapid growth of the Labour Party, arguing that Corbyn represents 'left populist strategy'. While not directly referring to postwork demands, Mouffe explains that the bold programme of the 2017 Manifesto drew a political frontier, and defined a rival. Additionally, the Momentum movement, established to support Corbyn's bid for leadership, has included activists from different social, cultural and political backgrounds, inaugurating a 'chain of equivalence between the different democratic struggles across British society', and turning the party into 'a large popular movement capable of articulating a new hegemony' (ibid). Mouffe is right to argue that this successful mobilisation (evidenced in a surge in membership and unexpected successes in the 2017 election), in stark contrast to the Party's struggling continental counterparts, lies in its capture of countercultural imaginaries. That said, these developments also hinge on the insistence on working-class politics with union support, which post-Marxists had decried as an antiquated effort. This is seen in the emphasis on infrastructure investment, progressive taxation, democratic ownership in the economy, and a host of similar measures associated with social democracy. That is not to say that the Party ignored other movements, but that its hegemonic project was anchored in a class-based exit from neoliberal imperatives that could also redress various forms of oppression. This bid for hegemony therefore targeted the mode of production, approaching Gramsci's original vision and not that of post-Marxism.

The integration of postwork demands such as UBI into working class politics within a programme of curtailing value-producing work could both enhance its public support, and prevent right-wing articulations. However, if the working class as a main beneficiary and political catalyst for transition is jettisoned as a category, it is hard to compose a political-economic program around a basic income. Advocacy of the measure without reference to the process of production would reduce it to a moral appeal for charity. As Weeks (2011: 228) argues, postwork politics is interwoven with postwork ethics, while a post-Marxist interpretation would sever the former from the latter since it invokes the mode of production, another concept deemed obsolete. The rejection of the productive underpinnings to politics relinquishes UBI to the free flow of discourse, but this time equalising the validity of all appropriations. Conversely, UBI ceases to be a floating signifier once it is positioned as part of a transitional program with basic services, which in turn addresses central issues of the work-centric society and those who shoulder its burden.

Once society is envisioned as a process of discursive articulations, where political actors lack any capacity save for that conferred by identity-formation, then the transitional horizon also recedes as a rupture between different societies. The outcome is the opposite of the liberation from fixed identities that the post-Marxists intended. A gambit of relinquishing class as a pregiven reality might appear to clear the ground for novel agencies. Yet, it unmoors the directionality of transition, culminating in a quasi-liberal support for progressive actors, whose 'progressiveness' is in the eye of the post-Marxist beholder, rather than based in the goal of recovering the means to build our society.

Marx (1977) had asserted it is forgotten that it is essential to 'educate the educator': people are subject to the circumstances they hope to change, thus revolutionary activity is essentially one of 'self-changing'. The revolutionary agent occupies a position where they are engulfed in transitions while intervening in them. The post-Marxist view, however, solely assumes an external intervention. The task of devising ways to properly side with the exploited, which is derived from class analysis, is dismissed as a pretension to contain complexity within prefabricated models. If all political agencies need to be discursively articulated, taking the immediate social reality as its point of departure, then this begs the question 'who will discursively articulate the discursive articulators?'. As far as post-Marxism is concerned, their charges of elitism and pretension to omniscience come full circle, placing themselves above society as the interlocutors of the left-right distinction.

In sum, agency should be considered through each of the temporally stratified social practices, and account for those with most to gain from its realisation. The post-Marxist separation of the political as an all-encompassing ground of contention and identity formation is not preferable to the relative autonomy of politics with respect to production. In addition, this account entirely marginalises the social, a space as political as economic and ideological, wherein the contents of political wills are generated. A case to transform the economy, including the process of production and resource allocation, needs to make use of contemporary possibilities and extend these in scale towards the desired society. Building cultural hegemony along such utopian lines is a stepping stone towards liberation from unnecessary work, creating space to consider what could be done with recovered time.

An advocacy of redistributive proposals and solidarity-based economics without this utopian orientation can lead to their appropriation for reactionary projects that operate along dystopian lines – the Hungarian right-wing government's pension cooperatives to 'help good Hungarians', Greek neo-Nazi party Golden Dawn's 'Greek only' food stands, or the Indian government's interest in UBI are among efforts that come to mind (Pitts and Dinerstein, 2017:

11; Buxton and Shipman, 2018: 6; Smith, 2013). On the other hand, the argument against postwork proposals on the grounds that they do not go far enough remain bound by an abstract utopianism and overlook the arduous transition process. In keeping with Wright's suggestion of 'real utopias', the postwork theorists refer to existing movements for measures that, while not sufficient in themselves, will be prefigurative of an alternative society built on principles of solidarity, freedom and equality. On this note of a temporally attuned, utopian formulation of agency, it is pertinent to consider the strategic and organisational side of transition.

3   Organising Transition: Prefiguration after Occupy

Postwork politics is positioned at a contradictory juncture, where the horizontal focus of anti-austerity movements overlaps with the resurgence of the party-form, taking shape as what have been called 'movement parties against austerity' (Della Porta et al., 2017). This is a welcome development, as a project to transform social relations cannot eschew a vertical ascendance to the commanding levers of political power. This further suggests that the party-form, even as a 'movement party' with roots in social movements, should not be cast aside as a redundant model. On the contrary, acknowledging that leaders emerge within mass movements, this form provides more structure and accountability, facilitating the execution of collective decisions and helping to maintain a democratic culture through clearly delineated procedures of leadership (Harvey, 2015). As Dean (2012: 210–211) argues, the party can add 'diagonal strength' to horizontality, translating the energy of social movements to official channels of representation, and leveraging these in their favour. Also, for better or worse, parties provide a lifeline between the wider public and political movements, helping to avoid isolation. This section argues that the horizontal and vertical distinction is inadequate for analysing paths to socialism, which Rahnema (2017: 19) correctly describes as 'no doubt the largest and most complicated project of human history'. Instead, I use Wright's concept of 'normative trade-offs' in enacting transitions to explain the need for strategic flexibility, and call for further theorisation of prefigurative politics, suggesting the addition of 'pragmatic prefiguration' to the problematic.

On 17 September 2011, the Occupy Wall Street demonstration began in Zucotti Park, within the financial district of New York City. This would be the forerunner of a global string of occupations and protests, described by Noam Chomsky (2012: 54) as 'the first major public response … to about thirty years of a really quite bitter class war'. Srnicek and Williams (2016: 2, 20–22, 36, 187) single out the horizontal orientation of the Occupy movement in their criticism of 'folk politics', arguing that while many of the classic demands of the left are more attainable than ever, this historically constructed common sense falls short of achieving them, since they are distanced from mechanisms of power. According to this designation, there has been a resistive, but not constructive, emphasis on spatio-temporal and conceptual 'immediacy'. Folk political actors favour the insurrectionary moment, the affective experience, and the fleeting occupation. Srnicek and Williams (ibid: 20–22) acknowledge folk politics as a corrective to the breakdown of social-democratic normalcy, and left parties' degeneration into insipid managers of capitalism, adding that a discussion of organisation should start from its contributions to the strategic repertoire. However, they also maintain that romanticizing the horizontal corners the left into a defensive position, receiving the concerted assaults of capital and the state, whereas it could proactively move from immediate to structural contestation.

The spatio-temporal immediacy idealised in horizontalism is indeed an impediment to left politics. Spontaneous uprisings attest to an undercurrent of melancholic and utopian temporalities, compounding past struggles with their incursion into the quantitative time of capital accumulation. Nonetheless, this spontaneity cannot fulfil its redemptive potential without taking on viable forms. This is reflected in the renewal of the debate on the party-form. As the Occupy movement unfolded, the rejection of representation and emphasis on process over results has shown that ultimately, those with more financial, educational, and other means to influence decision-making processes disproportionately impact the outcomes, sidelining the less-advantaged constituencies they seek to mobilise (Dean, 2012: 55; 2014: 830–831). This can sap the transgressive audacity of social opposition, leaving a lifeless husk of its ardour in defunct assemblies, discontinued blogs, and abandoned occupations.

In this context, Dean (2012) calls for an anticapitalist party, examples of which sprung up in the ensuing years with the emergence of Syriza in Greece and Podemos in Spain. According to Dean (Dean and Deseriis, 2012), the party introduces a vertical integration by drafting demands and considering what might happen in the proverbial 'morning after', once the pepper gas has cleared and the fervour has subsided (Žižek, 2017: 36–37). As the non-reformist reforms intend to have an imprint on the political future beyond their terms, the party cannot substitute for all political agencies, but it can facilitate their endurance. The defeat of Syriza against EU imposed austerity has marked an ignominious turn in its short lifespan, but there are also positive lessons to be drawn from the initial stratospheric ascendance of this movement-party. Following Dean's defence of the party-form, it could be maintained that it gave voice and structure to the popular opposition. The formation of a political will, engendering multiple currents, with a codified respect for movements' autonomy, has shown that organisational innovations can revitalise the party and reconfigure the possible. Dean also argues in a later article that the party could not sufficiently establish organic ties in the run-up to its election victory in 2015, which decreased further after accession to power (Spourdalakis et al., 2019). From this angle, Syriza dissipated the ecstatic social opposition in parliamentary triangulation, because it did not commit sufficiently to 'diagonalism' and trust its popular mandate to instigate a rupture, beginning to preach moderation and gradualism after acceding to the EU memorandum with a neoliberal thrust (Kouvelakis, 2019).

Considering these fluctuations between popular initiative and representation, it is more probable that the routine dichotomy of vertical and horizontal modes of organisation is an inadequate analytic of left strategy. As Dean (2016) reminds us: 'Political forms aren't pure'. They embody aspects of both forms of organisation, even if they may proclaim a support for one over the other. Social movements do not exist in a non-political vacuum; they have party activists among their most vocal members, at times forming the backbone of their defence against repression. Parties, on the other hand, condense the aspirations of amorphous multitudes, and bring these to national-level politics (Kouvelakis, 2015).

The organisational divide can be expressed more cogently in Wright's (2012) terminology. Wright argues real utopian impulses become transformative steps when they attend to unintended consequences and normative trade-offs. The latter is a valuable consideration, as it invokes the dichotomy of pragmatism and prefiguration, such as the exigency of winning elections as opposed to consolidating interstitial initiatives. Local considerations of these values can impose their reconfiguration, and expose the inadequacy of the horizontal and vertical dichotomy as an analytical frame. Conventionally, horizontalism is associated with solidarity along wills, particularly among disadvantaged communities, often to find ways to circumvent power relations. And vertical approaches are associated with party hierarchies and the bureaucratisation of protest, which can reach beyond the habitual locales of left agitation in a bid for national power. These approaches respectively overlap with prefiguration and pragmatism. However, this is the point where this model falls short. Prefigurative practices, embodied in a conduct that anticipates a desired future society, may be deprived of a wider reach and institutional support to their own detriment. Conversely, the normative trade-off of building longer lasting institutions to sustain such initiatives could empower them by enacting beneficial legislation, and scaling back state repression. Thus, it is more helpful to consider the normative trade-offs between pragmatic and prefigurative modes of engagement, rather than dogmatically elevate one over the other at any cost.

Since transitions are by definition liminal intervals with contradicting realities, it is more likely that decisions will be required that curtail some values and emphasise others. That being the case, there needs to be a prefigurative strain to any transitional demand and policy, such that there is a continuity between the desired outcomes and short term measures, yet this cannot be assumed in advance. As prefiguration is key to transitional politics, this can be formulated in terms of temporal lag between the ideological and political levels of social reproduction.

The June 2013 uprising in Turkey provides some indication of the utility of this temporal perspective. While the proposed redevelopment of Gezi Park, one of the last green spaces at the heart of İstanbul, was the spark that provoked a mass movement, encompassing millions of participants in all corners of the country, I shall refer to the occupation at the park itself. A 'commune' was founded here, maintained by volunteers and activists from all stripes of the Turkish and Kurdish left. Within the space of a few weeks, they created the vestiges of a new mode of life. A well-stocked library and a medical unit were founded, for all to benefit from freely, sustained solely by the ambience of solidarity that rode roughshod over factional differences and monetary concerns (Kuymulu, 2018: 46). The medical unit was active for twenty-four hours, treating protestors as well as the local homeless population, many of whom were receiving medical care for the first time (Turan, 2013: 70). Another striking development was the foundation of 'Revolution Market' (*Devrim Market*), providing necessities without charge. For the tens of thousands of protesters, with potential government agents in their ranks, this market at the centre of the park managed to function in a voluntary and non-commodified capacity, nullifying the cash-nexus and the hallowed 'supply-demand' model of exchange (Kuymulu, ibid; Sancar, 2013).

This act of urban commoning, at the centre of the largest city of a country that has been ruled by successive neoliberal regimes, embodies what is meant here with temporal lag. The proliferation of a non-capitalist mode of distribution within the commons does not account for a transition along economic lines, as this would also require a transformation of production. However, this experience shows a substantial ideological progress, engendered in the culture of safety, solidarity and egalitarianism that prevailed in the park (Yıldırım, 2013: 40). Thus, the fastidious refusal of monetary transactions only tangentially concerned the economic level. Additionally, the political trajectory, understood as the nature of state power, underwent minimal change, despite the cultural earthquakes in the ideological realm. Members of left parties, despite being numerically dwarfed, were unwavering participants, suffering casualties and providing the uprising with its most memorable slogans. However, the major opposition parties were slow to heed the calls from the street, most parliamentary support coming through the MPs' personal initiative. The sheer magnitude of the temporal lag between the economic and political trajectories on the one hand, and the ideological on the other, led to an unsustainable imbalance. The movement would dissipate into a steady trickle, finally leaving the core political groups without the surrounding social movements.

This episode indicates the significance of prefiguration for transitional politics, as its deliberations foreshadow a postcapitalist temporality. It is further necessary to consider organisation together with temporal lag, and the normative trade-offs of linking potentials in the present with their future actualisation. Horizontal and vertical tactics can both propel movements with roots in the future. Their spatio-temporal surrounding is a factor of their qualities, rather than holding intrinsic value. Pragmatic, short-term tactics may fall short of preserving these elements, but prefigurative practice, as in Gezi Park, may also lapse into the subterranean temporality of delayed redemption, where its disjunction with other trajectories is not bridged via hegemonic political action. Prefiguration is therefore necessary but insufficient, requiring a pragmatic aspect due to the normative trade-offs of enacting transitions. Thus, I follow Lara Monticelli (2018) in calling for more theorisation of the political, but also add that the possibility of 'pragmatic prefiguration' would reinvigorate the organisation debate.

The presence of multiple times, their manifestation as a visceral social unease with the moment, and the political ramifications of this unease – or lack thereof – can serve as an angle into this theorisation. Superimposing pragmatism and prefiguration onto the temporally stratified social formation, it is feasible to make the case that prefiguration attests to the qualitative, redemptive time that defies homogenising categorisations. This comes to sharp focus at points where the enactment of alternative societies registers a sense of untimeliness to their actors and the wider society. An example of this was the formation of a nearly self-reliant and autonomous community in Gezi Park, which simultaneously elicited homely and quaintly anachronistic sentiments among participants (Kumru and Toktamış, 2015: 18). It would not be amiss to say that the prefigurative arrangement is an enactment of the fleeting daydream. It takes it own political actors by surprise, and comes together spontaneously, outside the direct control of singular actors. Considered within the frame of multiple temporalities in social life, pragmatism refers to the – admittedly less glamorous and eye-catching – activities that concretise these sporadic defections from ingrained temporal scripts, as seen in the arguably successful efforts of Podemos at channelling energies into the halls of parliament.

Social opposition instils a futurity in the popular imaginary, and fissures the smoothness of the otherwise bland and timeless fluctuations marking capitalist flows. Going back through the preceding frames of temporal lag, utopia and melancholy can be glimpsed through the frustration and positive exertions that dot the global landscape, at times lapsing into regressive modes, at others coming to a halt as quickly as they have emerged. The third possibility, which has also shown some signs of realisation, is their ascendance to formal politics, with Syriza presenting the most successful, albeit ill-famed, case. What follows from this has so far been underwhelming. Burgeoning social movement-parties can introduce grains of a-temporality within the cogs of the state machinery, attenuating the pragmatism required to navigate these channels with a dose of prefiguration drawn from the loss of belonging to the dominant temporal frames. In this sense, temporal lag also chimes with techno-utopian postwork perspectives, which specifically advocate a recovery from the yoke of the working regime. This can counteract dynamics of alienation, which register production to an abstracted entity and obliterate alternate temporal subjectivities.

4   Transition as Prefiguration

Throughout a discussion of postwork demands, agency and general left strategy, this chapter has argued that these disparate spheres of enacting transitions are implied in each other as a prefiguration of a future mode of production. As much as the postwork demands' reasoned explanations, their contextual positioning and manner of presentation is a measure of their transitional capacity. Thus, the calls for UBI and automation need to be integrated into a wider hegemonic project with their beneficiaries in mind. Insofar as they envision their realisation within a series of non-reformist reforms, avoiding their reification as correctives to neoliberal excesses, these demands can maintain a temporal gap between faltering capitalism and a society compelled to shoulder its consequences.

Moreover, transitional demands are performative, implicating the agents of their realisation. An advocacy of UBI as a bulwark against social unrest presupposes a capitalist benevolence geared to restore profitability, while its defence in combination with UBS could unify the working majority and embolden further demands, shifting patterns of ownership and political power towards the working class. Postwork has been criticised for a narrow focus on work, at the expense of the socially reproductive labour that sustains it. This was shown to be an unfounded assertion, overlooking the impact that a reduction in toil and an expanded welfare system would have on the life-worlds of people outside the official workforce. While there is some slippage into techno-elitism and erasure of social struggle as the bearer of transition in some postwork literature, I have argued that a more persuasive techno-utopian current is also present.

Presenting postwork demands and revolutionary agency within the process-oriented sense of constructing a postcapitalist scaffold, is an argument for their prefigurative potential. In terms of left strategy, this means that flexibility is needed, disposing of one-sided idealisations of horizontal and vertical modes of organisation, and considering the normative trade-off involved in each. Furthermore, to assess these trade-offs within prefigurative politics, it is necessary to bring the theory of temporal lag into the equation, asking which strategic orientation is best poised to bind the loose ends of temporality at a point further than the present, where society as a whole can exercise more control over what, and how, it produces and survives. There is a subterranean temporality within each wave of social struggle, and this discussion is dedicated to calling for a theorisation of the pragmatic prefiguration *of* and *for* the future stages of rebellion.

SUMMARY

Transitional Politics and a Prefigurative Left Vision

Parts 1 and 2 of this book accounted for transitions as an ontological reality of historical change. Correspondingly, a historical materialist frame was outlined as an intelligible narrative to history, avoiding pitfalls of mechanic evolution and relativism. Furthermore, Part 2 explained that transitions can be recognised in the forms of melancholy and utopia, both of which attest to otherworldly temporalities through and beyond the present. For this reason, Part 3 has represented a break from this theoretical orientation to consider the practical side of enacting transitions. In order to put temporal lag as a theory of transition into effect, I have chosen a contemporary left vision that has been gaining traction, the postwork tendency. While there may be other candidates to consider, a sustained interaction with postwork theory has proven to be fruitful, suggesting how the temporal theory of transition can provide a critical vantage point, and be developed further as a result of this engagement.

Postwork theory has a broad family tree, extending from critiques of productivism of postmodern or autonomist inflections, to accelerationism. The influences on individual contributors to the paradigm are not limited to these currents, though these also resonate with all of their theoretical and policy output. Accordingly, Chapter 6 has explored these tendencies making up postwork theory, providing an account of their treatments – or lack thereof – of temporality as a socially and politically differentiated phenomenon. This chapter also charted the paths leading to postwork, with continuities and forks in the road. In this way, a judgment was formed on the merits of these predecessors of postwork, along with setting a scene to present this emergent paradigm against the conditions of its emergence.

The founding works of this paradigm respectively embody different theoretical antecedents. But a picture can be pieced together within a thematic map. In Chapter 7, it was found that there is a latent determinism to some accounts, manifested in the optimistic expectation of a technologically-assisted, networked postcapitalism. Against these approaches, this chapter has advanced the techno-utopian side of postwork politics, which is more involved in the discussion of political possibilities of a world without work, and less in a technocratic faith in an undifferentiated transition to postcapitalism.

Finally, Chapter 8 has concluded this Part, encapsulating the flow from theory to practice across this book, with an investigation of postwork demands and agency, as well as the question of strategy. With respect to this last subject, the net was cast wider, incorporating the most recent incarnation of the horizontalism-verticalism dichotomy following the Occupy movement, and the recent mobilisations against austerity. Postwork demands were considered on their own terms, with the merits of the positions in favour and against them, but also based on their social context and political intention. Thus, the letter of demands were subordinate to the question of whether they reiterate the past or anticipate the future. This consideration is in turn implicit in the manner of their defence, becoming explicit in the agencies they presuppose or seek to create. This was under consideration in the second section of this chapter, entertaining an agency-based criticism of postwork setting it apart from SRT, which is deemed to be more illuminating. This criticism was rejected, instead arguing for a complementarity between postwork and SRT, particularly in light of Weeks' authoritative use of this theory. Turning to strategy, it was argued that the previous findings suggest the importance of a future oriented, prefigurative streak to transition, and consequently that the dichotomy of horizontal and vertical models of left practice is not an effective template.

Conclusion

The 'short twentieth century', as Hobsbawm (1994) characterised it, culminated in the collapse of the Soviet Union, concluding a cycle of revolutions. However, the purported final victory for the neoliberal Washington Consensus began to peel away relatively quickly, reaching a period of sustained economic, social and political crises following the crash of 2008. It is therefore not surprising that online searches for the famous Gramscian (1971: 276; Achcar 2018) adage have seen a spike within the last decade: 'The crisis consists precisely in the fact that the old is dying but the new cannot be born; in this interregnum a great variety of morbid symptoms appear'. As much as a project to reanimate the concept of transition, this book was written as an eye-witness account of this liminal point, where events suggest a host of 'morbid symptoms', as well as a renewed reach for dignity, equality and solidarity.

While the present crisis-ridden historical moment may highlight the relevance of ideas about transition, it has been undertheorised in social and political theory. This is particularly curious for left theory, as it is has been and remains predicated on social progress and transformation. While there is a formidable amount of work on the survival of particular social formations, and instances of resistance, transitions in themselves have not received sufficient attention as a problem in their own right. This examination has sought to address this important lacuna.

Part 1 traced the concept of transition across classical and Western Marxist theory, drawing out the foundations for a more general theory. It was shown that the founders of historical materialism became increasingly aware of the importance of the transition concept, moving from an expectation of linear progress to an appreciation of the accidental and contingent in historical change. Thus, Marx's political works display a consideration of the multiple trajectories of social reproduction, differentiating the political and economic levels, although a theory of transition is not explicitly elaborated.

We then saw how transition had a troubled history among the theorists of Marxism after Marx: an expectation of inevitability took hold of prevalent left currents, postponing transition to a prospective future point. However, twentieth-century Marxism, with Gramsci as an interlocutor between its classical and Western variants, has also shown an interest in the subject, crucially with Balibar's essay on a theory of transition. I situated this pivotal work within the ambit of Althusserian theory, and together these formed the main elements of this book's theory of transition as a function of temporal contradictions. Taking a synthetic approach, I then incorporated Gramsci's concept of hegemony to shed light on the translations between the political, economic and ideological vectors of social reproduction. This has been a fruitful exercise in theorising the social more broadly, with further implications for a theory of the political beyond just state power. As seen in the examples of the Wages for Housework campaign, or the call for more automation investment, 'political' demands and debates gain their contents from outside of the political sphere, as grievances that emanate from the economic and ideological axes of social reproduction. This observation was enabled by the appreciation of the copresence of the economic, ideological, and political moments within each other, giving every turn of social reproduction a unique stamp of temporally uneven distribution. Additionally, hegemony as a theory of the interactions between these vectors was attenuated by contrasting it with its post-Marxist appropriation by Laclau and Mouffe. As a result, I emphasised the productive underpinnings of hegemony as its strength, accounting for the *relative* autonomy of the political. At the same time, I argued that in terms of the problematic of transition, a postcapitalist horizon is absent in the post-Marxist, discursive turn, primarily owing to its fundamental acceptance of liberal-democratic hegemony.

Having accounted for the dynamic ontology of transition in Part 1, Part 2 turned to its manifestations in left politics in terms of melancholy and utopianism. In particular, these concepts were reformulated as a potential resource for challenges against the socioeconomic order. Melancholy traverses these challenges, manifesting in the redemptive capacity of the calamitous defeats and wrong turns across episodes of social struggle. This served to illustrate that a subterranean temporality, as a qualitative time overarching the quantitative, congealed time of the prevalent order, is an immutable repository of experience, flashing as a transhistorical reach for alternative societies. The positive articulations of such societies are theorised as utopian impulses, transfiguring left melancholy into a rejuvenated ambition to transform society. Following an account of anti-utopianisms, present in right- and left-wing theory, we saw that the concept can be reclaimed as a sociologically grounded hermeneutic of transition. Furthermore, with an historical materialist consideration of utopianism in such manner, I explored the classical Marxist treatments of utopia, proposing much-needed revisions to the received wisdom that it is detrimental to the revolutionary project. Consequently, Part 2 sifted through conceptions of melancholy as a consequence of left defeats as well as a source of creativity, arguing that it is dialectically generative of utopian forays into the futures ensconced in the present.

With the aforementioned groundwork established in such wise, Part 3 involved a change of tack from the theory of transition to its actuality within left politics. Specifically, it focused on postwork as an emerging paradigm and an exemplar of the theoretical dilemmas of transition, with deep roots in left traditions. The analysis proceeded by identifying and critically analysing the contours of the postwork debate, and then examining its demands and their implications for a potential transition. Through a detailed comparative analysis of the key texts in postwork debates, it was concluded that a techno-utopian strain can be identified in this paradigm. I argued that this needs to be retained for the project not to devolve into a techno-determinist expectation of a frictionless transition to postcapitalism. Finally, the theoretical insights developed in Parts 1 and 2 were used to expand this study to left strategy in general. I criticised the routinely contrasted horizontal/vertical dichotomy of modes of organisation, by complicating their distinction through showing their copresence in transitional politics. In addition, I underlined the indispensability of prefiguration. Interest in prefiguration has been rekindled in left theory in light of the innovations of Occupy movements, and the subsequent emergence of 'movement parties'. Straddling the horizontal/vertical and pragmatic/prefigurative modes of organisation, this chapter has argued that we should look between them, at the upwards diagonal line that contains potentials of both. This attests to an uneven progress marking the movements of history, also engendered in the politics of transition as attempts to bridge its becoming. The anticipation of futures in the past that animated the discussion in Part 2 was thereby complemented in Part 3, with discussions of social and political movements in the present.

A salient conclusion of this investigation is that history, as a 'process without a subject', does not do the work of sustaining or supplanting social formations on behalf of social actors. Rather, it is open-ended, overflowing its structures in dominance, and fractured along multiple temporal lines. One has to be reminded that the original French title of Althusser's (1992) autobiography was *The Future Lasts Forever*. This, in my opinion, gets to the core of my problematisation of temporality, or an out of joint conjunction of a 'time of times'. The future menaces reactionary forces, and their perennially incomplete project of achieving a closure in the service of their interests. At the same time, it evades revolutionary efforts, who must constantly readjust their sails towards its regulative horizon. This tension at the heart of historical change provokes the conclusion that as the future is forever, so too are the ambushes into its heartlands, menacing the stability of the state of affairs and replenishing the desire for a better world. If and insofar as it provokes thought on such alternatives, this book will have achieved its purpose.

Bibliography

Acaroglu, O. 2019, 04/05-last update, *Review of 'The Transition from Capitalism: Marxist Perspectives'* [Homepage of Marx and Philosophy Review of Books], [Online]. Available: https://marxandphilosophy.org.uk/reviews/16747_the-transition-from-capitalism-Marxist-perspectives-by-rahnema-saeed-ed-reviewed-by-onur-acaroglu/ [2019, 07/05].

Acaroglu, O. 2018, "Paris 1871 and Fatsa 1979: Revisiting the Transition Problem", *Globalizations*, vol. 16, no. 4, pp. 404–423.

Acaroglu, O. 2016, "Anti-Capitalism Within and Beyond Capitalism: The Gramscian Bridge between Anti-Power and Statocentric Theories of Left Political Contestation", *New Birmingham Review*, vol. 2, no. 2, pp. 1–36.

Acaroglu, O. & Stronge, W. 2019. Forthcoming., "Antonio Gramsci: The Coherence Between Philosophy and Politics" in *The Bloomsbury Italian Philosophy Reader*, ed. M. Lewis, Bloomsbury, London.

Achcar, G. 2018, "Morbid Symptoms", *International Socialist Review*, no. 108.

Achcar, G. 2013, *Marxism, Orientalism, Cosmopolitanism,* Haymarket, Chicago.

Adamczak, B. 2017, *Communism for Kids,* MIT Press, Cambridge, MA.

Adamson, W. 1987, "Gramsci and the Politics of Civil Society", *Praxis International,* vol. 3, no. 4.

Adorno, T. 1973, *Negative Dialectics,* The Seabury Press, New York.

Allan, K. 2013, *Explorations in Classical Sociological Theory: Seeing the Social World,* Sage, Thousand Oaks.

Alquati, R. 1962, "Composizione organica del capitale e forza-lavoro alla Olivetti", *Quaderni Rossi,* vol. 2, pp. 62–62–98.

Althusser, L. 2015a, "From Capital to Marx's Philosophy" in *Reading Capital: The Complete Edition*, eds. L. Althusser & E. Balibar, Verso, London.

Althusser, L. 2015b, "The Object of Capital" in *Reading Capital: The Complete Edition*, eds. L. Althusser & E. Balibar, Verso, London.

Althusser, L. 2015c, "Letter to the Translator" in *Reading Capital: The Complete Edition*, eds. L. Althusser & E. Balibar, Verso, London.

Althusser, L. 2014, "On the Reproduction of Capitalism: Ideology and Ideological State Apparatuses" in Verso, London.

Althusser, L. 2007, "Reply to John Lewis" in *On Ideology* Verso, London.

Althusser, L. 2005, *For Marx,* Verso, London.

Althusser, L. 2003, *The Humanist Controversy and Other Writings,* Verso, London.

Althusser, L. 1997, *The Spectre of Hegel: Early Writings,* Verso, London.

Althusser, L. 1992, *The Future Lasts Forever: A Memoir,* The New Press, New York.

Althusser, L. 1976a, *Positions (1964–1975),* Sociales, Paris.

Althusser, L. 1976b, "Note on 'The Critique of the Personality Cult'" in *Essays in Self-criticism*. New Left Books, London.

Althusser, L. 1970, *Lenin and Philosophy and Other Essays*, Verso, London.

Anderson, P. 2017, *The H-Word: The Peripeteia of Hegemony*, Verso, London.

Anderson, P. 2000, "Renewals", *New Left Review*, vol. 1, pp. 1–20.

Anderson, P. 1976, "The Antinomies of Antonio Gramsci", *New Left Review*, vol. 1, no. 100.

Arditi, B. 2014, "Post-hegemony: Politics Outside the Usual Post-Marxist Paradigm" in *Radical Democracy and Collective Movements Today: The Biopolitics of the Multitude Versus the Hegemony of the People*, eds. G. Katsambekis & A. Kioupkiolis, Ashgate, London.

Armstrong, S. 2017, *The New Poverty*, Verso, London.

Ashton, T.H. & Philpin, C.H.E. (eds) 1985, *The Brenner Debate: Agrarian Class Structure and Economic Development in Pre-industrial Europe*, Cambridge University Press, Cambridge.

Avineri, S. 1968, *The Social and Political Thought of Karl Marx*, Cambridge University Press, Cambridge.

Badiou, A. 2012, *The Rebirth of History: Times of Riots and Uprisings*, Verso, London.

Badiou, A. 2010, *The Communist Hypothesis*, Verso, London.

Balestrini, N. 2016, *We Want Everything*, Verso, London.

Balibar, E. 2015, "Elements for a Theory of Transition" in *Reading Capital: The Complete Edition*, Verso, London.

Balibar, E. 2014, "Foreword: Althusser and the 'Ideological State Apparatuses'" in *On the Reproduction of Capitalism: Ideology and Ideological State Apparatuses* Verso, London, pp. i–xviii.

Balibar, E. 2007, *The Philosophy of Marx*, Verso, London.

Balibar, E. 1977, *On the Dictatorship of the Proletariat*, New Left Books, London.

Barron, A. 2013, "Free Software Production as Critical Social Practice", *Economy and Society*, vol. 42, no. 4, pp. 597–625.

Bastani, A. 2019, *Fully Automated Luxury Communism: A Manifesto*, Verso, London.

Bastani, A. 2015, 06/12-last update, *We Don't Need More Austerity: We Need Luxury Communism* [Homepage of Vice], [Online]. Available: https://www.vice.com/en_uk/article/ppxpdm/luxury-communism-933 [2019, 05/08].

Baudrillard, J. 1998, *The Consumer Society: Myths and Structures*, Sage, London.

Baudrillard, J. 1981, *For a Critique of the Political Economy of the Sign*, St. Louis, Telos Press.

Baudrillard, J. 1975, *The Mirror of Production*, Telos Press, St. Louis.

Beckert, J. 2016, *Imagined Futures*, Harvard University Press, Cambridge.

Beckett, A. 2017, 05/11-last update, *Accelerationism: how a fringe philosophy predicted the future we live in* [Homepage of The Guardian], [Online]. Available: https://www.theguardian.com/world/2017/may/11/accelerationism-how-a-fringe-philosophy-predicted-the-future-we-live-in [2019, 05/03].

Beecher, J. & Bienvenu, R. 1971, "Introduction" in *The Utopian Vision of Charles Fourier: Selected Texts on Work, Love and Passionate Attraction*, eds. J. Beecher & R. Bienvenu, Beacon Press, Boston.

Behan, T. 2009, *The Italian Resistance: Fascists, Guerrillas and the Allies*, Pluto, London.

Bell, D. 2000, *The End of Ideology: On the Exhaustion of Political Ideas in the Fifties*, Harvard University Press, London.

Benjamin, W. 1999, "The Author as Producer" in *Walter Benjamin: Selected Writings Volume 2, Part 2 1931–1934*, eds. M.W. Jennings, H. Eiland & Gary Smith, Harvard University Press, Cambridge, MA.

Benjamin, W. 1999, *Selected Writings Volume 2 Part 1 1927–1930*, Harvard University Press, Cambridge, MA.

Benjamin, W. 1994, "Left-Wing Melancholy" in *The Weimar Republic Sourcebook*, eds. A. Kaes, M. Jay & E. Dimendberg, University of California Press, Berkeley.

Benjamin, W. 1989, *Reflections: Essays, Aphorisms, Autobiographical Writings*, Schocken Books, New York.

Benjamin, W. 1980, "Conversations with Brecht" in *Aesthetics and Politics*, Verso Editions edn, Verso, London, pp. 86–99.

Benjamin, W. 1968, *Illuminations: Essays and Reflections*, Schocken Books, New York.

Bernstein, E. 2011, *Evolutionary Socialism*, Prism Key, New York.

Bhattacharya, T. 2018, 02/15/2018-last update, *Mapping Social Reproduction Theory* [Homepage of Verso], [Online]. Available: https://www.versobooks.com/blogs/3555-mapping-social-reproduction-theory [2019, 06/28].

Bhattacharya, T. 2017, "Introduction: Mapping Social Reproduction Theory" in *Social Reproduction Theory: Remapping Class, Recentring Oppression*, ed. T. Bhattacharya, Pluto, London, pp. 1–1–20.

Bhattacharya, T. 2015, 10/31/2015-last update, *How Not To Skip Class: Social Reproduction of Labor and the Global Working Class* [Homepage of Viewpoint Magazine], [Online]. Available: https://www.viewpointmag.com/2015/10/31/how-not-to-skip-class-social-reproduction-of-labor-and-the-global-working-class/ [2019, 25/06/2019].

Bloch, E. 1995a, *The Principle of Hope: Volume 1*, MIT Press, Cambridge, MA.

Bloch, E. 1995b, *Principle of Hope: Volume 2*, MIT Press, Cambridge, MA.

Bloch, E. 1990, *Heritage of our Times*, University of California Press, Berkeley.

Bloch, E. 1977, "Nonsynchronism and the Obligation to its Dialectics", *New German Critique*, vol. 11, pp. 22–38.

Bloodworth, J. 2018, *Hired: Six Months Undercover in Low-wage Britain*, Atlantic Books, London.

Boer, R. 2016, "Concerning the 'Warm Stream' within Marxism", *International Critical Thought*, vol. 6, no. 1, pp. 13–28.

Bollinger, S. & Koivisto, J. 2009, "Hegemonic Apparatus", *Historical Materialism,* vol. 17, pp. 301–308.

Bonefeld, W. 2001, *The Politics of Europe: Monetary Union and Class,* Palgrave, London.

Bourdieu, P. 1998, "The Utopia (Becoming Reality) of Unlimited Exploitation" in *Acts of Resistance: Against the New Myths of Our Time,* ed. P. Bourdie, Polity Press, Cambridge.

Bowman, P. 2007, *Post-Marxism versus Cultural Studies,* Edinburgh University Press, Edinburgh.

Brand, U. 2012, "Contradictions and Crises of Neoliberal-imperial Globalization and the Political Opportunity Structures for the Global Justice Movements", *Innovation: The European Journal of Social Science Research,* vol. 25, no. 3, pp. 283–298.

Braverman, H. 1974, *Labor and Monopoly Capital The Degradation of Work in the Twentieth Century,* Monthly Review Press, London.

Bregman, R. 2017, *Utopia for Realists and How We Can Get There,* Bloomsbury, London.

Brenner, R. 1977, "The Origins of Capitalist Development: a Critique of Neo-Smithian Marxism", *New Left Review,* no. 104, pp. 25–93.

Brewster, B. 1972, "Notes on Machines", *Economy and Society,* vol. 1, no. 3, pp. 235–243.

Brewster, B. 1969, "Althusser Glossary" in *For Marx* The Penguin Press, London.

Brody, R. 2012, *The Inadequacy of Berlin's "Memorial to the Murdered Jews of Europe"* [Homepage of The New Yorker], [Online]. Available: https://www.newyorker.com/culture/richard-brody/the-inadequacy-of-berlins-memorial-to-the-murdered-jews-of-europe [2018, 08/25].

Brown, W. 1999, "Resisting Left Melancholy", *boundary 2,* vol. 26, no. 3, pp. 19–27.

Bruno, V.A. & Downes, J.F. 2018, 07/08/2018-last update, *The Electoral Success of the Radical Right in Europe* [Homepage of Public Seminar], [Online]. Available: http://www.publicseminar.org/2018/08/the-electoral-success-of-the-radical-right-in-europe/ [2018, 10/29].

Buber, M. 1949, *Paths in Utopia,* Routledge and Kegan Paul, London.

Butler, J. 2016, "One Time Traverses Another: Benjamin's 'Theological- Political Fragment'" in *Walter Benjamin and Theology,* eds. C. Dickinson & S. Symons, Fordham University Press, New York.

Butler, J. 2015, 12/01/2015-last update, *What's Wrong With 'All Lives Matter'?* [Homepage of The New York Times], [Online]. Available: https://opinionator.blogs.nytimes.com/2015/01/12/whats-wrong-with-all-lives-matter/?_r=0 [2017, 22/09/2017].

Butler, J. 1990, *Gender Trouble: Feminism and the Subversion of Identity,* Routledge, New York.

Butler, P. 2018, 16/09-last update, *New study finds 4.5 million UK children living in poverty* [Homepage of The Guardian], [Online]. Available: https://www.theguardian.com/society/2018/sep/16/new-study-finds-45-million-uk-children-living-in-poverty [2019, 04/20].

Buttigieg, J. 2006, "The Prison Notebooks: Antonio Gramsci's Work in Progress", *Rethinking Marxism*, vol. 18, no. 1, pp. 37–42.

Buxton, N. & Shipman, P. 2018, *Building Post-capitalist Futures*, Transnational Institute, Amsterdam.

Caffentzis, G. 2013, "Why Machines Cannot Create Value: Marx's Theory of Machines" in *In Letters of Blood and Fire: Work, Machines, and the Crisis of Capitalism*, ed. G. Caffentzis, PM Press, Oakland, pp. 139–139–163.

Carey, J. 1999, "Introduction" in *The Faber Book of Utopias*, ed. J. Carey, Faber and Faber, London.

CCRU 2015, *CCRU Writings 1997–2003*, Time Spiral Press, 2015.

Chakelian, A. 2018, 24/09/2018-last update, *"Slaveroo": How riders are standing up to Uber, Deliveroo and the gig economy* [Homepage of New Statesman], [Online]. Available: https://www.newstatesman.com/politics/uk/2018/09/slaveroo-how-riders-are-standing-uber-deliveroo-and-gig-economy [2019, 04/01].

Chakrabortty, A. & Weale, S. 2016, 10/16/2016-last update, *Universities accused of 'importing Sports Direct model' for lecturers' pay* [Homepage of The Guardian], [Online]. Available: https://www.theguardian.com/uk-news/2016/nov/16/universities-accused-of-importing-sports-direct-model-for-lecturers-pay [2019, 04/01].

Chambers, S. 2011, "Untimely Politics avant la lettre: The Temporality of Social Formations", *Time and Society*, vol. 20, no. 2, pp. 197–223.

Chomsky, N. 2012, *Occupy*, Zucotti Park Press, New York.

Claeys, G. 1985, "The Political Ideas of the Young Engels, 1842–1845: Owenism, Chartism and the question of violent revolution in the transition from 'Utopian' to 'Scientific' Socialism", *History of Political Thought*, vol. VI, no. 3, pp. 455–478.

Cohen, G.A. 2013, "Complete Bullshit" in *Finding Oneself in the Other*, ed. M. Otsuka, Princeton, Princeton University Press, pp. 94–94–95.

Cole, G.D.H. 1958, *A History of Socialist Thought 4: Communism and Social Democracy*, MacMillan, London.

Cole, G.D.H. 1935, *Principles of Economic Planning*, Macmillan, London.

Comte, A. 2009, *A General View of Positivism*, Cambridge University Press, Cambridge.

Corlett, A. 2019, *The Living Standards Outlook 2019*, Resolution Foundation, London.

Corlett, A., Clarke, S. & Tomlinson, D. 2017, *The Living Standards Audit 2017*, Resolution Foundation, London.

Credit Suisse 2018, *Research Institute: Global Wealth Databook 2018*, Credit Suisse.

Crehan, K. 2002, *Gramsci, Culture and Anthropology*, Pluto, London.

Critchley, S. & Marchart, O. 2004, "Introduction" in *Laclau: A Critical Reader* Routledge, London.

Crouch, C. 2011, *The Strange Non-death of Neo-liberalism*, Polity, London.

Cutler, A., Hindess, B., Hirst, P. & Hussain, A. 1977, *Marx's Capital and Capitalism Today Volume I*, Routledge & Kegan Paul Ltd., London.

Dadwal, V. 2018, 07/12-last update, *4 reasons cities should embrace Universal Basic Income* [Homepage of World Economic Forum], [Online]. Available: https://www.weforum.org/agenda/2018/07/why-cities-should-embrace-universal-basic-income/ [2019, 06/21].

Dardot, P. & Laval, C. 2013, *The New Way of the World: On Neoliberal Society*, Verso, London.

David, I. & Toktamış, K. 2015, "Gezi in Retrospect" in *'Everywhere Taksim': Sowing the Seeds for a New Turkey at Gezi*, eds. I. David & K. Toktamış, Amsterdam University Press, Amsterdam, pp. 15–24.

Davies, W. 2017, "The Moral Economies of the Future – The Utopian Impulse of Sustainable Prosperity", *Center for the Understanding of Sustainable Prosperity Working Paper No 5*, [Online], pp. 2018–1–23. Available from: http://research.gold.ac.uk/23504/1/WP05-WD-2017-Moral-Economies-of-the-Future.pdf. [01/11/2018].

Davis, A., Hirsch, D. & Padley, M. 2018, *A Minimum Income Standard for the UK 2008–2018*, Joseph Rowntree Foundation, London.

Dawala, S., Jhabvala, R., Standing, G. & Mehta, S.K. 2015, *Basic Income: A Transformative Policy for India*, Bloomsbury, London.

Dawson, M. 2016, *Social Theory for Alternative Societies*, Palgrave, London.

Dean, J. 2016, *Crowds and Party*, Verso, London.

Dean, J. 2014, "Response: The Question of Organization", *South Atlantic Quarterly*, vol. 113, no. 4, pp. 821–835.

Dean, J. 2012, *The Communist Horizon*, Verso, London.

Dean, J. 2005, "Communicative Capitalism: Circulation and the Foreclosure of Politics", *Cultural Politics*, vol. 1, no. 1, pp. 51–74.

Dean, J. & Deseriis, M. 2012, 01/03/2012-last update, *A Movement Without Demands?* [Homepage of Social Science Research Council], [Online]. Available: https://www.possible-futures.org/2012/01/03/a-movement-without-demands/ [2019, 08/08].

Della Porta, D., Fernández, J., Kouki, H. & Mosca, L. 2017, *Movement Parties Against Austerity*, Polity, London.

Desmoulières, R.B. 2017, 06/01/2017-last update, *Chantal Mouffe, the philosopher who inspires Jean-Luc Mélenchon*. Available: https://www.versobooks.com/blogs/3037-chantal-mouffe-the-philosopher-who-inspires-jean-luc-melenchon [2017, 07/21].

Deutscher, I. 1955, *Heretics and Renegades, and Other Essays*, Jonathan Cape, London.

Diefenbach, K. 2006, 01/01/2006-last update, *The Spectral Form of Value: Ghost-Things and Relations of Forces* [Homepage of European Institute for Progressive Cultural Politics], [Online]. Available: http://transform.eipcp.net/transversal/1106/diefenbach/en/print [2019, 06/28].

Douzinas, C. & Zizek, S. 2010, "Introduction" in *The Idea of Communism*, eds. C. Douzinas & S. Zizek, Verso, London.

Duménil, G. & Lévy, D. 2011, *The Crisis of Neoliberalism,* Harvard University Press, Harvard.

Düzenli, F.E. 2016, "Did Marx Fetishize Labor?", *Rethinking Marxism,* vol. 28, no. 2, pp. 204–219.

Duzgun, E. 2019, "The Political Economy of the Transition to Capitalism in the Ottoman Empire and Turkey: Towards a New Interpretation" in *Case Studies in the Origins of Capitalism*, eds. X. Lafrance & C. Post, Palgrave Macmillan, London, pp. 265–290.

Eagleton, T. 1991, *Ideology: An Introduction,* Verso, London.

Eaton, G. 2018, 09/19-last update, *Corbynism 2.0: the radical ideas shaping Labour's future* [Homepage of The New Statesman], [Online]. Available: https://www.newstatesman.com/politics/uk/2018/09/corbynism-20-radical-ideas-shaping-labour-s-future [2019, 04/02].

Eisenman, P. 2018, *Peter Eisenman about the Memorial*. Available: https://www.stiftung-denkmal.de/en/memorials/the-memorial-to-the-murdered-jews-of-europe/peter-eisenman.html [2018, 25/08].

Elliott, G. 1987, *Althusser: The Detour of Theory,* Brill Publishers, Leiden.

Engels, F. 2012, *Socialism: Utopian and Scientific,* Charles H. Kerr & Company, Chicago.

Engels, F. 1987, *The Condition of the Working Class in England,* Penguin, London.

Engels, F. 1987, "Dialectics of Nature" in *Marx-Engels Collected Works* International Publishers, New York.

Engels, F. 1975a, "Speeches in Elberfeld" in *Marx and Engels Collected Works* Lawrence and Wishart, London, pp. 385–387.

Engels, F. 1975b, "Engels to Marx, 17 March 1845" in *Marx and Engels Collected Works* Lawrence and Wishart, London.

Engels, F. 1975c, "The Peasant War in Germany" in *Marx and Engels Collected Works* Lawrence and Wishart, London.

Engels, F. 1959, "Preface" in *Capital Volume III* Progress Publishers, Moscow.

Errejón, Í. 2011, "Política, conflicto y populismo (I): La construcción discursiva de identidades populares", *Viento Sur*, no. 114.

Errejón, Í. & Mouffe, C. 2015, *Construir Pueblo: Hegemonía y Radicalización de la Democracia,* Icaria, Barcelona.

Evans-Prichard, A. 2018, "The Next Downturn Could Rival the Great Depression and Wipe $10 Trillion off US Household Assets", *The Telegraph*, London.

Fay, B. 1981, "Positivist Social Science and Technological Politics" in *Society and the Social Sciences*, ed. D.C. Potter, Routledge and Kegan Paul, London, pp. 425–434.

Fisher, M. 2009, *Capitalist Realism: Is There No Alternative?* Zero Books, London.

Flatley, J. 2008, *Affective Mapping: Melancholia and the Politics of Modernism,* Harvard University Press, Cambridge, MA.

Forgacs, D. 1985, "Dethroning the Working Class?", *Marxism Today*, no. May.

Foucault, M. 2005, *The Order of Things: An Archaeology of the Human Sciences*, Routledge, London.

Foundation Memorial to the Murdered Jews of Europe 2018, *Memorial to the Murdered Jews of Europe with exhibition at the Information Centre*. Available: https://www.stiftung-denkmal.de/en/memorials/the-memorial-to-the-murdered-jews-of-europe.html#c694 [2018, 08/25].

Fourier, C. 1996, "1808 Introduction" in *The Theory of the Four Movements*, eds. I. Patterson & G. Steadman Jones, Cambridge University Press, Cambridge, pp. 3–3–4.

Fourier, C. 1971b, "General Conditions and Descriptions" in *The Utopian Vision of Charles Fourier: Selected Texts on Work, Love, and Passionate Attraction*, eds. J. Beecher & R. Bienvenu, Beacon Press, Boston, pp. 274–274–275.

Fourier, C. 1971a, "The Phalanstery" in *The Utopian Vision of Charles Fourier: Selected Texts on Work, Love, and Passionate Attraction*, eds. J. Beecher & R. Bienvenu, Beacon Press, Boston, pp. 240–240–242.

Fraser, N. 1995, "From Redistribution to Recognition? Dilemmas of Justice in a 'Post-Socialist' Age", *New Left Review*, no. 212.

Frayne, D. 2015, *The Refusal of Work,* Pluto, London.

Freud, S. 1957, "Mourning and Melancholia" in *The Standard Edition of the Complete Psychological Works of Sigmund Freud Volume XIV (1914–1916): On the History of the Psychoanalytic Movement Papers on Metapsychology*, ed. J. Strachey, The Hogarth Press, London, pp. 243–258.

Frosini, F. 2015, "Time and Revolution in Gramsci's 'Prison Notebooks'", *PAST AND PRESENT. Philosophy, Politics, and History in the Thought of Gramsci.* London.

Fuchs, C. 2016, "Henryk Grossmann 2.0: A Critique of Paul Mason's Book 'Postcapitalism: A Guide to Our Future'", *TripleC*, vol. 14, no. 1, pp. 232–243.

Fuchs, C. 2014, *Social Media: A Critical Introduction,* Sage, London.

Fukuyama, F. 1992, *The End of History and the Last Man,* The Free Press, New York.

Fukuyama, F. 1989, "The End of History?", *National Interest*, no. 16.

Gallagher, S. 2019, 04/23-last update, *The Rise Of 'Slashies': How Many People Actually Want To Hold Down Multiple Jobs?* [Homepage of The Huffington Post], [Online]. Available: https://www.huffingtonpost.co.uk/entry/the-rise-of-slashies-are-people-holding-down-multiple-jobs-because-they-want-to-or-have-to_uk_5cbedbd8e4b0f7a84a749495 [2019, 05/29].

Geddes, J.M. 1979, *New Vogue for Critic of Keynes*, The New York Times, New York.

Geoghegan, V. 2008, *Utopianism and Marxism,* Peter Lang, Oxford.

Geras, N. 1987, "Post-Marxism?", *New Left Review*, no. 163.

Geras, N. 1983, *Marx and Human Nature: Refutation of a Legend,* Verso, London.

Gerratana, V. 1977, "Althusser and Stalinism", *New Left Review*, no. 101, pp. 110–121.

Gill, S. 1993, "Epistemology, Ontology and the 'Italian School'" in *Gramsci, Historical Materialism and International Relations*, ed. S. Gill, Cambridge University Press, Cambridge.

Gorz, A. 1982, *Farewell to the Working Class*, Pluto Press, London.

Graeber, D. 2018, *Bullshit Jobs: A Theory*, Simon & Schuster, New York.

Gramsci, A. 2000, *The Gramsci Reader: Selected Writings 1916–1935*, New York University Press, New York.

Gramsci, A. 1987, "Revolution Against 'Capital'" in *Selections from Political Writings: 1910–1920*, ed. Q. Hoare, Lawrence & Wishart, London, pp. 34–37.

Gramsci, A. 1977, "Unions and Councils" in *Selections from Political Writings: 1910–1920*, ed. Q. Hoare, Lawrence and Wishart, London.

Gramsci, A. 1971, *Selections from the Prison Notebooks*, International Publishers, New York.

Gramsci, A. 1968, "Soviets in Italy", *New Left Review*, no. 1.

Gray, J. 2007, *Black Mass: Apocalyptic Religion and the Death of Utopia*, London, Allen Lane.

Gunnel, J.G. 1968, "Social Science and Political Reality: The Problem of Explanation", *Social Research*, vol. 35, no. 1.

Habermas, J. 1970, "Ernst Bloch – A Marxist Romantic", *Salmagundi*, no. 10, pp. 311–325.

Hall, S. & O'Shea, A. 2013, "Common-sense Neoliberalism", *Soundings*, vol. 55, pp. 8–24.

Hall, S., Lumley, R. & McLennan, G. 2006, "Politics and Ideology: Gramsci" in *On Ideology*, ed. Centre for Contemporary Cultural Studies, Routledge, London, pp. 45–76.

Hall, S. 1988, *Hard Road to Renewal*, Verso, London.

Hardt, M. & Negri, A. 2009, *Commonwealth*, Cambridge, Harvard University Press.

Hardt, M. & Negri, A. 2004, *Multitude: War and Democracy in the Age of Empire*, Penguin, New York.

Hardt, M. & Negri, A. 2000, *Empire*, Harvard University Press, Cambridge.

Harnecker, M. 1994, "Althusser and the 'Theoretical Antihumanism' of Marx", *Nature, Society and Thought: A Journal of Dialectical and Historical Materialism*, vol. 7, no. 3, pp. 325–342.

Hartsock, N. 1983, *Money, Sex and Power: Toward a Feminist Historical Materialism*. Northeastern University Press, Boston.

Harvey, D. 2015, 01/10-last update, *Listen, Anarchist! A personal response to Simon Springer's "Why a radical geography must be anarchist"*. Available: http://davidharvey.org/2015/06/listen-anarchist-by-david-harvey/ [2019, 08/07].

Harvey, D. 2005, *A Brief History of Neoliberalism*, Oxford University Press, Oxford.

Harvey, D. 2000, *Spaces of Hope*, Edinburgh University Press, Edinburgh.

Hatherley, O. 2016, 06/30/2016-last update, *One Click at a Time* [Homepage of London Review of Books], [Online]. Available: https://www.lrb.co.uk/v38/n13/owen-hatherley/one-click-at-a-time [2019, 07/06].

Hawkins, K. 2009, "Is Chávez Populist? Measuring Populist Discourse in Comparative Perspective", *Comparative Political Studies,* vol. 42, no. 8.

Henderson, W.O. 1976, *The Life of Friedrich Engels,* Frank Cass, London.

Hertz, R. 1960, *Death and the Right Hand,* Glencoe, New York.

Hindess, B. & Hirst, P. 1977, *Mode of Production and Social Formation: An Auto-Critique of Pre-Capitalist Modes of Production*, Macmillan Press, London.Hinton, R.H. (ed) 1978, *The Transition from Feudalism to Capitalism*, Verso, London.Hoare, Q. & Smith, G.N. 1971, "Introduction" in *Selections from the Prison Notebooks* International Publishers, New York.

Hobsbawm, E. 2012, "Introduction" in *The Communist Manifesto*, A Modern Edition edn, Verso, London, pp. 5–30.

Hobsbawm, E. 1997, *On History,* The New Press, New York.

Hobsbawm, E. 1994, *The Age of Extremes: The Short Twentieth Century, 1914–1991,* Michael Joseph, London.

Hobsbawm, E. 1964, "Introduction" in *Pre-Capitalist Economic Formations*, ed. K. Marx, International Publishers, New York.

Holloway, J. 2002, *Change the World without Taking Power: The Meaning of Revolution Today,* Pluto Press, London.

Howarth, D. 2015, "Discourse, Hegemony and Populism: Ernesto Laclau's Critical Theory" in *Ernesto Laclau: Post-Marxism, Populism, and Critique*, ed. D. Howarth, Routledge, London.

Huws, U., Spencer, N., Syrdal, D.S. & Holts, K. 2018, "Working in the Gig Economy: Insights from Europe" in *Working in the Digital Age* Rowman & Littlefield International, London, pp. 153–162.

Iglesias, P. 2014, *The Left Can Win* [Homepage of Jacobin], [Online]. Available: https://www.jacobinmag.com/2014/12/pablo-iglesias-podemos-left-speech/ [2017, 07/21].

Institute for Global Prosperity 2017, *Social prosperity for the future: A proposal for Universal Basic Services*, University College London, London.

ITUC 2019, *ITUC Global Rights Index 2019*, International Trade Union Confederation.

Jablonka, F. 1998, "War Gramsci ein Poststrukturalist 'avant la lettre'? (Zum 'linguistic turn' bei Gramsci)" in *Gramsci-Perspektiven*, ed. U. Hirschfeld, Argument, Berlin-Hamburg.

Jameson, F. 1996, "Walter Benjamin" in *London Review of Books: An Anthology*, ed. J. Hindle, Verso, London.

Jay, M. 1999, "Against Consolation: Walter Benjamin and the Refusal to Mourn" in *War and Remembrance in the Twentieth Century*, eds. J. Winter & E. Sivan, Cambridge University Press, Cambridge.

Jefferies, B. 2019, 11/06/2019-last update, *Fully Automated Luxury Communism: A Manifesto* [Homepage of Marx and Philosophy Review of Books], [Online]. Available: https://marxandphilosophy.org.uk/reviews/17006_fully-automated-luxury-communism-a-manifesto-by-aaron-bastani-reviewed-by-bill-jefferies/ [2019, 06/21].

Jeffries, S. 2011, *Did Stalin's Killers Liquidate Walter Benjamin?*, Guardian, London.

Jessop, B. 1982, *The Capitalist State: Marxist Theories and Methods*, Martin Robinson, Oxford.

Johnson, P. 2012, *Some reflections on the relationship between utopia and heterotopia* [Homepage of Heterotopian Studies], [Online]. Available: http://www.heterotopiastudies.com/wp-content/uploads/2012/05/Reflections-on-the-relationship-between-utopia-and-heterotopia.pdf [2018, 01/11].

Kerr, C., Dunlop, J.T., Harbison, F.H. & Myers, C.A. 1960, *Industrialism and Industrial Man: The Problem of Labor and Management in Economic Growth*, Harvard University Press, Cambridge.

Keucheyan, R. 2013, *The Left Hemisphere: Mapping Critical Theory Today*, Verso, London.

Kilcoyne, M. 2018, 19/01/2018-last update, *Rising Evidence for Universal Basic Income* [Homepage of Adam Smith Institute], [Online]. Available: https://www.adamsmith.org/news/rising-evidence-basic-income [2019, 05/08].

Kolakowski, L. 1971, "Althusser's Marx", *Socialist Register*, vol. 8, pp. 111–128.

Kouvelakis, S. 2019, 06/11-last update, *Syriza's Failure Has Hurt Us All* [Homepage of Jacobin], [Online]. Available: https://www.jacobinmag.com/2019/06/syriza-greece-elections-tsipras-varoufakis [2019, 09/20].

Kouvelakis, S. 2015, 01/22/2015-last update, *Greece: Phase One* [Homepage of Jacobin], [Online]. Available: https://www.jacobinmag.com/2015/01/phase-one/ [2019, 08/08].

Kristal, T. 2010, "Good Times, Bad Times: Postwar Labor's Share of National Income in Capitalist Democracies", *American Sociological Review*, vol. 75, no. 5, pp. 729–763.

Kuymulu, M.B. 2018, "Confronting 'Aggressive Urbanism': Frictional Heterogeneity in the 'Gezi Protests' in Turkey" in *Worldwide Mobilisations: Class Struggles and Urban Commoning*, eds. D. Kalb & M. Mollona, Barghahn, London, pp. 31–51.

Laclau, E. 2014, "The Impossibility of Society" in *The Discourse Studies Reader: Main Currents in Theory and Analysis*, eds. J. Angermuller, D. Maingueneau & R. Wodak, John Benjamins Publishing Company, Amsterdam.

Laclau, E. 2006, "Ideology and Post-Marxism", *Journal of Political Ideologies*, vol. 11, no. 2, pp. 103–114.

Laclau, E. 2005, *On Populist Reason*, Verson, London.

Laclau, E. 1977, *Politics and Ideology in Marxist Theory: Capitalism, Fascism, Populism*, New Left Books, London.

Laclau, E. & Mouffe, C. 1990, "Post-Marxism without Apologies" in *New Reflections on the Revolution of our Time*, ed. E. Laclau, Verso, London, pp. 97–134.

Laclau, E. & Mouffe, C. 1985, *Hegemony and Socialist Strategy: Towards a Radical Democratic Politics*, Verso, London.

Land, N. 2018, *Fanged Noumena: Collected Writings 1987–2007*, Urbanomic, Falmouth.

Land, N. 2017, 05/25-last update, *A Quick-and-Dirty Introduction to Accelerationism* [Homepage of Jacobite], [Online]. Available: https://jacobitemag.com/2017/05/25/a-quick-and-dirty-introduction-to-accelerationism/ [2019, 05/07].

Land, N. 2014, *Templexity: Disordered Loops through Shanghai Time*, Urbanatomy.

Land, N. 2010, *Shanghai Expo Guide 2010*, Urbanatomy.

Lansley, S. & Reed, H. 2019, *Basic Income for All: From Desirability to Feasibility*, Compass, London.

Lefebvre, H. 2009, "Theoretical Problems of Autogestion" in *Henri Lefebvre: State, Space, World Selected Essays*, eds. N. Brenner & S. Elden, University of Minnesota Press, Minnesota, pp. 138–152.

Le Guin, U. 1999, *The Dispossessed*, SF Masterworks edn, Orion, London.

Leggett, W. 2017, *Politics and Social Theory: The Inescapably Social, the Irreducibly Political*, Palgrave, London.

Leggett, W. 2013, "Restoring Society to Post-structuralist Politics: Mouffe, Gramsci and Radical Democracy", *Philosophy and Social Criticism*, vol. 39, no. 3, pp. 299–315.

Lenin, V.I. 1977, "The Three Sources and Three Component Parts of Marxism" in *Collected Works Volume 19* Progress Publishers, Moscow, pp. 21–28.

Lenin, V.I. 1976, *Collected Works: Volume 38*, Progress Publishers, Moscow.

Lenin, V.I. 1974, "Left-wing Communism: An Infantile Disorder" in *Lenin Collected Works: Volume 31*, ed. J. Katzer, Progress Publishers, Moscow, pp. 17–104.

Lenin, V.I. 1972, "The Taylor System – Man's Enslavement by the Machine" in *Lenin Collected Works: Volume 20* Progress Publishers, Moscow, pp. 152–154.

Lenin, V.I. 1971, "Immediate Tasks of the Soviet Government', 28 April 1918" in *Selected Works, One-Volume ed.* Lawrence and Wishart, London.

Lenin, V.I. 1966, *'Left-Wing' Communism: An Infantile Disorder*, Progress Publishers, Moscow.

Lenin, V.I. 1960, "What is to be Done: Burning Questions of our Movement" in *Collected Works: Volume 5* Progress Publishers, Moscow.

Levitas, R. 2013, *Utopia as Method: The Imaginary Reconstitution of Society*, Palgrave, London.

Levitas, R. 2010, "In Eine Bess're Welt Entruckt: reflections on Music and Utopia", *Utopian Studies*, vol. 21, no. 2, pp. 215–231.

Levitas, R. 2007, "Looking for the Blue: The Necessity of Utopia", *Journal of Political Ideologies*, vol. 12, no. 3, pp. 289–306.

Levitas, R. 2005, *Imaginary Reconstitution of Society, or Why Sociologists and Others Should Take Utopia more Seriously.* Available: http://www.bristol.ac.uk/media-library/sites/spais/migrated/documents/inaugural.pdf?_ga=2.103851584.1767444649.1547403745-835728908.1547403745 [2018, 01/13].

Levitas, R. 1990, *The Concept of Utopia,* Peter Lang, Oxford.

Lewis, K. & Stronge, W. 2018, 01/19/2018-last update, *A right-wing think tank is now supporting Universal Basic Income – but they've missed the point* [Homepage of The Independent],[Online].Available:https://www.independent.co.uk/voices/universal-basic-income-adam-smith-institute-austerity-libertarian-a8167701.html [2019, 05/08].

Lind, M. 1997, *Up From Conservatism: Why the Right is Wrong for America,* Simon & Schuster, New York.

Lotringer, S. & Marazzi, C. (eds) 1980, *Autonomia: Post-Political Politics,* semiotext(e), Los Angeles.

Lovell, D. 2004, "Marx's Utopian Legacy", *The European Legacy,* vol. 9, no. 5, pp. 629–640.

Löwy, M. 2005, *Fire Alarm: Reading Walter Benjamin's 'On the Concept of History',* Verso, London.

Luxembourg, R. 2008, "Reform or Revolution" in *The Essential Rosa Luxembourg: Reform or Revolution and The Mass Strike,* ed. H. Scott, Haymarket Books, Chicago, pp. 41–104.

MacDougald, P. 2016, 04/14/2016-last update, *Accelerationism, Left and Right.* Available: https://pmacdougald.wordpress.com/2016/04/14/accelerationism-left-and-right/ [2019, 05/07].

Mackay, R. 2012, "Nick Land – An Experiment in Inhumanism", *Umělec Magazine,* no. 1.

Marcuse, H. 1974, *Eros and Civilisation: A Philosophical Inquiry into Freud,* Beacon Press, Boston.

Marcuse, H. 1970, "The End of Utopia" in *Five Lectures* Beacon Press, Boston, pp. 62–82.

Marx, K. 2009, *The Eighteenth Brumaire of Louis Napoleon,* Dodo Press, Gloucester.

Marx, K. 1990, *Capital: A Critique of Political Economy,* Penguin, London.

Marx, K. 1978, "Theses on Feuerbach" in *The Marx-Engels Reader,* ed. R.C. Tucker, Second Edition edn, W.W. Norton & Company, New York, pp. 143–145.

Marx, K. 1975a, "Letter from Marx to Pavel Vasilyevich Annenkov" in *Marx-Engels Collected Works Vol. 38* International Publishers, New York, p. 95.

Marx, K. 1975b, "A Contribution to the Critique of Hegel's Philosophy of Right" in *Early Writings* Penguin, London, pp. 243–259.

Marx, K. 1975c, "Notes on Adolph Wagner" in *Karl Marx: Texts on Method,* ed. T. Carver, Basil Blackwell, Oxford, p. 190.

Marx, K. 1974, "Critique of Hegel's Doctrine of the State" in *Early Writings* Penguin, London, pp. 57–198.

Marx, K. 1973, *Grundrisse: Foundations of the Critique of Political Economy (Rough Draft)*, Penguin Books, London.

Marx, K. 1940, *The Civil War in France,* International Publishers, New York.

Marx, K. 1959, *Economic and Philosophical Manuscripts of 1844,* Progress Publishers, Moscow.

Marx, K. 1962, *The Poverty of Philosophy: Answer to the "Philosophy of Poverty" by M. Proudhon,* Foreign Languages Publishing House, Moscow.

Marx, K. 1964, *Pre-capitalist Economic Formations,* International Publishers, New York.

Marx, K. 1968, *A Critique of The German Ideology,* Progress Publishers, Moscow.

Marx, K. 1972a, *The Eighteenth Bruimaire of Louis Bonaparte,* Progress Publishers, Moscow.

Marx, K. 1972b, *Critique of the Gotha Programme,* Foreign Languages Press, Beijing.

Marx, K. & Engels, F. 2012, *The Communist Manifesto,* A Modern Edition edn, Verso, London.

Marzani, C. 1957, "Antonio Gramsci" in *The Open Marxism of Antonio Gramsci* Cameron Associates, Inc., New York.

Mason, P. 2015, *Postcapitalism: A Guide to our Future,* Penguin, London.

Mazzucato, M. 2013, *The Entrepreneurial State: Debunking Public vs. Private Sector Myths,* Anthem, London.

McCarney, J. 1990, *Social Theory and the Crisis of Marxism,* Verso, London.

McDonnell, J. (ed) 2018, *Economics for the Many,* Verso, London.

McLellan, D. 1969, "Marx's View of the Unalienated Society", *The Review of Politics,* vol. 31, no. 4, pp. 459–465.

McNally, D. 2017, "Intersections and Dialectics: Critical Reconstructions in Social Reproduction Theory" in *Social Reproduction Theory: Remapping Class, Recentring Oppression,* ed. T. Bhattacharya, Pluto, London, pp. 94–111.

Medina, E. 2011, *Cybernetic Revolutionaries: Technology and Politics in Allende's Chile,* MIT Press, Cambridge.

Meriç, C. 1995, *Saint-Simon: İlk Sosyolog İlk Sosyalist,* İletişim, Istanbul.

Mirowski, P. 2013, *Never Let a Serious Crisis Go To Waste: How Neoliberalism Survived the Financial Meltdown,* Verso, London.

Molina, V. 1977, "Notes on Marx and the Problem of Individuality" in *On Ideology,* ed. Center for Contemporary Cultural Studies, Routledge, London.

Monbiot, G. 2016, 15/04/2016-last update, *Neoliberalism – the ideology at the root of all our problems* [Homepage of The Guardian], [Online]. Available: https://www.theguardian.com/books/2016/apr/15/neoliberalism-ideology-problem-george-monbiot [2018, 10/21].

Monticelli, L. 2018, "Embodying Alternatives to Capitalism in the 21st Century", TripleC, vol. 16, no. 2, pp. 501–517.

More, T. 2016, *Utopia,* Verso, London.

Mosès, S. 1989, "The Theological-Political Model of History in the Thought of Walter Benjamin", *History and Memory*, vol. 1, no. 2, pp. 5–33.
Mouffe, C. 2005, *On the Political*, Routledge, London.
Mouffe, C. 2018, 04/21-last update, *Corbyn represents the implementation of a left populist strategy* [Homepage of The New Pretender], [Online]. Available: http://newpretender.com/2018/04/21/chantal-mouffe-corbyn-represents-left-populist-strategy/ [2019, 07/08].
Mouzelis, N. 1978, "Ideology and Class Politics: A Critique of Ernesto Laclau", *New Left Review*, no. 112.
Mumford, L. 1922, *The Story of Utopias*, Boni and Liveright, New York.
Negri, A. 2002, "Approximations towards an Ontological Definition of the Multitude", *Multitudes*, vol. 9, pp. 36–48.
Negri, A. 1991, *Marx Beyond Marx – Lessons on the Grundrisse*, Autonomedia, New York.
Nelson, C. & Grossberg, L. (eds) 1988, *Marxism and the Interpretation of Culture*, Macmillan, Houndmills.
Nicolaus, M. 1973, "Foreword" in *Grundrisse: Foundations of the Critique of Political Economy (Rough Draft)*, Penguin, London.
Novara Media 2014, 11/10-last update, *Fully Automated Luxury Communism!*. Available: https://www.youtube.com/watch?v=dmQ-BZ3eWxM [2019, 21/06].
Noys, B. 2010, *The Persistence of the Negative: A Critique of Contemporary Continental Theory* (Edinburgh: Edinburgh University Press, Edinburgh).
Noys, B. 2014, *Malign Velocities: Capitalism and Accelerationism*, Zero Books, London.
Ollman, B. 1971, *Alienation: Marx's Conception of Man in Capitalist Society*, 2nd edn, Cambridge University Press, London.
Ollman, B. 1977, "Marx's Vision of Communism: A Reconstruction", *Critique: Journal of Socialist Theory*, vol. 8, no. 1, pp. 4–41.
Ostry, J.D., Loungani, P. & Furceri, D. 2016, "Neoliberalism: Oversold?", *IMF Finance and Development*, vol. 53, no.2, pp. 38–41.
Özselçuk, C. 2006, "Mourning, Melancholy, and the Politics of Class Transformation", *Rethinking Marxism*, vol. 18, no. 2, pp. 225–240.
Pansa, G. 1980, "Fiat Has Branded Me" in *Autonomia: Post-political Politics*, eds. S. Lotringer & C. Marazzi, semiotext(e), Los Angeles, pp. 24–28.
Pateman, C. 2004, "Democratising Citizenship: Some Advantages of a Basic Income", *Politics and Society*, vol. 32, no. 1, pp. 89–105.
Peck, J. 2010, *Constructions of Neoliberal Reason*, Oxford University Press, Oxford.
Petri, E. 1971, *The Working Class Goes to Heaven*, New Line Cinema, Novara.
Pfaller, R. 2015, "Althusser's Best Tricks", *Crisis and Critique*, vol. 2, no. 2, pp. 25–45.
Pilling, G. 1972, "The Law of Value in Ricardo and Marx", *Economy and Society*, vol. 1, no. 3, pp. 281–307.

Pipes, R. 1990, *The Russian Revolution: 1899–1919*, Collins Harvill, London.
Pitts, F.H. 2017, "Beyond the Fragment: Postoperaismo, Postcapitalism and Marx's 'Notes on machines', 45 Years On", *Economy and Society*, vol. 46, no. 3–4, pp. 1–22.
Pitts, F.H. 2018, "A crisis of measurability? Critiquing post-operaismo on labour, value and the basic income", *Capital & Class*, vol. 42, no. 1, pp. 3–21.
Pitts, F.H. & Dinerstein, A.C. 2017a, "Corbynism's conveyor belt of ideas: Postcapitalism and the politics of social reproduction", *Capital & Class*, vol. 41, no. 3, pp. 423–434.
Pitts, F.H. & Dinerstein, A.C. 2017b, *Postcapitalism, Basic Income and the End of Work: A Critique and Alternative*, Centre for Development Studies University of Bath, Bath.
Pitts, F.H., & Dinerstein, A.C. 2018, "From post-work to post-capitalism? Discussing the basic income and struggles for alternative forms of social reproduction", *Journal of Labour and Society*, vol. 21, pp. 471–491.
Plehwe, D., Walpen, B. & Neunhöffer, G. (eds) 2006, *Neoliberal Hegemony: A Global Critique. London and New York: Routledge.*, Routledge, London.
Popper, K. 1947, *The Open Society and Its Enemies*, Routledge, London.
Popper, K. 1948, "Utopia and Violence", *Hibbert Journal*, no. 46.
Popper, K. 2002, *Conjectures and Refutations: The Growth of Scientific Knowledge.* Routledge, London.
Poulantzas, N. 1975, *Classes in Contemporary Capitalism*, New Left Books, London.
Press Association 2019, 05/12-last update, *Labour would trial universal basic income if elected, John McDonnell says* [Homepage of The Guardian], [Online]. Available: https://www.theguardian.com/society/2019/may/12/labour-would-trial-universal-basic-income-if-elected-john-mcdonnell-says [2019, 08/02].
Rabinbach, A. 1977, "Unclaimed Heritage: Ernst Bloch's Heritage of Our Times and the Theory of Fascism", *New German Critique*, no. 11, pp. 5–21.
Rahnema, S. (ed) 2017, *The Transition from Capitalism: Marxist Perspectives*, Palgrave, London.
Riley, B. 2016, 02/29/2016-last update, *Boots Riley – How Capitalism Needed Racism To Operate (247HH Exclusive)*. Available: https://www.youtube.com/watch?v=Jmy WvjszBOw [2019, 04/23].
Russell, B. 1918, *Proposed Roads to Freedom*, Blue Ribbon Books, New York.
Russell, B. 1945, *History of Western Philosophy and Its Connection with Political and Social Circumstances from the Earliest Times to the Present Day*, Simon and Schuster, New York.
Rustin, M. 1988, "Review: Absolute Voluntarism: Critique of a Post-Marxist Concept of Hegemony", *New German Critique*, no. 43.
Sabbagh, D. 2018, 10/09-last update, *John McDonnell shapes Labour case for four-day week* [Homepage of The Guardian], [Online]. Available: https://www.theguardian.com/politics/2018/nov/09/john-mcdonnell-shapes-labour-case-for-four-day-week [2019, 04/02].

Saint-Simon, H.d. 1976, "Letters from an Inhabitant of Geneva to His Contemporaries" in *The Political Thought of Saint-Simon*, ed. G. Ionescu, Oxford University Press, London.

Sancar, N. 2013, *Sıcak Haziran*, Evrensel, İstanbul.

Sargent, L.T. 2010, *Utopianism: A Very Short Introduction*, Oxford University Press, Oxford.

Sassoon, A.S. 1987, *Gramsci's Politics*, Minnesota University Press, Minneapolis.

Schäfer, A. 2013, "Liberalization, Inequality and Democracy's Discontent" in *Politics in the Age of Austerity*, eds. A. Schäfer & W. Streeck, Polity, London, pp. 169–195.

Schecter, D. 2007, *The History of the Left from Marx to the Present: Theoretical Perspectives*, Continuum, London.

Schecter, D. 2010, "Gramsci's Unorthodox Marxism: Political Ambiguity and Sociological Relevance", Modern Italy, no. 15.

Scheppele, K.L. 2012, "Liberalism Against Neoliberalism: Resistance to Structural Adjustment and the Fragmentation of the State in Russia and Hungary" in *Ethnographies of Neoliberalism*, ed. C.J. Greenhouse, University of Pennsylvania Press, Philadelphia.

Sennett, R. 2006, *The Culture of New Capitalism*, Yale University Press, New Haven.

Shanin, T. 1983, *Late Marx and the Russian Road: Marx and the 'Peripheries of Capitalism'*, Monthly Review Press, New York.

Shaviro, S. 2015, *No Speed Limit: Three Essays on Accelerationism*, University of Minnesota Press, Minneapolis.

Smith, H. 2013, 05/01/2013-last update, *Golden Dawn food rally raises tensions in Athens* [Homepage of The Guardian], [Online]. Available: https://www.theguardian.com/world/2013/may/01/golden-dawn-food-rally-athens [2019, 06/30].

Smith, N. 2009, "The Revolutionary Imperative", *Antipode*, vol. 41, no. 1, pp. 50–65.

Smith, T. 1990, "The Critique of Marxism in Baudrillard's Later Writings", *Rethinking Marxism*, vol. 3, no. 3–4, pp. 275–286.

Sochor, Z. 1981, "Soviet Taylorism Revisited", *Soviet Studies*, vol. XXXIII, no. 2, pp. 246–264.

Sorel, G. 1999, *Reflections on Violence*, Cambridge University Press, Cambridge.

Spanos, W.V. 2006, "Cuvier's Little Bone: Joseph Buttigieg's English edition of Antonio Gramsci's *Prison Notebooks*", *Rethinking Marxism*, vol. 18, no. 1, pp. 23–36.

Spivak, G.C. 2000, "From Haverstock Hill Flat to U.S. Classroom, What's Left of Theory?" in *What's Left of Theory? New Work on the Politics of Literary Theory*, ed. J. Butler, Routledge, New York, pp. 1–39.

Spourdalakis, A., Pitsili-Chatzi, D., Panitch, L., Wainwright, H. & Dean, J. 2019, 01/16-last update, *New Democracy Against Democracy* [Homepage of Jacobin], [Online]. Available: https://jacobinmag.com/2019/01/syriza-new-democracy-greece-far-right [2019, 08/08].

Srnicek, N. & Williams, A. 2014, "#Accelerate: Manifesto for an Accelerationist Politics" in *#Accelerate: The Accelerationist Reader*, eds. R. Mackay & A. Avenassian, Urbanomic, Falmouth.

Srnicek, N. & Williams, A. 2015, *Inventing the Future: Postcapitalism and a World Without Work*, Verso, London.

Srnicek, N. 2017a, 08/15-last update, *Would you support the introduction of a Universal Basic Income? If so, how should it be implemented?* [Homepage of Autonomy], [Online]. Available: http://autonomy.work/portfolio/3-support-introduction-universal-basic-income-dr-nick-srnicek/ [2019, 05/08].

Srnicek, N. 2017b, *Platform Capitalism,* Polity, London.

Srnicek, N. 2018, "Platform Monopolies and the Political Economy of AI" in *Economics for the Many*, ed. J. McDonnell, Verso, London, pp. 152–163.

Standing, G. 2011, *The Precariat: The New Dangerous Class,* Bloomsbury, London.

Standing, G. 2014, 01/18-last update, *Basic income paid to the poor can transform lives* [Homepage of The Guardian], [Online]. Available: https://www.theguardian.com/business/economics-blog/2014/dec/18/incomes-scheme-transforms-lives-poor [2019, 05/08].

Standing, G. 2019, *Basic Income as Common Dividends: Piloting a Transformative Policy*, Progressive Economy Forum, London.

Steadman Jones, G. & Patterson, I. 1996, "Introduction" in *The Theory of Four Movements*, ed. C. Fourier, Cambridge University Press, Cambridge, pp. vii–xxvi.

Streeck, W. 2011, "The Crises of Democratic Capitalism", *New Left Review*, no. 71, pp. 5–29.

Stronge, W. 2019, 02/01-last update, *Work isn't working – but a four-day week would help fix it* [Homepage of The Guardian], [Online]. Available: https://www.theguardian.com/commentisfree/2019/feb/01/work-four-day-week-workloads-stress-economy [2019, 04/02].

Stronge, W. & Hester, H. forthcoming, "Towards Post-Work Studies: Identifying Misconceptions in an Emerging Field", *Political Quarterly.*

Syal, R. 2018, 05/01/2018-last update, *'McStrike': McDonald's workers walk out over zero-hours contracts* [Homepage of The Guardian], [Online]. Available: https://www.theguardian.com/business/2018/may/01/mcstrike-mcdonalds-workers-walk-out-over-zero-hours-contracts [2019, 04/01].

Szymanski, A. 1984, *Human Rights in the Soviet Union,* Zed Books, London.

Talmon, J.L. 1952, *The Origins of Totalitarian Democracy,* Sphere, London.

The Economist 2017, 02/02/2017-last update, *Bonfire of the subsidies: India debates the case for a universal basic income.* Available: https://www.economist.com/leaders/2017/02/02/india-debates-the-case-for-a-universal-basic-income [2019, 06/30].

Thomas, P.D. 2009, *The Gramscian Moment: Philosophy, Hegemony, and Marxism,* Brill,Leiden.

Thomas, P.D. 2012, "Althusser's Last Encounter: Gramsci" in *Encountering Althusser Politics and Materialism in Contemporary Radical Thought*, eds. K. Diefenbach, S.R. Farris, G. Kirn & P.D. Thomas, Bloomsbury, London, pp. 137–151.

Thompson, E.P. 1978, *The Poverty of Theory and Other Essays*, Merlin Press, London.

Thompson, E.P. 1980, *The Making of the English Working Class*, Penguin, London.

Thompson, E.P. 2000, *The Poverty of Theory: or an Orrery of Errors*, Verso, London.

Thompson, P. 2013, 04/29/2013-last update, *The Frankfurt school, part 6: Ernst Bloch and the Principle of Hope* [Homepage of The Guardian], [Online]. Available: https://www.theguardian.com/commentisfree/belief/2013/apr/29/frankfurt-school-ernst-bloch-principle-of-hope [2018, 12/17].

Timur, T. 2007, *Marksizm, İnsan ve Toplum: Balibar, Sève, Althusser, Bourdieu*, Yordam, İstanbul.

Torfing, J. 1999, *New Theories of Discourse: Laclau, Mouffe and Zizek*, Wiley & Blackwell, Hoboken, NJ.

Toscano, A. 2013, "Transition Deprogrammed", *South Atlantic Quarterly*, vol. 113, no. 4, pp. 761-775.

Toscano, A. 2014, "Reformism and Melancholia: Economic Crisis and the Limits of Sociology", *Sociology*, vol. 48, no. 5, pp. 1024–1038.

Tosel, A. 2008, "The Development of Marxism: From the End of Marxism-Leninism to a Thousand Marxisms – France-Italy, 1975–2005" in *Critical Companion to Contemporary Marxism*, eds. J. Bidet & E. Kouvelakis, Brill, Leiden, pp. 39–78.

Traverso, E. 2016, *Left-Wing Melancholia: Marxism, History and Memory*, Columbia University Press, New York.

Tronti, M. 1971, *Operai e capitale,* 2nd edn. Einaudi, Turin.

Trotsky, L. 1969, *The Permanent Revolution and Results and Prospects,* Pathfinder Press, New York.

Trotsky, L. 1977, *The History of the Russian Revolution,* Pluto, London.

Tucker, R.C. 1972, *Philosophy and Myth in Karl Marx,* Second Edition edn, Cambridge University Press, Cambridge.

Turan, Ö. 2013, "Gezi Parkı Direnişi ve Armağan Dünyası", *Toplumsal Tarih*, vol. 238, pp. 62–73.

Turchetto, M. 2008, "From 'Mass Worker' to 'Empire': The Disconcerting Trajectory of Italian Operaismo" in *Critical Companion to Contemporary Marxism*, eds. J. Bidet & E. Kouvelakis, Brill, Leiden, pp. 285–308.

Turner, F. 2018, 07/31/2018-last update, *Fred Turner: Silicon Valley Thinks Politics Doesn't Exist* [Homepage of 032c], [Online]. Available: https://032c.com/fred-turner-silicon-valley-thinks-politics-doesnt-exist [2018, 05/04].

Uetricht, M. 2019, 30/01/2019-last update, *The Beginning of the End of Capitalist Realism* [Homepage of Jacobin], [Online]. Available: https://www.jacobinmag.com/2019/01/capitalist-realism-mark-fisher-k-punk-depression [2019, 02/05].

Valdivielso, J. 2017, "The Outraged People: Laclau, Mouffe and the Podemos hypothesis", *Constellations,* vol. 24, no. 3, pp. 296–309.
Vasina, L. & Vasin, Y. 1988, "Historical Background to Marx's Critique of the Gotha Programme" in *Marx's 'Critique of the Gotha Programme',* eds. L. Vasina & Y. Vasin, Progress Publishers, Moscow, pp. 5–22.
Virno, P. 1990, "Citazioni di fronte al pericolo", *Luogo commune,* vol. 1, pp. 9–13.
Virno, P. & Hardt, M. 1996, "Glossary of Concepts" in *Radical Thought in Italy: A Potential Politics,* eds. P. Virno & M. Hardt, University of Minnesota Press, Minneapolis, pp. 260–264.
Virno, P. 2001, "General Intellect" in *Lessico Postfordista: Dizionario di idee della mutazione,* eds. U. Fadini & A. Zanini, Feltrinelli, Milan.
Weber, M. 1958, *From Max Weber: Essays in Sociology,* Oxford University Press, Oxford.
Weeks, K. 2011, *The Problem with Work: Feminism, Marxism, Antiwork Politics, and Postwork Imaginaries,* Duke University Press, Durham.
Widerquist, K. 2018, *A Critical Analysis of Basic Income Experiments for Researchers, Policymakers, and Citizens,* Palgrave, London.
Williams, A. 2013, "Escape Velocities", *e-flux,* no. 46.
Wolff, R.P. 1988, *Moneybags Must Be So Lucky: On the Literary Structure of Capital,* University of Massachusetts Press, Amhurst.
Wood, E.M. 1986, *The Retreat from Class: A New True Socialism,* Verso, London.
Wood, E.M. 2002, *The Origin of Capitalism: A Longer View,* Verso, London.
Wood, E.M. 2016, "The separation of the 'economic' and the 'political' in capitalism" in *Democracy Against Capitalism: Renewing Historical Materialism* Verso, London, p. 20.
Wright, E.O. 1985, *Classes,* Verso, London.
Wright, E.O. 1989, *The Debate on Classes,* Verso, London.
Wright, E.O. 2004, "Basic Income, Stakeholder Grants and Class Analysis", *Politics and Society,* vol. 32, no. 1, pp. 79–87.
Wright, E.O. 2010, *Envisioning Real Utopias,* Verso, London.
Wright, E.O. 2012, "Transforming Capitalism through Real Utopias", *American Sociological Review,* vol. 78, no. 1, pp. 1–12.
Wright, S. 2002, *Storming Heaven Class Composition and Struggle in Italian Autonomist Marxism,* Pluto Press, London.
Yıldırım, B. 2014, *Sanki Devrim: Bir Devrim Gezi'sinden Notlar,* Notabene, İstanbul.
Žižek, S. 2000, "Melancholy and the Act", *Critical Inquiry,* vol. 26, no. 4, pp. 657–681.
Žižek, S. 2006, "Against the Populist Temptation", *Critical Inquiry,* vol. 32, no. 3, pp. 551–574.

Žižek, S. 2008, *In Defense of Lost Causes,* Verso, London.
Žižek, S. 2010, *Living in the End Times,* Verso, London.
Žižek, S. 2017, "Introduction: Remembering, Repeating, and Working Through" in *Lenin 2017: Remembering, Repeating, and Working Through,* ed. S. Zizek, Verso, London, pp. 8–56.

Index

2008 financial crash   90, 103, 108, 199

accelerationism   9, 145–148
alienation   21–25, 140
Althusser, Louis   14, 29, 62, 70–71, 145, 168, 177, 187
   'Althusser effect'   57–58

Baldwin, James   36
Balestrini, Nanni   142–144
Balibar, Etienne   14, 39, 45
base and superstructure   31–32, 53, 77
Bastani, Aaron   174, 177, 186
Baudrillard, Jean   8, 136–139
Benjamin, Walter   92–93, 176
Bhattacharya, Tithi   181–182, 185
Bloch, Ernst   4, 28, 118–123
Bolshevism   1, 38–39, 50–51
Brown, Wendy   92–96

Capital   15, 155
capitalism   42–43, 45, 74–75
   post-capitalism   148–149, 155, 161
communism   1, 24–25, 90
Communist Manifesto   110–111, 117
Comte, Auguste   115–116
Cybernetic Culture Research Unit
   See accelerationism
Cybersyn   166–169, 175

Dean, Jodi   92, 96–97, 157–158, 191
décalage   6, 41, 44–45
determinism   2–3, 17, 80, 84
   economic determinism   35
   techno-determinism   9, 169, 180
diagonalism   192
dialectics   20
Dobb-Sweezy debate   2

economy   26, 40–41, 46, 70
Eurocentrism   42

Feuerbach, Ludwig   18
Fourier, Charles   112–114
Freud, Sigmund   91
   See also left melancholy
Fukuyama, Francis   105–106

Gramsci, Antonio   47, 76, 135, 177, 187
   See also hegemony

Harvey, David   103n, 123–124
Hegel, G.W.F.   29
hegemony   28, 40–41, 48–51, 57
historical materialism   17–18, 80, 93
Hobsbawm, Eric   22, 199
horizontal-vertical organisation   190, 201
human nature   19, 107
humanism   34–36

ideology   30–31, 40–41, 55, 61–62, 145, 168
immediacy   31

Klee, Paul   99

Labour Party   154, 173, 177, 183, 188
labour-power   21, 45, 161
   and capital   21–22
labour theory of value (LTV)   158, 181
Laclau, Ernesto   62, 105, 174, 179
   See also populism
Land, Nick
   See accelerationism
left melancholy   73, 78, 90
Le Guin, Ursula   124–125
Lenin, Vladimir Ilyich   4, 33, 52–53, 65, 134
Levitas, Ruth   120, 125–126

Marx, Karl   15–16, 67, 187, 189
Marxism   33, 119, 138
   autonomist Marxism   132, 141–145
   post-Marxism   60, 68, 78, 187–189
   and utopia   110
Mason, Paul   135, 155–164, 166, 174, 180
Memorial to the Murdered Jews of Europe   100
mode of production   17, 24, 46, 75
Mouffe, Chantal   188
Müntzer, Thomas   117

neoliberalism   1, 123, 151–154, 170, 176, 192
network-hierarchy
   See horizontal/vertical organisation
New Left   2, 152

INDEX

Occupy   164, 171, 190–192
Ollman, Bertell   21
Owen, Robert   114–115

Paris Commune   5n, 187
Petri, Elio   145
politics   22–23, 40–41, 63, 75
Popper, Karl   104
populism   63–66,78
postwork   151, 172, 178
prefiguration   195
   prefigurative pragmatism   194
problématique   15, 118
productive activity   4–5, 17–22
   See also productivism
productive essentialism   29, 81–82
productivism   132, 139–140
Proudhon, Pierre-Joseph   17

radical democracy   73, 78
reductionism, economic   13
relations of production   16,31
Russia   26

Saint-Simon, Henri de   112
social democracy   1, 93
social reproduction theory (SRT)
   171, 180

Soviet Union   34–35, 40, 47–48, 93n, 134n,
   199
species-being   19
Srnicek, Nick   9, 145–146, 161–162, 173,
   190
status quo   25, 77, 107
suture   71, 105

temporal lag
   See *décalage*
temporality   46, 48–49, 58, 79, 184, 194–195
transition   67–69, 80
   and Marx   25–27
   as a research agenda   3
Turkey   193–194, 43–45

Universal Basic Income (UBI)   170, 173–179,
   183, 195–196
utopia   120, 151
   anti-utopianism   104–110, 173
   techno-utopianism   164, 167–169, 176, 184

Weeks, Kathi   134, 170
Williams, Alex   148
Wright, Eric Olin   190, 192–193
   See also utopia

Žižek, Slavoj   90, 106, 135, 191

CPSIA information can be obtained
at www.ICGtesting.com
Printed in the USA
JSHW041230291121
20834JS00005B/5